COLLEGE MAJORS & CAREERS

SIXTH EDITION

A Resource Guide for Effective Life Planning

Paul Phifer

Checkmark Books

An imprint of Infobase Publishing

College Majors and Careers: A Resource Guide for Effective Life Planning,
Sixth Edition

Checkmark Books
An imprint of Infobase Publishing
132 West 31st Street
New York NY 10001

Library of Congress Cataloging-in-Publication Data

Phifer, Paul.
  College majors and careers : a resource guide for effective life planning / Paul
Phifer. -- 6th ed.
      p. cm.
  Includes bibliographical references and index.
  ISBN-13: 978-0-8160-7664-2 (hardcover : alk. paper)
  ISBN-10: 0-8160-7664-2 (hardcover : alk. paper)
  ISBN-13: 978-0-8160-7665-9 (pbk. : alk. paper)
  ISBN-10: 0-8160-7665-0 (pbk. : alk. paper) 1. Vocational guidance--United
States. 2. Vocational interests--United States. 3. College majors--United
States. 4. Professions--United States. I. Title.
  HF5382.5.U5P445 2008
  331.7020973--dc22
                            2008026061

Checkmark Books are available at special discounts when purchased in bulk
quantities for businesses, associations, institutions, or sales promotions.
Please call our Special Sales Department in New York at (212) 967-8800 or
(800) 322-8755.

You can find Facts On File on the World Wide Web at http://www.factsonfile.com

Text design adapted by Annie O'Donnell
Cover design by Takeshi Takahashi

Printed in the United States of America

Sheridan MSRF 10 9 8 7 6 5 4 3 2 1

This book is printed on acid-free paper.

To my wife, Margaret, for her continuing support
of whatever I have endeavored to seriously pursue.

Contents

Appendixes

Index of Occupations

About the Author

Acknowledgments

I would like to express my gratitude for the advice and support given to me over the years by Robert Calvert, Andy Morkes, and recently, by Jim Chambers and Jennifer Way. In addition, I am grateful to the Grand Rapids Community College administration for their support of my various professional development requests over the years. I am also thankful for the many career writers from whose research and publications I was privileged to draw. Although not mentioned in bibliographical form, their works provided this resource with the degree of accuracy and quality required. But most importantly, I must acknowledge my Savior, Jesus Christ, whose indwelling spirit deserves all the credit for anything I might have included within these pages that may serve to enable the user to live a more directed and fulfilling life.

Introduction

College Majors and Careers is designed to help students and prospective students of all ages with the critical decision of choosing a focus in a collegiate program. Whether you are just graduating from high school, preparing to enter a college or university, or planning a midlife career change, this book can help.

You will find descriptions of 63 college majors along with a list of careers each major commonly leads to, skills and personality traits best suited for those careers, degree requirements, ways to enhance your knowledge and skills outside the classroom, and resources for more information.

Why is there a need for a guide of this type? To answer this question requires a closer look at the society in which we live. It is a society that is changing at a phenomenal pace. In the last 35 years, computerization has transformed the United States from a primarily industrial nation to one with an overwhelming emphasis on information and services.

Such changes have brought unprecedented comforts, conveniences, and leisure time, but they also have created a more complex and stressful lifestyle for many Americans. The cost of living has skyrocketed. New concerns have arisen about crime, the quality of education, and the condition of our environment, and family structures have changed dramatically.

The job security enjoyed by previous generations has become a fading memory for many as companies downsize and make other short-term economic decisions in an increasingly competitive and global marketplace. The hiring of temporary workers and outsourcing have become routine, and job turnover rates are high.

These factors, combined with the unfulfilled personal needs experienced by many, are spurring increasing numbers of people to return to school or change careers. As a result, the business of career development services is booming.

In this environment, it is more important than ever to start early in determining a career path. This means not only choosing the college major that is right for you, but also recognizing that an occupation alone will not lead to a fulfilling life. In your educational pursuits, it is important to consider life's other major aspects, such as family, religion, and leisure activities. Today's society demands a comprehensive sense of direction, including a healthy balance of professional and personal activity.

This does not mean that you should make a mad rush to select the right curriculum or job. What it does mean is that you should become thoughtfully involved in the process of determining the educational, occupational, and leisure-time activities that most strongly support your basic values and bring the deepest meaning and purpose to your life. This is a lifelong process, and when approached correctly, it will reflect your unique personality configuration and lead to true fulfillment.

But the process of choosing a college major can be daunting. *College Majors and Careers* aims to motivate students to begin a realistic assessment of their lives and career goals. Its special mission is to help students who are saturated with information or experiencing apprehension from a lack of career awareness or direction. By linking the selection of a college major and associated occupations with your personality traits and preferences, the book should help you to narrow your focus and choose an academic and occupational direction that is likely to be most fulfilling for you.

Keep in mind that this book is intended as a starting point only. People are complex, and each individual has his or her own personality, needs, talents, and goals. Further research and a consultation with a career counselor is highly recommended. Additional career information can be found in career resource centers, counseling offices, libraries, and departmental offices.

May you have success on your journey!

Section I
Clusters of Majors

The majors are presented alphabetically, but each one may be viewed as a member of a family of related majors. History and political science, for example, are both in the social science field. Here's how the majors cluster in general fields:

Agriculture and Horticulture
Agriculture
Forestry
Horticulture

Architecture, Construction, and Technology
Architecture
Construction
Electrical/Electronic Technology
Industrial and Precision Production/Technology
Mechanics and Related Services
Transportation

Business and Related Areas
Accounting
Banking and Finance
Business Administration and Management
Hotel/Motel Management
Marketing and Distribution
Secretarial (Management and Administrative) Services

Culinary Arts, Food Service, and Recreation
Culinary Arts
Food and Beverage Management/Service
Home Economics
Recreation and Leisure

Engineering
Aerospace Engineering
Chemical Engineering
Civil Engineering
Electrical/Electronic Engineering
Industrial Engineering
Mechanical Engineering
Metallurgical and Mining Engineering

Fine and Performing Arts

Art

Performing Arts

Government, Public Service, and Related Areas

Criminal Justice

Education

Law

Legal and Protective Services

Library and Information Science

Military Science

Religion and Theology

Social Work

Health Care, Medicine, and Nursing

Allied Health Assisting and Technology

Allied Health Sciences

Health Administration, Management, and Related Services

Medicine

Nursing and Related Services

Language Arts

Communications

English

Foreign Language

Philosophy

Rehabilitation Therapy and Related Services

Life Sciences

Biology

Botany

Physiology

Zoology

Physical Sciences and Math

Astronomy

Chemistry

Computer Science

Geology

Mathematics

Physics

Social Sciences

Anthropology

Economics

Geography

History

Political Science

Psychology

Sociology

Connecting College Majors to Career Clusters

The following table shows how the college majors presented in this book connect to two popular career cluster systems. Each system is a valuable tool in translating an individual's strengths and interests into a college or career plan.

First, college majors are connected to one or more of the four major work areas: Data-People-Ideas-Things. These areas describe the primary work tasks typical to that field. The Data work area covers tasks including facts, numbers, files, and business procedures. The Ideas work area covers tasks including gaining knowledge and insight and developing new theories and ways of doing things. The People work area covers tasks including service, care, leadership, and sales. The Things work area covers tasks including tools, machinery, raw materials, and living things.

Next, college majors are connected to career clusters drawn from the States' Career Clusters Initiative (SCCI). Their 16 career clusters are broad groupings of related occupations designed to help people define an area of interest and develop career goals.

Table 1: Connecting College Majors to Career Clusters

College Major	Data-Things-Ideas-People	National Career Clusters
Accounting	Data	Finance
Aerospace Engineering	Ideas-Things	Science, Technology, Engineering, and Mathematics
Agriculture	Ideas-Things	Agriculture, Food, and Natural Resources
Allied Health Assisting and Technology	People	Health Science
Allied Health Sciences	People	Health Science
Anthropology	People	Education and Training

(continues)

Table 1: Connecting College Majors to Career Clusters
(continued)

Architecture	Ideas-Things	Architecture and Construction
Art	Ideas-Things	Arts, Media, Technology, and Communications
Astronomy	Ideas-Things	Science, Technology, Engineering, and Mathematics
Banking and Finance	Data	Finance
Biology	Ideas-Things	Agriculture, Food, and Natural Resources
Botany	Ideas-Things	Agriculture, Food, and Natural Resources
Business Administration and Management	Data-People	Business, Management, and Administration
Chemical Engineering	Ideas-Things	Science, Technology, Engineering, and Mathematics
Chemistry	Ideas-Things	Science, Technology, Engineering, and Mathematics
Civil Engineering	Ideas-Things	Science, Technology, Engineering, and Mathematics
Communications	Data-Ideas	Arts, Media, Technology, and Communications
Computer Science	Data-Things	Information Technology
Construction	Ideas-Things	Architecture and Construction
Criminal Justice	Data-People	Law, Public Safety, and Security
Culinary Arts	People-Things	Human Services
Economics	Data-People	Education and Training
Education	People	Education and Training
Electrical/Electronic Engineering	Ideas-Things	Science, Technology, Engineering, and Mathematics
Electrical/Electronic Technology	Ideas-Things	Science, Technology, Engineering, and Mathematics

(continues)

English	Data-Ideas	Arts, Media, Technology, and Communications
Food and Beverage Management/Service	Data-People	Human Services
Foreign Language	Data-People	Arts, Media, Technology, and Communications
Forestry	Ideas-Things	Agriculture, Food, and Natural Resources
Geography	People-Things	Government and Public Service
Geology	Ideas-Things	Agriculture, Food, and Natural Resources
Health Administration, Management, and Related Services	People	Health Science
History	People	Education and Training
Home Economics	People-Things	Human Services
Horticulture	Ideas-Things	Agriculture, Food, and Natural Resources
Hotel/Motel Management	Data-People	Hospitality and Tourism
Industrial Engineering	Ideas-Things	Science, Technology, Engineering, and Mathematics
Industrial and Precision Production/Technology	Ideas-Things	Science, Technology, Engineering, and Mathematics
Law	Data-People	Law, Public Safety, and Security
Legal and Protective Services	Data-People	Law, Public Safety, and Security
Library and Information Science	Data-People	Education and Training
Marketing and Distribution	Data-People	Marketing, Sales, and Service
Mathematics	Data	Science, Technology, Engineering, and Mathematics
Mechanical Engineering	Ideas-Things	Science, Technology, Engineering, and Mathematics
Mechanics and Related Services	Ideas-Things	Manufacturing
Medicine	People	Health Science

(continues)

Table 1: Connecting College Majors to Career Clusters
(continued)

Metallurgical and Mining Engineering	Ideas-Things	Science, Technology, Engineering, and Mathematics
Military Science	Data-People	Law, Public Safety, and Security
Nursing and Related Services	People	Health Science
Performing Arts	People-Ideas	Arts, Media, Technology, and Communications
Philosophy	Ideas	Education and Training
Physics	Ideas-Things	Science, Technology, Engineering, and Mathematics
Physiology	Ideas-Things	Science, Technology, Engineering, and Mathematics
Political Science	People	Government and Public Service
Psychology	People	Education and Training
Recreation and Leisure	People-Things	Hospitality and Tourism
Rehabilitation Therapy and Related Services	People	Health Science
Religion and Theology	People	Human Services
Secretarial (Management and Administrative) Services	Data-Things	Business, Management, and Administration
Social Work	People	Human Services
Sociology	People	Education and Training
Transportation	Things	Transportation, Distribution, and Logistics
Zoology	Ideas	Agriculture, Food, and Natural Resources

Section II

Who Will Be Helped by This Book?

College Majors and Careers is a valuable reference guide for:

Students

- Introduces them to a wide variety of college courses, giving them an overview of their content and how they relate to other fields of study.
- Emphasizes personal traits associated with success in each major and in careers that most logically follow that major.
- Lists leisure activities associated with various majors.
- Gives the approximate length and level of education required for employment in related occupations.
- Provides a sampling of preparatory high school courses for each major.
- Offers answers to many career-related questions.
- Provides a summary description of each major field.
- Lists transferable skills useful in pursuing various academic programs.
- Serves as a springboard and motivation for more in-depth and focused career exploration.
- Cites resources and organizations that provide more information about each field and provides a sampling of key characteristics of selected occupations.

Junior and Senior High School Counselors

- Augments existing data on college study and occupational life.
- Helps motivate students by clearly showing the relationships between study and later life.
- Serves as a resource for teacher in-service and counselor training sessions.
- Provides valuable information for assisting students with college major planning, helping to reduce curriculum, program, and course misplacement.
- Lists organizations and books for more background information.
- Offers a sampling of preparatory courses to help students plan an appropriate four-year program.
- Provides answers to career-related questions asked by many students as well as responses to concerns of students with special needs.

Parents

- Helps to clearly define the relationship between college study and work.
- Provides background for discussing college plans with children who are current or prospective college students.
- Cites references and resources for additional exploration.

Teachers

- Highlights the importance of career guidance. Makes it easier to motivate students by citing jobs related to their studies. Provides information useful in course orientation and introductions.
- Provides information to help suggest career options to students.
- Encourages use of the classroom as a laboratory for career exploration activities.
- Provides information that may help misplaced or misguided students.
- Encourages high school and college academic departments to become more aware of and sensitive to the career activities of their graduates.
- Provides a textbook for use in career education classes or as a referral source in libraries.
- Provides answers to many questions frequently asked by students.

College Counselors and Other Student Personnel Workers

- Offers valuable help in counseling, attracting, and recruiting students in the admissions process.
- Provides background for building closer links between the counseling staff and academic departments.
- Provides a base of knowledge useful in meeting student questions about educational programs and career options.
- Answers many questions frequently asked by students, including those with special needs.
- Suggests part-time and summer job options that may be closely related to students' academic training and potential career choices.
- Serves as a useful resource for counseling center clients as a part of their self-development research.
- Shows employers how various aspects of college support services help educate and prepare future employees.
- Provides information related to career direction suitability that should be useful for Upward Bound and Special Services (and similar programs) personnel in meeting governmental guidelines.

Section III

How This Book Is Organized and How to Use It

Each of the college majors and career briefs featured contains information presented in a consistent format for easy reference. Each entry begins with a general definition of the major field, then continues with the sections described below.

High School Courses

Lists high school courses or areas that are closely related to the major or considered useful background for that field. Course titles and grade levels vary greatly among high schools. Courses cited are not all-inclusive and are intended to be used as a general guideline by students, parents, teachers, and counselors. Educators will need to exercise professional expertise and include local courses that may apply to a particular field but are not listed. It is strongly suggested that students consult with counselors concerning preparatory courses related to particular fields of study.

Related Majors

Lists college majors that are closely related to the subject of the entry. While many options are included, the list is not all encompassing. Students are advised to consult with counselors to get the fullest view of potential college majors in their areas of interest.

Related Occupations

Lists jobs appropriate for graduates with that major, followed by the average minimum level of education required. Some occupations listed in this section require additional, specialized academic training for licensure and/or full professional status. Interested students are encouraged to contact a career counselor or academic advisor about these requirements before making a decision.

Following is a key for the codes used in this section:

AA: Associate's degree (or two full years of college study after high school) is generally required or very helpful. In some cases, people enter the field after taking specialized courses that may not require two full years.

B: Bachelor's degree (four or more full years of college study after high school) generally required or helpful. This may be a BA (Bachelor of Arts) or BS (Bachelor of Science) degree.

C: Certificate, normally awarded following successful completion of one year or less of training and/or formal college education.

M: Master's degree is preferred for the field; usually requires one or two years of study after the bachelor's degree. This may be an MA (Master of Arts) or MS (Master of Science) degree.

P: First professional degree is required; usually after completion of bachelor's degree. Some professional degrees include the BD (Bachelor of Divinity), LLB (law school degree), MD (Doctor of Medicine), and DDS (Doctor of Dental Science).

D: Doctoral degree is preferred for full professional status in the field. These include the PhD (Doctor of Philosophy) and EdD (Doctor of Education), which usually take from three to five years after the bachelor's degree. However, interested students often enter their field as Research Assistants (RA) or Administrative Assistants (AA).

V: Requirements vary greatly and/or vocational training is generally required; may include a combination of academic and work experience.

Sometimes, two or more codes appear after an occupation, which means that employers may hire candidates with different levels of education for the same job. For example, under Communications, employers might hire a news photographer with either a two-year certificate or a four-year bachelor's degree, depending on the candidate's other characteristics and qualifications. Definitions for the least familiar of the cited occupations appear in Appendix B.

Leisure Activities

Identifies hobbies, interests, and activities related to the major as well as to many of the occupations cited. This list provides a clearer picture of how extracurricular activities are related to majors, occupations, and other life endeavors.

Skills

Presents a partial list of skills that may be related to success in the major or related occupations or are frequently used in either. Some are natural inborn traits (aptitudes); others are acquired through practice, study, or extra effort (abilities). Some of the skills may be developed or discovered while a student is advancing in a course of study or occupation. The list of skills also provides a valuable and time-saving stop-check for students who may be mistakenly moving in an unsuitable direction. Definitions of skill statements that may be unfamiliar or difficult to understand appear in Appendix C.

Values and Attributes

Lists some of the motivations and personal characteristics generally associated with the field of study. This is not to imply that other values are not present or that these values are held by everyone interested in the subject. The values listed should help students determine if the subject, and subjects related to it, will move them closer to what is really most important to them in life. Definitions of some of the values and attributes that may be unfamiliar or hard to interpret can be found in Appendix D.

Resources

Lists books and/or professional associations that can provide additional information related to the major. For names of other associations in the major field of interest, see the *Encyclopedia of Associations* (published by Gale Research Company) or *National Trade and Professional Associations of the United States* (published annually by Columbia Books). These should be available in the reference section of most public libraries. Readers should augment the resources cited in this book with references recommended by a local counselor or teacher. Obviously, some of the references cited are subject to change due to books going out of print, revisions and updates, and address changes. Information provided by the references cited does not necessarily reflect the viewpoints of the author or publisher.

Be aware that due to similarities in definition, the words major, college major, field of study, field, subject, and like terms are used interchangeably and all refer to a student's major area of study.

Helpful Information

This section features a typical occupation associated with this career brief area along with information about projected growth, number employed, and salary range. Several related occupations and their salary ranges are also included. Each Helpful Information section includes:

Growth Outlook (2006–2016)

Provides the name of one or more selected occupations related to the career brief to be highlighted. In some instances, an asterisk (*) is placed before an occupation if it is currently considered by the U.S. Department of Labor, Bureau of Labor Statistics (BLS) to be "In Demand."

Projected

Shows the expected percent of growth or decline for the occupation between the years 2006–2016, according to the BLS.

Number Employed (2006)

Provides the number of people said to be employed in this occupation in 2006 and the number estimated to be employed by 2016, according to the BLS.

Salary Range (2006)

Provides the salary range for the cited occupation(s) for the year 2006. EXAMPLE: $32,000–$87,200. The first amount means the lowest 10 percent of the workers in this occupation earned this amount or less for the year 2006. The second amount means the highest 10 percent earned this amount or more for the year 2006. Figures were provided by the BLS.

Related Occupations

Provides a sampling of the salary ranges for three or four additional occupations related to the career brief. An asterisk placed before the occupation means it is considered to be "In Demand," according to the BLS.

Source Code(s)

Provides the full name of the source code(s) used in this section.

Career-Related Questions and Answers

Provides answers to key career-related questions either frequently asked by students or considered to be important for certain populations. As a career counselor, I have been asked the same or similar questions dozens of times by students, parents, and other professionals over the years. Included in this section are the most common questions along with their answers.

The 4-Step Career Development Process

While it is possible to browse the career briefs and supporting material in the traditional chronological way (and then proceed to identify majors that seem to be most interesting, and eventually, select the one believed to be the best fit), this book's content attempts to help you with much more.

The sixth edition of *College Majors and Careers* places primary emphasis on the first step of the career development process. Career counselors some-time elect to present the career-development process in three-, four-, five-, and even six-step models. The model presented here is a four-step approach to the traditional career-development process, which has been commonly used by career development professionals for years. This process, in brief, encourages the individual to conduct a *self-assessment* followed by an *exploration of career fields*; narrowing down to the best options or *decision making*, and then *placement* or taking action on the decisions made.

There are a few important aspects about Step 1. First, the understanding and accurate application of Step 1 is critical to a person being able to engage in effective career decision making. Secondly, Step 1 generates motivation as well as establishes or confirms direction in life. This direction then becomes a blueprint to be used in the remaining three steps. Therefore, in light of these realities, *College Majors and Careers* provides the reader with an opportunity in Appendix A to complete a Step 1 activity, the results of which should help the individual to determine or confirm a career or college major selection.

What follows are brief descriptions of each step of the 4-Step Career Development Process followed by an illustration showing how the direction established or confirmed in Step 1 serves as a gauge for all four steps. It represents a useful, easy-to-understand model for students as well as adults of differing ages, backgrounds, and educational levels.

STEP 1
INSIDE

Step 1 helps a person to base important decisions on his or her *life direction* rather than simply planning for a good job or a college major. Step 1 focus is on the *inside* of a person. It entails an identification of a life mission and then gathering information to find out just who he or she is and what is most important to him or her in life. Accurately identifying, gathering information about, and then determining the above is commonly referred to by career counselors as a *self-assessment*, and in essence becomes for the individual a "rough blueprint." Whenever a person has a big decision to make, such as selecting a career or college major, the strongest influence will most likely be determined by one's unique personality configuration and most cherished values on the inside. Therefore, it is strongly recommended that the interested reader complete the Step 1 activity (or self-assessment) in Appendix A. In other words, at minimum, the results of Step 1 should be applied before finalizing one's decision(s) about which major or career is the best fit. If an individual is still undecided about a career or major after he or she has completed the above, it may be necessary to contact a qualified high school or college counselor to assist in this effort.

STEP 2
OUTSIDE

In Step 2, the individual is made aware of common characteristics of significant areas *outside* of him or her (such as family, leisure-time, faith, occupations, education and training, etc.) on which big decisions will have an impact and therefore will need to be considered before a final decision is made. The individual is then encouraged to explore aspects within each that both support and do not support Step I results. Activities that involve the identification of suitable occupations along with the requirements for performing them are usually initiated during this step.

STEP 3
CLOSER LOOK

In Step 3, the individual *narrows down* options identified within significant areas on the outside, particularly in regards to the occupation and the education and training required to prepare for entry. Eventually, the individual selects the occupation and/or education he or she determines to be most reflective of his or her Step 1 results. This *decision* becomes the *goal*. Finally, the individual creates a *plan* to follow and achieve his or her goal.

STEP 4
MATCHING UP

In Step 4, the individual *takes action*, actually putting into practice the decision he or she made in Step 3. The decision to select one career and/or college major rather than another resulted in the occupation and/or the education and training goal that the individual's actions will seek to reach. In addition, the decision and goal determined in Step 3 should be reflected in one's plan and serve as a guideline for the person's continuing "follow-through" actions in this step.

THE 4-STEP CAREER DEVELOPMENT PROCESS

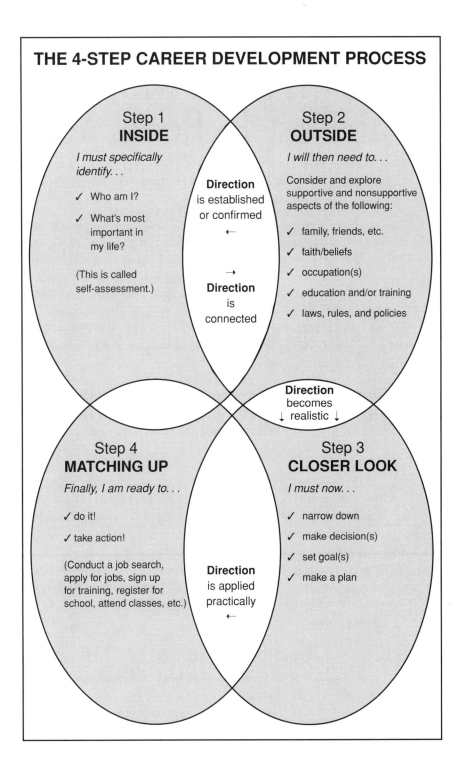

Step 1
INSIDE

I must specifically identify...

✓ Who am I?

✓ What's most important in my life?

(This is called self-assessment.)

Direction
is established or confirmed

←

→

Direction
is connected

Step 2
OUTSIDE

I will then need to...

Consider and explore supportive and nonsupportive aspects of the following:

✓ family, friends, etc.

✓ faith/beliefs

✓ occupation(s)

✓ education and/or training

✓ laws, rules, and policies

Direction
becomes
↓ realistic ↓

Step 4
MATCHING UP

Finally, I am ready to...

✓ do it!

✓ take action!

(Conduct a job search, apply for jobs, sign up for training, register for school, attend classes, etc.)

Direction
is applied practically

←

Step 3
CLOSER LOOK

I must now...

✓ narrow down

✓ make decision(s)

✓ set goal(s)

✓ make a plan

Choosing the Major That Best Reflects You

This section describes and offers pertinent information about 63 of the most popular college majors today.

Most of you will be able to acquire valuable insight by simply browsing through and identifying those majors that most interest you. However, it is suggested that you use this popular approach as a stop-check measurement only. To obtain a more accurate self-appraisal in terms of choosing a suitable major, it is recommended that you complete the Self-Assessment in Appendix A. Doing a self-assessment consists of identifying and summarizing your most pronounced personality attributes and most cherished life and work values. After completing the self-assessment, browse through this chapter and select the top two majors you believe most closely reflect the answers on your self-assessment summary page. Make sure to also consider your weaknesses. Finally, while the self-assessment activity will more than likely prove to be extremely beneficial, it is strongly recommended that you consult a qualified career counselor to confirm your findings.

Useful Tips

You may want to use the following questions as you explore the possibilities of each major in this section. These questions are arranged to follow the structure of the listings in this section.

General Description

Does __(Name of Major)__ sound like a field I would like to go into?

Should I look at some related areas or engage in formalized career planning? (See Clusters of Majors)

Do I need to explore this area further? (See Resources and Helpful Information)

Should I complete a self-assessment before making my decision about a career or major? (See Appendix A)

Should I take basic courses required to obtain my diploma or degree before engaging in a more in-depth career exploration?

Do most of the activities, skills, and attributes listed for this major relate to my interests and abilities?

Career Briefs

High School Courses:
Do I currently take or have I taken courses such as the ones listed in this brief?

Related Majors:
Are there any majors listed in this section that I am curious to learn more about?

Related Occupations:
Should I look up any of the occupations in this section? (See Index of Occupations or O*NET OnLine http://www.online.onetcenter.org)

Am I aware of and am I prepared to undertake the amount of education required for the occupation I have interest in?

Leisure Activities:
Is there some related activity or hobby I can engage in right now that might help me decide or give me valuable exposure/experience?

Are there any activities listed in this section that I have experienced or am currently involved in that further confirm my interest?

Skills:
Do I already have some of the skills cited in this section?

Do I want to acquire and believe I am capable of acquiring the skills that I lack?

Do I need to find out the meaning of some of these skills? (See Appendix C or O*NET OnLine)

Values and Attributes:
Do I have the personality traits suitable to or similar to those cited in this section? (See Appendix C or O*NET OnLine)

Do I need to find out the meaning of some of these values and attributes? (See Appendix D)

Resources:
Should I explore the Web sites listed in this section, as well as other related resources, before making a final decision?

Helpful Information:
Do the salary ranges and outlook of occupations help me in making a final decision? (See also America's Career InfoNet: http://www.acinet.org)

Accounting

Accounting involves the examination, organization, management, and design of accurate recording and reporting procedures of financial and business transactions. The study of accounting helps you learn the various ways of maintaining accurate, up-to-date financial and business records. This includes methods of compilation, verification, supervision, revision, examination, efficiency recording, designing, and reporting of such practices for both individuals and businesses. Knowledge and implementation of good accounting procedures are required to achieve success in finance or business, whether it be for an individual, family, or corporation. Some of the major specializations include tax accounting, management accounting, environmental accounting, forensic accounting, government accounting, international accounting, and consulting.

High School Courses

Accounting	Computer Operations
Banking	Computer Programming
Bookkeeping	Consumer Math
Business	Economics
Business Law	Math
Business Math	Statistics

Related Majors

Assurance Services	International Accounting
Auditing	Management Accounting
Environmental Accounting	Personal Financial Planning
Forensic Accounting	Public Accounting
Government Accounting	Tax Accounting

Related Occupations

See page 11 for detailed explanation of key.

Accountant—B	Internal Auditor—B
Actuary—B	Internal Revenue Agent—B
Auditor—B	International Accountant—B
Bank Officer—AA/B	Investment Banker—B
Bookkeeper—V/AA	Management Accountant—B
Budget Analyst—B/M	Management Consultant—B/M
Controller—B/M	Market Research Analyst—B
Cost Estimator—V	Public Accountant—B

Credit Manager—AA/B	Purchasing Agent—B
Economist—B	Statistician—B
Educator—B/M/D	Tax Accountant—AA/B
Financial Analyst—B	Tax Preparer—V/B
Financial Planner—B	Treasurer—B
Insurance Agent—V/B	Underwriter—B

Leisure Activities

- Working as a part-time or volunteer treasurer or income tax preparer
- Joining a professional accounting organization
- Reading accounting-related publications
- Joining a financial advisory board
- Solving problems involving analytical and logical processes
- Attending accounting-related lectures, trade shows, or conventions
- Working as a student aide in a high school or college accounting department
- Working with a personal computer

Skills

- Proficiency in written and oral communication
- Ability to organize, analyze, and interpret numerical data
- Aptitude for accuracy and detail
- Proficiency with computers

HELPFUL INFORMATION
*Accountants and Auditors
Growth Outlook (2006–2016)

Projected: Grow faster than the average (increase 14% to 20%)
Number Employed (2006): 1,274,000   **(By 2016)** 1,500,000 (+9%)
Salary Range (2006): $34,740–$94,050
Related Occupations: *AIN*

	SALARY RANGE:
*Budget Analysts	$40,100–$93,100
*Financial Analysts	$40,400–$130,100
*Personal Financial Advisors	$32,300–$145,600
Tax Examiners	$27,300–$81,900

*According to the BLS, workers in these occupations are currently in high demand and thus have been designated as "In Demand."

SOURCE CODE(S):
Department of Labor, Bureau of Labor Statistics = *BLS*
Occupational Outlook Handbook, 2008–2009 = OOH
America's Career InfoNet (Online) = *AIN*
O*NET (Online) = *NET*

- Ability to work alone and concentrate for long periods of time
- Ability to make sound judgments and decisions and to solve quantitative problems
- Ability to explain complex financial data to others
- Intellectual capacity to do well in most undergraduate and graduate college programs
- Ability to lead, supervise, and direct others

Values and Attributes

- Achievement
- Tendency toward analytical and logical thinking
- Patience
- Intellectual growth
- Integrity
- Independence
- Capacity for precision, detail, and order
- Thoroughness
- Recognition and appreciation from others
- Ability to frame inquiry and respond objectively
- Resourcefulness
- Skill with numbers
- Imagination

Resources

- **American Accounting Association**
  5717 Bessie Drive
  Sarasota, FL 34233-2399
  941-921-7747
  http://aaahq.org
  (offers student membership, job placement service, and a helpful list of links and organizations)
- **American Institute of Certified Public Accountants**
  1211 Avenue of the Americas
  New York, NY 10036
  212-596-6200
  http://aicpa.org
  (publishes preparation information for CPA examinations, provides job posting services, career path and internship information; see Career Development and Workplace links)
- **American Society of Women Accountants**
  8405 Greensboro Drive, Suite 800
  McLean, VA 22102
  800-326-2163
  http://www.aswa.org
  (offers scholarships and employment opportunities)

Aerospace Engineering

Aerospace engineering is the practical application of physical science and mathematics in the research, design, development, testing, launching, and production of aircraft, spacecraft, navigational systems, and related equipment, systems, and processes in an efficient and economical manner. It involves the design and production of power units, vehicle structure, aerodynamics and guidance control as well as airplane, rocket, missile, and satellite launching. Specialties include aircraft design, guidance systems, instrumentation, fluid mechanics, thermodynamics, satellites, helicopters, rockets, and military aircraft.

High School Courses

Algebra	Math
Calculus	Mechanical Drawing
Chemistry	Mechanics
Computer Science	Physical Science
Computers	Physics
Drawing	Trigonometry
Geometry	Statistics
Intro. to Blueprint Reading	

Related Majors

Agricultural Engineering	Environmental Engineering
Architectural Engineering	Manufacturing Engineering
Bioengineering	Marine Engineering
Biomedical Engineering	Mechanical Engineering
Chemical Engineering	Metallurgical Engineering
Civil Engineering	Nuclear Engineering
Computer Engineering	Petroleum Engineering
Electrical/Electronic Engineering	Systems Engineering

Related Occupations

See page 11 for detailed explanation of key.

Aerodynamist—B	Marine Engineer—B
Aeronautical Engineer—B/D	Mechanical Engineer—B
Aerospace Airplane Pilot—AA/B	Metallurgical Engineer—B
Aerospace Engineer—B/D	Nuclear Engineer—B/D
Astronomer—D	Petroleum Engineer—B
Astrophysicist—B/D	Physicist—B/D

Computer Programmer—B
Computer Science Engineer—B
Consulting Engineer—B/M/D
Electrical Engineer—B
Environmental Engineer—B

Research Engineer—B/D
Safety Engineer—B
Systems Analyst—B
Systems Engineer—B

Leisure Activities

- Reading publications related to flying or space
- Viewing aircraft or space-related documentaries and programs on TV or at the movies
- Browsing the Internet for aviation-related topics
- Developing hobbies or collections related to model airplanes, cars, mechanics, or electronic games and equipment
- Air travel
- Attending lectures or conferences related to aviation or engineering
- Visiting science museums and exhibits
- Belonging to a club or organization such as the American Institute of Aeronautics and Astronautics
- Solving analytic and logic problems

Skills

- High proficiency in mathematics and physical sciences
- Ability to analyze, organize, and interpret scientific data
- Ability to work well with others
- Ability to make keen observations and sound judgments
- Aptitude for accuracy and detail, spatial perception, and abstract reasoning
- Sensitivity to economic considerations and human needs
- Proficiency in an area of specialization and in current practices and trends
- Ability to conduct and clearly communicate results of scientific research
- Intellectual capacity to perform well in most undergraduate and graduate college programs
- Proficiency with computers

Values and Attributes

- Creativity
- Knowledge
- Achievement
- Desire to help others live better
- Strong interest in aviation and space
- Interest in seeing ideas developed into practical use
- Curiosity
- Imagination
- Perseverance
- Responsibility
- Capability

HELPFUL INFORMATION
*Aerospace Engineers
Growth Outlook (2006–2016)

Projected: Grow about as fast as the average (increase 7% to 13%)
Number Employed (2006): 90,000 **(By 2016)** 90,000 (+10%)
Salary Range (2006): $59,610–$124,550
Related Occupations: *AIN*

	SALARY RANGE:
*Chemical Engineers	$50,060 and up
*Electrical Engineers	$49,120–$115,240
*Nuclear Engineers	$65,220–$124,510
*Computer Hardware Engineers	$53,190–$135,260

*According to the BLS, workers in these occupations are currently in high demand and thus have been designated as "In Demand."

SOURCE CODE(S):
Department of Labor, Bureau of Labor Statistics = BLS
Occupational Outlook Handbook, 2008–2009 = OOH
America's Career InfoNet (Online) = *AIN*
O*NET (Online) = *NET*

Resources

■ **American Institute of Aeronautics and Astronautics**
1801 Alexander Bell Drive, Suite 500
Reston, VA 20191-4344
703-264-7500
http://www.aiaa.org
(offers student membership, see AIAA Career Center)

■ **Junior Engineering Technical Society**
1420 King Street, Suite 405
Alexandria, VA 22314
703-548-5387
http://www.jets.org
(offers a helpful list of links, printed resources, accredited schools, and student-related information; see the publication on aerospace engineering)

■ **Society of Women Engineers**
230 East Ohio Street, Suite 400
Chicago, IL 60611-3265
312-576-5223
http://www.swe.org
(provides an array of helpful information, such as scholarships, college programs, and much more)

Agriculture

Agriculture is the science of growing crops and raising livestock. It involves planting, cultivating, fertilizing, harvesting, processing, and distributing fruits, vegetables, and nursery stock. It also includes the raising, feeding, breeding, and marketing of livestock. In addition, agricultural study exposes you to the various by-products of livestock, such as dairy products, eggs, honey, and fur. Agricultural research related to increasing the yield and quality of products and by-products, sanitation, diseases, methods of efficiency, and other areas is another important part of the field.

High School Courses

Algebra	Geometry
Biology	Landscape Gardening
Chemistry	Math
Computer Applications	Trigonometry
Earth Science	Zoology
Food Science	

Related Majors

Agricultural Economics	Fisheries and Wildlife
Agricultural Engineering	Food Science
Animal Science	Forestry
Botany	Horticulture
Crop/Soil Sciences	Natural Resources Management
Entomology	Park and Recreation Administration

Related Occupations

See page 11 for detailed explanation of key.

Agricultural Engineer—B	Feed Store Operator—V
Agronomist—B/D	Fish Farmer—V/B
Agricultural Scientist—B/D	Florist—V
Biochemist—B/D	Food Scientist—B
Biologist—B/D	Horticulturist—B/D
Botanist—B/D	Laboratory Assistant—AA
Cattle Farmer—V/B	Landscape Gardener—AA
Chemical Lab Technician—AA	Microbiologist—B/D
Cooperative Extension Agent—B	Nursery Manager—V
Dairy Farmer—V/B	Parasitologist—B/D
Educator—B/D	Physiologist—D
Entomologist—B/D	Soil Conservationist—B/D
Farm Equipment Mechanic—AA/V	Soil Scientist—B/D
Farmer—V/B	Veterinarian—P

Leisure Activities

- Working part time or as a volunteer on a farm, ranch, pet shop, garden center, or zoo
- Gardening
- Owning and caring for pets
- Belonging to the National Future Farmers of America Organization (FFA) or 4-H
- Scouting
- Attending farm shows and fairs
- Working as a student aide or volunteer in a school science or college agriculture department
- Attending clinics, lectures, and workshops related to agriculture
- Reading agriculture-related publications
- Developing hobbies and collections related to gardening, horses, or raising livestock

Skills

- Good understanding of and familiarity with agricultural techniques and applications
- Physical stamina, good vision, and manual dexterity
- Ability to recognize differences in shapes, shading, and color
- Proficiency in reading and writing
- Ability to make keen observations and sound judgments
- Ability to organize, analyze, and interpret scientific data
- Ability to make appropriate decisions and apply scientific methods to agricultural concerns
- Ability to manage and supervise others
- Ability to work both alone and with others
- General knowledge of farm supplies, equipment, services, and business/ marketing practices
- Aptitude for science and mathematics

Values and Attributes

- Independence
- Desire to help people
- Achievement
- Strong interest in agriculture
- Fondness for outdoor activities
- Ability to adapt to frequent changes
- Patience
- Responsibility
- Perseverance
- Resourcefulness

Resources

- **American Farm Bureau Federation**
  600 Maryland Avenue SW, Suite 1000W
  Washington, DC 20024
  202-406-3600
  http://www.fb.org

(sponsors a Young Farmer's and Rancher's Program for ages 18 to 35; Web
site also provides an extensive list of links to various agricultural sites)

- **American Society of Agronomy**
677 South Segoe Road
Madison, WI 53711
608-273-8080
http://www.agronomy.org
(offers an excellent career placement link)

- **National FFA Organization**
6060 FFA Drive
PO Box 68960
Indianapolis, IN 46268-0960
317-802-6050
http://www.ffa.org
(features an agricultural career center that includes scholarship and job
opportunities)

- **U.S. Department of Agriculture**
Higher Education Program
14th Street and Independence SW
Washington, DC 20250
202-720-2791
http://www.usda.gov (click on "Agriculture")
(offers information on agriculture, conservation, food and nutrition, weather,
and employment)

HELPFUL INFORMATION
Agricultural and Food Scientists
Growth Outlook (2006–2016)

Projected: Grow about as fast as the average (increase 7% to 13%)
Number Employed (2006): 33,000   **(By 2016)** 36,000 (+9%)
Salary Range (2006): $343,650–$93,460
Related Occupations: *AIN*

	SALARY RANGE:
*Farmers/Ranchers	$22,800–$76,000
*Biological Scientists	$34,300–$95,100
*Conservation Scientists	$24,900–$80,300
*Agricultural Engineers	$42,400–$96,300

*According to the BLS, workers in these occupations are currently in high
demand and thus have been designated as "In Demand."

SOURCE CODE(S):
Department of Labor, Bureau of Labor Statistics = *BLS*
Occupational Outlook Handbook, 2008–2009 = *OOH*
America's Career InfoNet (Online) = *AIN*
O*NET (Online) = *NET*

Allied Health Assisting and Technology

Allied health assisting and technology involves the study of areas of technological support and health-related assistance to physicians, dentists, and other health professionals. The skills and services in this field are considered essential to effective health care programs. Among the various specializations are dental assisting, hygiene, and technology; medical laboratory technology and assisting; radiography; dietetics and nutrition; and physical and occupational therapy.

High School Courses

Biology	Psychology
Chemistry	Physical Education/Fitness
Computer Applications	Physiology
First Aid	Science
Health	Sociology

Related Majors

Cardiovascular Technology	Radiologic Technology
Health Information Technology	Respiratory Technology
Medical Assisting	Surgical Technology
Orthotic/Prosthetic Program	

Related Occupations

See page 11 for detailed explanation of key.

Biomedical Equipment Technician—AA	Occupational Therapy Assistant—AA
Cytotechnologist—AA/B	Operating Room Technician—AA
Dental Assistant—AA	Ophthalmic Medical Assistant—AA
Dental Hygienist—AA	Optician—AA
Dental Lab Technician—AA	Optometric Assistant—AA
Diagnostic Medical Sonographer—AA	Orthotics/Prosthetics Technician—AA
Dietetic Technician—AA	Perfusionist—V
EEG Technologist—AA	Physical Therapy Assistant—AA
EKG Technician—AA	Physician Assistant—AA/B
Emergency Medical Technician—AA	Podiatric Assistant—AA
Environmental Health Technician—AA	Radiological Technologist—AA

Medical Assistant—AA	Respiratory Therapy Technician—AA
Medical Lab Technician—AA	Surgical Technician—AA
Medical Records Technician—AA	Veterinary Technician—AA
Mental Health Technician—AA	X-Ray Technician—AA

Leisure Activities

- Attending science fairs
- Visiting science museums and exhibits
- Reading health-related publications
- Serving as an aide in a church or community health agency
- Working part time in a hospital, medical center, or nursing home
- Attending lectures and workshops related to health care services
- Watching health-related documentaries, movies, or TV dramas
- Actively supporting health care expansion and medical research drives

Skills

- Ability to react quickly and maintain emotional and physical composure in stressful situations
- High proficiency for accuracy and detail
- Proficiency in interpersonal communication

HELPFUL INFORMATION
*Occupational Therapist Assistants
Growth Outlook (2006–2016)

Projected: Grow much faster than the average (increase 21% or more)
Number Employed (2006): 25,000 **(By 2016)** 31,000 (+25%)
Salary Range (2006): $26,050–$58,270
Related Occupations: *AIN*

	SALARY RANGE:
*Physical Therapist Assistants	$26,200–$57,200
*Dental Hygienists	$40,500–$86,500
*Radiologic Technologists and Technicians	$32,800–$68,900
*Medical Records and Health Information Technicians	$19,100–$45,300

*According to the BLS, workers in these occupations are currently in high demand and thus have been designated as "In Demand."

SOURCE CODE(S):
Department of Labor, Bureau of Labor Statistics = *BLS*
Occupational Outlook Handbook, 2008–2009 = *OOH*
America's Career InfoNet (Online) = *AIN*
O*NET (Online) = *NET*

- Proficiency in memorization and giving and receiving directions
- Physical stamina, good vision, and manual dexterity
- Ability to make keen observations, sound judgments, and appropriate decisions
- Ability to work cooperatively with people of differing backgrounds
- Good motor coordination

Values and Attributes

- Achievement
- Desire to help others
- Health
- Wisdom
- Interest in challenges and working directly with people
- Helpful and friendly attitude
- Sensitivity to the needs and pain of others
- Willingness to work irregular hours and on weekends
- Industriousness
- Capability
- Poise
- Dependability
- Resourcefulness

Resources

- Damp, Dennis V. *Health Care Job Explosion: High Growth Health Care Careers and Job Locator*. McKee's Rock, PA: Bookhaven Press, 2006.
- **American Medical Technologists Association**
  10700 West Higgins Road, Suite 150
  Rosemont, IL 60018
  847-823-5169
  http://www.amt1.com
  (offers information about certification exams for lab assistants, phlebotomists, and dental assistants, as well as job search assistance)
- **American Society of Radiologic Technologists**
  15000 Central Avenue SE
  Albuquerque, NM 87123-3917
  800-444-2778
  http://www.asrt.org
  (offers student scholarships and job placement services)
- **Commission on Accreditation of Allied Health Education Programs**
  1361 Park Street
  Clearwater, FL 33756
  http://www.caahep.org/index.htm
  (highlights accredited allied health programs)

Allied Health Sciences

Allied health sciences is the study of health science areas that are related to and supportive of medical services provided by physicians and dentists. You learn ways of supporting and maintaining health care and medical services for individuals and populations. In addition, you study scientific, educational, and social approaches to identification, evaluation, prevention and control of disease, sickness, disorders, and injury. Special areas of concentration include environmental health, occupational safety and health, dental and medical technology, research, health education, diet/nutrition, and rehabilitation.

High School Courses

Algebra	Physical Education/Fitness
Biology	Physiology
Chemistry	Psychology
Computer Applications	Science
Geometry	Sociology
Health	Trigonometry

Related Majors

Athletic Training	Medical Technology
Biomedical Engineering	Microbiology
Dietary/Nutrition	Occupational Safety
Health Administration	Pharmacy
Health Education	Physician Assistant
Medical Illustration	Technical Writing
Medical Research	

Related Occupations

See page 11 for detailed explanation of key.

Athletic Trainer—B	Hospital Administrator—M
Biomedical Engineer—B	Medical Engineer—B
Biostatistician—B/M	Medical/Scientific Illustrator—B
Blood Bank Specialist—B	Medical Technologist—B
Clinical Chemist—B	Nuclear Medicine Technologist—B
Cytologist—B	Nutritionist—V
Dental Hygienist—AA/B	Pharmacist—B
Dietitian—B	Physician Assistant—AA/B
Endoscopy Technician—AA	Radiation Therapy Technologist—AA
Health Care Administrator M/D	Radiologic Health Specialist—B
Health Educator—B/D	Technical Writer—B
Health Microbiologist—B	Tissue Technologist—V
Histotechnologist—AA/B	

Leisure Activities

- Attending science fairs, health exhibits, and visiting museums
- Reading health science-related publications
- Doing lab experiments and researching health science-related topics
- Working part time or as a volunteer for a health agency, hospital, or school health science department
- Writing reports and summaries
- Watching TV programs and documentaries related to the health sciences
- Attending health-related lectures and workshops
- Belonging to a health science club, health guild, or professional organization
- Actively supporting health care expansion and medical research drives

Skills

- Ability to concentrate for long periods of time
- Ability to conduct and clearly explain scientific research
- Ability to make keen observations and appropriate decisions
- Ability to work under pressure and meet deadlines
- High proficiency for accuracy and detail
- Proficiency in observing, collecting, and analyzing scientific data
- Proficiency in reading, writing, speaking, and memorization
- General knowledge of health sciences
- Physical stamina, good vision, and manual dexterity
- Intellectual capacity to perform well in most undergraduate and graduate college programs
- Proficiency with computers

Values and Attributes

- Intellectual growth
- Achievement
- Wisdom
- Health
- Desire to help others and make a contribution to humanity
- Interest in public health and safety
- Sensitivity to the needs and pain of others
- Scientific inquiry
- Patience
- Self-discipline
- Thoroughness

Resources

- **American Health Information Management Association**
  233 North Michigan Avenue, 21st Floor
  Chicago, IL 60601-5800
  312-233-1100

http://www.ahima.org
(good career and accredited program information)

■ **American Hospital Association**
1 North Franklin
Chicago, IL 60606
312-422-3000
http://www.aha.org
(provides information on careers in medicine and health care)

■ **Commission on Accreditation of Allied Health Education Programs**
1361 Park Street
Clearwater, FL 33756
727-210-2350
http://www.caahep.org/index.aspx
(highlights 17 accredited allied health programs)

Anthropology

Anthropology is the study of the origin and development of humans. It provides students with a better understanding of human physical differences, language systems, and the way cultures today compare with cultures of the past. Anthropology is sometimes considered a branch of archaeology. Specialties include cultural anthropology, physical anthropology, linguistic anthropology, and various ethnosciences.

High School Courses

Anatomy/Physiology	History
Anthropology	Math
Art	Psychology
Computer Applications	Social Studies
Computer Science	Sociology
English	Statistics
Foreign Languages	World History
Geography	

Related Majors

Archaeology	History
Art History	Linguistics
Biological Anthropology	Medical Anthropology
Foreign Language	Museology
Geography	Psychology
Geology	Sociology

Related Occupations

See page 11 for detailed explanation of key.

Anthropologist—D	Geographer—B/D
Archaeologist—M/D	Historian—M/D
Archivist—M/D	Linguistic Anthropologist—D
Art Conservator—B	Museum Worker—V
Bibliographer—M	Paleontologist—B/D
Cultural Anthropologist—D	Research Associate—B
Curator—M/D	Social Worker—M/D
Educator—B/M/D	Sociologist—D
Ethnologist—M/D	Technical Writer—B
Genealogist—B/D	

Leisure Activities

- Visiting libraries and museums
- Participating in historical preservation efforts
- Doing historical research
- Camping, backpacking, and exploring
- Participating in archaeological field experiences
- Reading publications related to anthropology
- Joining an organization such as the American Anthropological Association
- Collecting relics, antiquities, and artifacts
- Working part time or as a volunteer in an antique shop, museum, or college anthropology department
- Serving as a graduate research assistant

Skills

- Background of general knowledge
- Aptitude for foreign language
- Intellectual capacity to perform well in most undergraduate and graduate college programs
- Proficiency in reading comprehension, writing, and public speaking
- Ability to conduct and explain scientific research clearly
- Good vision, spatial perception, and manual dexterity
- Proficiency with computers
- Ability to accurately interpret and evaluate events, information, and ideas related to the past
- Interpersonal communication skills

Values and Attributes

- Achievement
- Appreciation for and understanding of other cultures
- Desire for recognition and to influence humanity
- Desire to research and explore the human past
- Interest in learning about the similarities and differences between cultures
- Patience
- Alertness
- Curiosity
- Resourcefulness
- Integrity
- Imagination
- Analytical thought

HELPFUL INFORMATION
*Anthropologists and Archeologists
Growth Outlook (2006–2016)

Projected: Grow about as fast as the average (increase 7% to 13% or more)
Number Employed (2006): 5,500   **(By 2016)** 6,400 (+15%)
Salary Range (2006): $29,000–$81,500
Related Occupations: *AIN*

	SALARY RANGE:
Geographers	$37,500–$93,900
Sociologists	$36,800–$115,800
*Urban and Regional Planners	$35,600–$86,900
Historians	$23,500–$89,900

*According to the BLS, workers in these occupations are currently in high demand and thus have been designated as "In Demand."

SOURCE CODE(S):
Department of Labor, Bureau of Labor Statistics = *BLS*
Occupational Outlook Handbook, 2008–2009 = *OOH*
America's Career InfoNet (Online) = *AIN*
O*NET (Online) = *NET*

Resources

- **American Anthropological Association**
  4350 North Fairfax Drive, Suite 640
  Arlington, VA 22203-1620
  703-528-1902
  http://www.aaanet.org
  (provides information on careers in anthropology, publishes a career brochure; see sections on jobs, careers, and student resources

- **Society for Applied Anthropology**
  PO Box 2436
  Oklahoma City, OK 73101-2436
  405-843-5113
  http://www.sfaa.net
  (provides job opportunity information, student membership, and other helpful assistance)

Architecture

Architectural study includes design, construction, and development of both physical structures and elements of the natural environment. It exposes you to the combined skills of creative aesthetics and practical function. The field of architecture involves planning layout, drawing, research, design, making modifications, selecting materials and equipment, estimating time requirements and costs, determining specifications, supervising inspecting, and writing reports. The results of architectural design are evident in houses, churches, office buildings, hospitals, airports, bridges, highways, parkways, recreational facilities, and community developments. Landscape architecture, naval architecture, design theory, preservation, and health care facility design are a few of the major specialties in this area.

High School Courses

Algebra	Drafting
Architectural Drawing	Drawing
Art Interior	Geometry
Blueprint Reading	Math
Calculus	Physics
Chemistry	Sculpture
Computer Graphics	Trigonometry
Decorating	

Related Majors

Cartography	Landscape Architecture
Civil Engineering	Naval Architecture
Environmental Design	Solar Design
Graphic Design	Structural Engineering
Industrial Design	Urban Planning
Interior Design	

Related Occupations

See page 11 for detailed explanation of key.

Aeronautical Drafters—AA	Educator—B/M/D
Architect—B/M	Graphic Designer—AA
Architectural Drafter—AA	Illustrator—V
Architectural Technician—AA	Industrial Designer—V
Building Contractor—V	Interior Designer—V
Cartographer—B	Landscape Architect—V
Civil Engineer—B	Model Maker—V
Civil Engineering Technician—AA	Structural Engineer—B
Commercial Artist—AA/B	Surveyor—AA
Computer Graphics Technician—AA	Technical Illustrator—AA

Contractor Administrator—B Technical Photographer—AA/B
Design/Building Specialist—V Technical Writer—B
Drafter—AA Urban Planner—V/M

Leisure Activities

- Taking art classes
- Drawing and sketching
- Developing hobbies related to building models
- Working part time or as a volunteer on a construction project or in an architectural firm
- Joining an architecture-related organization such as the American Institute of Architects
- Reading architecture publications
- Doing jigsaw puzzles and playing games of strategy
- Designing house furniture and landscapes
- Taking elective courses in geometry, mechanical drawing, and blueprint reading
- Attending architecture-related lectures, workshops, trade shows, or conventions
- Serving as a student aide in a high school or college architecture department

Skills

- Aptitude for accuracy and detail
- Ability to apply complex mathematical and engineering concepts to practical, real-life problems
- Strong spatial and form perception
- Ability to work with others as well as alone for long periods of time
- Ability to make keen observations and appropriate decisions
- Aptitude for drawing and sketching
- Ability to recognize differences in shapes, shading, and color
- Intellectual capacity to perform well in most undergraduate or graduate college programs
- Ability to work under pressure and meet deadlines
- Aptitude for math
- Ability to communicate ideas both orally and in writing
- Ability to conduct and clearly explain scientific research
- Proficiency with computers

Values and Attributes

- Creativity
- Achievement
- Desire for recognition and appreciation from others
- Aesthetic awareness
- Ability to adapt to fluctuations and deadlines
- Ability to accept public scrutiny and criticism
- Analytical thought
- Imagination
- Artistic nature
- Practical mind
- Perseverance

Resources

- Piper, Robert, J. *Opportunities in Architecture Careers*. New York, NY: McGraw-Hill, 2006.
- **American Institute of Architects**
  1735 New York Avenue NW
  Washington, DC 20006-5292
  202-626-7300
  http://www.aia.org
  (provides information about accredited schools, job placement service, internships, and career development)
- **Association of Collegiate Schools of Architecture**
  1735 New York Avenue NW
  Washington, DC 20006
  202-785-2324
  http://www.acsa-arch.org
  (sponsors student design competitions; publishes a brochure of architecture schools and information for prospective students)
- **National Architectural Accrediting Board**
  1735 New York Avenue NW
  Washington, DC 20006
  202-783-2007
  http://www.naab.org/index.htm
  (provides list of accredited programs in the United States)

HELPFUL INFORMATION
*Architects
Growth Outlook (2006–2016)

Projected: Grow faster than the average (increase 14% to 20%)
Number Employed (2006): 132,000   **(By 2016)** 155,000 (+18%)
Salary Range (2006): $39,420–$104,970
Related Occupations: *AIN*

	SALARY RANGE:
Landscape Architects	$34,200–$95,400
*Construction Managers	$43,200–$135,800
*Civil Engineers	$44,800–$104,400
*Urban and Regional Planners	$35,600–$86,900

*According to the BLS, workers in these occupations are currently in high demand and thus have been designated as "In Demand."

SOURCE CODE(S):
Department of Labor, Bureau of Labor Statistics = *BLS*
Occupational Outlook Handbook, 2008–2009 = *OOH*
America's Career InfoNet (Online) = *AIN*
O*NET (Online) = *NET*

Art

Art is the study of the various creative visual ways to express human thoughts, interests, attitudes, emotions, and ideas. It includes both fine art and commercial art. Fine art includes painting and drawing, sculpture, photography, printmaking, and crafts, such as ceramics, weaving, textile design, fashion design, jewelry design, interior decorating, and metalsmithing. Commercial art includes advertising and publishing and encompasses design, illustration, film, videography, and TV and the making of murals, cards, and posters. Art history, art education, art therapy, journalism, and public relations are other key areas of concentration.

High School Courses

Art	Painting
Art History	Photography
Computer Graphics	Pottery
Crafts	Sketching
Drawing	Watercolors
Jewelry Design	

Related Majors

Advertising	Graphic Design
Architecture	Industrial Design
Art Education	Interior Design
Art History	Medical Illustration
Art Therapy	Photography
Cinematography	Studio Art
Commercial Art	

Related Occupations

See page 11 for detailed explanation of key.

Antique Dealer—V	Fine Artist—B
Architect—B/M	Film Producer—B
Archivist—B	Freelance Artist—AA
Art Appraiser—B	Graphic Designer—AA/B
Art Director—B	Industrial Designer—V
Art Therapist—B/M	Jeweler—AA/V
Cartoonist—AA/V	Medical/Scientific Illustrator—B
Cinematographer—V/B	Model Maker—V
Computer Animator—AA	Motion Picture Photographer—V
Curator—M/D	Multimedia Artist—V
Craft Artist—V	Painter—V/B
Designer—V/B	Photojournalist—AA/B

Educator—B/M/D	Sculptor—V
Fashion Illustrator—AA	Sign Painter—V
Film Editor—AA	TV Director—V/B

Leisure Activities

- Entering art contests
- Working part time or volunteering in an art studio, museum, or advertising agency
- Collecting art, jewelry, or crafts
- Working as a photographer or artist for a school newspaper
- Attending art shows, festivals, and art exhibits
- Collecting antiques
- Developing skills in weaving, sculpture, macramé, furniture restoration, or photography
- Freelance drawing and painting
- Sewing, knitting, and crocheting
- Making and editing movies
- Helping to develop advertising material for local community service organizations and other groups

Skills

- Proficiency for accuracy and detail
- Ability to concentrate intensely for long periods
- Ability to communicate ideas and emotions creatively

HELPFUL INFORMATION
Multimedia Artists
Growth Outlook (2006–2016)

Projected: Grow faster than the average (increase 14% to 20%)
Number Employed (2006): 87,000   **(By 2016)** 110,000 (+26%)
Salary Range (2006): $30,390–$92,720
Related Occupations: AIN

	SALARY RANGE:
Art Directors	$37,920–$135,090
Craft Artists	$14,130–$46,700
Fine Artists	$18,350–$79,390

*According to the BLS, workers in these occupations are currently in high demand and thus have been designated as "In Demand."

SOURCE CODE(S):
Department of Labor, Bureau of Labor Statistics = BLS
Occupational Outlook Handbook, 2008–2009 = OOH
America's Career InfoNet (Online) = AIN
O*NET (Online) = NET

- Ability to recognize difference in shapes, shading, and color
- Familiarity with computer-aided design (CAD) techniques
- Aptitude for spatial relationships
- Ability to meet deadlines
- Good finger and manual dexterity
- Ability to make keen observations and appropriate decisions

Values and Attributes

- Aesthetic awareness
- Independence
- Self-expression and personal fulfillment
- Desire to influence others
- Creativity
- Feel for design and form
- Ability to adjust to creative ups and downs
- Ability to adjust to close public scrutiny and criticism
- Imagination
- Curiosity
- Patience
- Perseverance
- Dedication
- Flexibility
- Self-discipline

Resources

- Clark, Richard R, Pamela Fehl, and Brad Holland. *Career Opportunities in the Visual Arts*. New York, NY. Facts On File, Inc., 2006.
- **Americans for the Arts**
  1000 Vermont Avenue NW, 12th Floor
  Washington, DC 20005
  202-371-2830
  http://www.americansforthearts.org
  (serves as a clearinghouse; advocates for creating opportunities for every American to participate in and appreciate all forms of art)
- **National Art Education Association**
  1916 Association Drive
  Reston, VA 20191-1590
  703-860-8000
  http://www.naea-reston.org
  (offers general information on arts study)

Astronomy

Astronomy, a branch of the physical sciences, is the study of our universe: its origin, its physical properties, its changes, and the distribution of its physical phenomena. An astronomer observes the planets, sun, solar system, and galaxies and then analyzes, interprets, and reports the findings. Astronomy is closely related to mathematics and is usually considered a subdivision of physics.

High School Courses

Algebra	Geometry
Calculus	Math
Chemistry	Physical Science
Computer Applications	Physics
Computer Science	Science
Earth Science	Trigonometry

Related Majors

Aeronautical Engineering	Electrical/Electronic Engineering
Aerospace Engineering	Geology
Astrophysics	Geophysics
Chemistry	Meteorology
Computer Science	Physical Science
Earth Science	Physics

Related Occupations

See page 11 for detailed explanation of key.

Acoustical Engineer—V	Geologist—V
Acoustical Physicist—B	Geophysicist—B/D
Aerospace Engineer—B/D	Mathematician—B/D
Aerospace Engineering Technician—AA	Metallurgical Engineer—B
	Meteorologist—V/D
Astronomer—D	Mineralogist—B/D
Astrophysicist—B/D	Oceanographer—B/D
Biophysicist—B/D	Optical Physicist—B
Cartographer—B	Radiographer—V
Computer Programmer—B	Research Technician—AA
Educator—B/M/D	Seismologist—V
Electrical/Electronics Engineer—B	Systems Analyst—B

Leisure Activities

- Visiting planetariums, observatories, and science museums
- Involvement in outdoor activities
- Attending science fairs and exhibits
- Joining a photography club, the American Association of Amateur Astronomers, or another astronomy club
- Watching TV programs on natural science
- Doing lab experiments and projects
- Reading astronomy or science publications
- Working part time or as a volunteer in a planetarium, observatory, campus astronomy department, or weather station
- Operating a ham radio
- Computer programming
- Repairing radios/TVs

Skills

- Ability to analyze and solve quantitative problems and make appropriate decisions
- Proficiency in reading, writing, speaking, and memorization
- Ability to concentrate for long periods of time
- Aptitude for accuracy and detail
- Acute spatial and form perception

- Proficiency in mathematics
- Intellectual capacity to perform well in most undergraduate and graduate college programs
- Ability to conduct and clearly explain scientific research
- Good vision, finger dexterity, and mechanical ability
- Proficiency with computers
- Ability to make keen observations

Values and Attributes

- Achievement
- Independence
- Intellectual growth
- Recognition
- Analytical and logical thinking
- Intellectual curiosity about the atmosphere, space, and universal phenomena
- Fondness for physics and mathematics
- Imagination
- Self-discipline
- Perseverance
- Patience
- Precision

Resources

- **American Association of Amateur Astronomers**
  PO Box 7981
  Dallas, TX 75209-0981
  http://www.astromax.com
  (see the Web site's FAQ section to read the online article, "Career Profile: Astronomy.")
- **American Astronomical Society**
  2000 Florida Avenue, Suite 400
  Washington, DC 20009-1231
  202-328-2010
  http://www.aas.org
  (maintains job register, has a résumé posting service, and publishes a career brochure)
- **Astronomical League**
  9201 Ward Parkway, Suite 100
  Kansas City, MD 64114
  937-678-5032
  http://www.astroleague.org
  (composed of 250 amateur astronomical societies; encourages amateur astronomy)

Banking and Finance

Banking and finance is a major field in business that involves the study of how money is stored, protected, received, distributed, and generally managed. Banking and finance is a broad area and overlaps with a number of more specialized fields, such as securities and insurance. Study in this area focuses on methods of deposits and withdrawals, checking and savings accounts, loans, interest rates, credit, trusts, investments, accounting procedures, budgets and financing, and securities. Areas of specialization are numerous and include savings and loans, checking, customer service, clerical, accounting, credit cards, computer systems, research, budget, expenditures and cost analysis, supervision and administration, trust services, and securities.

High School Courses

Accounting	Consumer Math
Bookkeeping	Economics
Business Math	Introduction to Business
Computer Applications	Math
Computer Programming	

Related Majors

Accounting	Economics
Actuarial Science	Financial Planning
Business	Insurance and Risk Management
Business Economics	International Business
Business Management	Management Information Systems
Computer Programming	Mathematics
Computer Science	Statistics

Related Occupations

See page 11 for detailed explanation of key.

Accountant—B	Educator—B/M/D
Account Executive—B	Financial Aid Officer—B
Actuary—B	Financial Analyst—B
Advertising Manager—V	Financial Planner—B
Appraiser/Assessor—B	Insurance Agent—V/B
Bank Economist—B/D	Internal Auditor—B
Bank Teller—V	International Banking Officer—B
Branch Manager—B	Investment Banker—B
Budget Analyst—B	Loan Officer—B
Computer Programmer—B	Securities Clerk—AA/V

Controller-Accountant—B	Statistician—B
Correspondent Banking Officer—B	Stockbroker—B
Cost Accountant—B	Systems Analyst—B
Credit Analyst—AA/B	Treasurer—B
Credit Manager—AA/B	Trust Administrator—V

Leisure Activities

- Working as a part time or volunteer treasurer or tax preparer
- Sitting on a financial advisory board
- Reading publications related to banking and finance
- Attending finance-related lectures, workshops, or conventions
- Participating in investment activities (real or virtual)
- Solving problems involving analytical and logical processes
- Joining a professional organization such as the American Bankers Association
- Working part time in a bank, savings and loan agency, or credit union
- Serving as a student aide in an accounting or business department

Skills

- Ability to organize, analyze, and interpret numerical data
- Aptitude for accuracy and detail
- Ability to make sound judgments and decisions and to solve quantitative problems

---

HELPFUL INFORMATION
*Financial Managers
Growth Outlook (2006–2016)

Projected: Grow about as fast as the average (increase 7% to 13%)
Number Employed (2006): 506,000   **(By 2016)** 570,000 (+13%)
Salary Range (2006): $50,00–$145,000
Related Occupations: *AIN*

	SALARY RANGE:
*Accountants	$34,500–$94,100
*Financial Analysts	$40,400–$130,100
*Budget Analysts	$40,100–$93,100
*Loan Officers	$29,600–$107,000

*According to the BLS, workers in these occupations are currently in high demand and thus have been designated as "In Demand."

SOURCE CODE(S):
Department of Labor, Bureau of Labor Statistics = BLS
Occupational Outlook Handbook, 2008–2009 = *OOH*
America's Career InfoNet (Online) = *AIN*
O*NET (Online) = *NET*

- Ability to explain complex financial transactions and data to others
- Proficiency with computers
- Proficiency in written and oral communication
- Ability to communicate and get along with people of different personalities and backgrounds
- Knowledge of financial and economic history, practices, and trends

Values and Attributes

- Wealth
- Recognition and appreciation from others
- Achievement
- Good eyesight and emotional well-being
- Tendency to be organized, confident, and businesslike
- Ability to handle money
- Interest in working with both people and data
- Integrity
- Alertness
- Ambition
- Discretion
- Trustworthiness

Resources

- **American Bankers Association**
  1120 Connecticut Avenue NW
  Washington, DC 20036
  800-226-5377
  http://www.aba.com
  (sponsors job résumé bank and online courses)
- **Association for Financial Professionals**
  7315 Wisconsin Avenue, Suite 600 West
  Bethesda, MD 20814
  301-907-2862
  http://www.afponline.org
  (has information on careers, certification, and industry news)
- **Credit Union National Association**
  PO Box 431
  Madison, WI 53701-0431
  800-356-9655
  http://www.cuna.org
  (offers training assistance; see Self-Study Certificate Programs in the Services section of the Web site)

Biology

Biology is the study of life, from the simplest forms of plants and animals (including one-celled animals and algae) to the highly complex structure of the human being. It includes the study of how organisms are structured as well as how they function and relate to each other. Among the major branches of biology are human anatomy and physiology, botany (the study of plants), microbiology (the study of microscopic organisms), zoology (the study of animals), and ecology (the study of the relationship between organisms and the environment). You may elect to concentrate in one or more of the subdivisions.

High School Courses

Algebra	Health
Biology	Physiology
Chemistry	Science
Computer Applications	Trigonometry
Earth Science	Zoology

Related Majors

Agriculture	Genetics
Biochemistry	Horticulture
Biophysics	Marine Biology
Botany	Medicine
Chemistry	Microbiology
Environmental Science	Molecular Biology
Forestry	Zoology

Related Occupations

See page 11 for detailed explanation of key.

Biochemist—B/D	Microbiologist—B/D
Bioinformatics Scientist—B/D	Mycologist—D
Biologist—B/D	Nutritionist—B
Botanist—B/D	Occupational Therapist—B
Dietitian—B	Paramedic—AA
Ecologist—B/D	Parasitologist—B/D
Educator—B/M/D	Physical Therapist—B
Florist—V	Physician—P
Food Scientist—B	Physiologist—D
Forester—B	Public Health Director—B
Funeral Director—AA/B	Research Assistant—B/M
Geneticist—B/D	Respiratory Therapist—AA

Horticulturist—B/D   Taxonomist—B

Medical/Scientific Illustrator—B   Veterinarian—P

Medical Lab Technician—AA   Zoologist—B/D

Medical Librarian—M/D

Leisure Activities

- Attending science exhibits, county and state fairs, and 4-H shows
- Participating in Camp Fire Girls, Bluebirds, or Scouts
- Belonging to an environmental group, the Humane Society, a health club, or a community social group
- Browsing in floral shops or nature centers
- Working part time or as a volunteer in a greenhouse or nursery
- YMCA/YWCA involvement
- Hiking, fishing, trapping, backpacking, or gardening
- Visiting zoos or museums
- Owning or caring for pets
- Reading science magazines, books, and other related publications
- Performing lab experiments
- Taking nature walks
- Bird-watching
- Developing hobbies or collections related to leaves, butterflies, trees, flowers, or other natural items

Skills

- Ability to concentrate for long periods of time
- Ability to make keen observations and appropriate decisions
- Proficiency in reading, writing, thinking, questioning, analyzing, and problem solving
- Ability to operate scientific equipment
- Intellectual capacity to perform well in most undergraduate and graduate college programs
- Proficiency for accuracy and detail
- Ability to organize and maintain accurate records
- Proficiency in speaking and memorization
- Ability to conduct and clearly explain scientific research
- Good vision and manual dexterity
- Thorough knowledge of basic biological theories and practices

Values and Attributes

- Achievement
- Creativity
- Desire to help humanity
- Intellectual growth
- Precision
- Enthusiasm for exploring

- Spirit of scientific inquiry
- Strong interest in living organisms
- Diligence
- Endurance
- Interest in challenges
- Patience
- Perseverance

Resources

- **American Institute of Biological Sciences**
  Communications Office
  1444 Eye Street NW, Suite 200
  Washington, DC 20005
  202-628-1500
  http://www.aibs.org
  (offers student membership, outreach programs and publishes *Guide to Non-Traditional Careers in Science*)
- **American Society for Microbiology**
  1752 N Street NW
  Washington, DC 20036
  202-737-3600
  http://www.asmusa.org
  (offers job search assistance as well as information for minorities and women)

Botany

Botany is a major branch of the biological sciences and involves the study of plants. Plant groups typically included are bacteria, algae, fungi, lichens, mosses, ferns, conifers, and flowering plants. Botany focuses on plant growth, structure, function, classification, distribution, and reproduction. Within the field of botany are a number of specialized areas, including morphology (microscopic and macroscopic plant structure), horticulture (the cultivation of ornamental plants and fruit and vegetable crops), and forestry. Plant habitat and the relationship of plants to humans and to our general environment are other important areas of botanical study.

High School Courses

Algebra	Landscape Gardening
Biology	Math
Chemistry	Physiology
Computer Applications	Science
Earth Science	Trigonometry

Related Majors

Agriculture	Economic Botany
Agronomy	Food Science and Technology
Biochemistry	Forestry
Biology	Horticulture
Biophysics	Landscape Architecture
Biotechnology	Molecular Biology
Chemistry	Plant Science

Related Occupations

See page 11 for detailed explanation of key.

Agronomist—B/D	Food Service Technician—AA/B
Bacteriologist—B/D	Groundskeeper—V
Biochemist—B/D	Horticulturist—B/D
Botanist—B/D	Landscape Gardener—AA
Cooperative Extension Worker—B	Mycologist—D
Curator—M/D	Nursery Manager—V
Cytologist—B/D	Nutritionist—V
Dietitian—B	Phycologist—M/D
Ecologist—B/D	Plant Breeder—V
Educator—B/M/D	Range Manager—AA/B
Farmer—V/B	Seed Analyst—B
Farm/Ranch Manager—B/V	Soil Scientist—B/D
Florist—V	Taxonomist—B

Food Scientist—B/D Virologist—M/D

Forester—B Wood Technologist—B

Geneticist—B/D

Leisure Activities

- Visiting nature centers, botanical gardens, conservatories, farms, parks, and museums
- Attending flower shows and fairs
- Browsing through floral shops, 4-H exhibits, and science displays
- Hiking, exploring, camping, sightseeing, and nature photography
- Gardening, canning, and freezing foods
- Sailing, canoeing, and swimming
- Developing hobbies and collections related to flowers, leaves, house plants, or floral design
- Working part time or as a volunteer in a greenhouse, nursery, state park, or camp
- Joining a science club, orchid club, or conservation group
- Reading science publications
- Supporting or participating in natural resource preservation efforts
- Undertaking nature studies or rural expeditions

Skills

- Proficiency in observing, collecting, and analyzing data
- Physical stamina, good vision, and manual dexterity
- Ability to concentrate for long periods of time
- Proficiency in reading, writing, speaking, and memorization
- Ability to conduct and clearly explain scientific research
- Proficiency for accuracy and detail
- Intellectual ability to perform well in most undergraduate or graduate college programs
- Proficiency in problem solving and decision making
- Thorough knowledge of general biology

Values and Attributes

- Aesthetic awareness
- Independence
- Intellectual growth
- Interest in public health and safety
- Fondness for outdoor activities
- Deep appreciation for nature
- Green thumb
- Thoroughness
- Perseverance
- Patience
- Curiosity

Resources

■ **American Society for Horticultural Science**
113 South West Street, Suite 200
Alexandria, VA 22314-2851
703-836-4606
http://www.ashs.org
(offers student membership job search assistance, career information, and
much more)

■ **Botanical Society of America**
Attn: Business Manager
P.O. Box 299
St. Louis, MO 63166-0299
614-292-3519
http://www.botany.org
(Provides an extensive list of resources; see Careeer Opportunities link)

Business Administration and Management

The field of business administration and management involves the coordination, implementation, promotion, supervision, and direction of the activities of individuals, organizations, and businesses. Effective techniques of business management constitute the backbone of strong economic, political, and social systems at all levels. Study in this major exposes you to methods of operation, coordination, sales and marketing, finance and budget, personnel, property and equipment management/maintenance, and security. Other key areas of concentration are organization, leadership, planning, interpersonal communications, delegating, supervising community resources, employee organizations, and policy making/implementation.

High School Courses

Accounting	Management
Business	Marketing
Business Law	Psychology
Computer Applications	Sociology
Economics	Speech
Entreprenuership	

Related Majors

Accounting	International Business
Business Communications	Labor/Personnel Relations
Business Education	Management Information
Entrepreneurship	Marketing
Finance and Banking	Operations Management and
Human Resources Management	Supervision

Related Occupations

See page 11 for detailed explanation of key.

Accountant—B/M	Hotel/Motel Manager—V/B
Advertising Executive—B	Human Resources Manager—B
Airport Manager—B	Production Superintendent—B
Chamber of Commerce President—B	Public Relations Specialist—B
Chief Executive Officer—B	Recreation Director—B

City Manager—B	Restaurant Manager—AA/V
College Dean—M/D	Sales Manager—V
Comptroller—B/M	School Administrator—M/D
Consultant—B/D	Traffic Manager—V
Convention Manager—B	TV Director—V
Database Manager—B	Warehouse Manager—AA/V
Department Store Manager—B	Wholesaler—B
Director of Career Placement—B/M	YMCA/YWCA Director—B
Director of Food Services—B	

Leisure Activities

- Working part time in a local business establishment
- Participating in oratory contests
- Planning, starting, or managing a part time business endeavor
- Assisting in the planning of a civic or social event
- Playing games of strategy, competition, or achievement
- Attending lectures, workshops, and conferences related to business management
- Serving as a student aide in a college business department
- Participating in a management training program
- Serving as a volunteer in a social agency
- Belonging to a Junior Achievement Club or a professional business organization

Skills

- Ability to clearly communicate ideas and concepts to others
- Proficiency in reading, writing, and speaking
- Ability to solve problems and make appropriate decisions
- Strong background in business, marketing, and human relations
- Proficiency in organizing, planning, coordinating, and directing activities
- Ability to inspire productivity and exact loyalty from others
- Ability to respond spontaneously and work well under pressure
- Intellectual capacity to perform well in most undergraduate and graduate college programs
- Aptitude for leadership
- Proficiency in interpersonal communication
- Proficiency with computers

Values and Attributes

- Achievement
- Wealth
- Prestige
- Willingness to work beyond expectations
- Tendency to be responsible, show initiative, and exercise patience
- Leadership
- Decisiveness
- Resourcefulness
- Diplomacy

- Integrity
- Ambition

Resources

- **American Management Association**
  1601 Broadway
  New York, NY 10019
  212-586-8100
  http://www.amanet.org
  (offers an array of helpful information)
- **Junior Achievement**
  One Education Way
  Colorado Springs, CO 80906
  719-540-8000
  http://www.ja.org
  (nonprofit organization that teaches young people about business, free enterprise, and the workforce)
- **U.S. Small Business Administration**
  409 Third Street SW
  Washington, DC 20416
  800-U-ASK-SBA
  http://www.sbaonline.sba.gov
  (Web site has information on starting your own business and much more)

HELPFUL INFORMATION
*Advertising and Promotion Managers
Growth Outlook (2006–2016)

Projected: Grow about as fast as the average (increase 7% to 13%)
Number Employed (2006): 47,000   **(By 2016)** 50,000 (+16%)
Salary Range (2006): $36,200–$145,600
Related Occupations: *AIN*

	SALARY RANGE:
Administrative Services Managers	$35,000–$117,600
Chief Executives	$62,000–$145,600
Educational Administrators Postsecondary	$41,100–$137,900
*Food Services Managers	$27,400–$70,800

*According to the BLS, workers in these occupations are currently in high
demand and thus have been designated as "In Demand."

SOURCE CODE(S):
Department of Labor, Bureau of Labor Statistics = *BLS*
Occupational Outlook Handbook, 2008–2009 = *OOH*
America's Career InfoNet (Online) = *AIN*
O*NET (Online) = *NET*

Chemical Engineering

Chemical engineering is the the practical application of science and mathematics in the process, manufacture, equipment design, and development related to raw and synthetic substances and energy in an economical and efficient manner. It contributes to the development of products that affect nearly every aspect of life, including foods, fuels, drugs, plastics, glass, soaps, paints, paper, and much more. Areas of special concentration include plastics, petroleum, research and development, environmental control, food, energy, pharmaceuticals, and education.

High School Courses

Algebra	Geometry
Calculus	Math
Chemistry	Physical Science
Computer Applications	Physics
Computer Science	Science
Earth Science	Trigonometry

Related Majors

Agronomy	Material Engineering
Chemistry	Mathematics
Electrical Engineering	Metallurgical Engineering
Engineering Physics	Mining/Mineral Engineering
Environmental Engineering	Petroleum Engineering
Food Science	Pharmacy

Related Occupations

See page 11 for detailed explanation of key.

Agricultural Engineer—B	Food Scientist—B
Agronomist—B	Geological Engineer—B
Biochemist—B/D	Materials Handling Engineer—B
Ceramic Engineer—B	Metallurgical Engineer—B
Chemical Engineer—B	Metallurgist—B
Chemical Technician—AA	Nuclear Engineer—B/D
Chemical Research Engineer—B/D	Petroleum Engineer—B
Chemist—B/D	Pharmacist—B
Computer Science Engineer—B	Pharmacologist—D
Consulting Engineer—B/M/D	Plastics Engineer—B
Electrical Engineer—B	Safety Engineer—B
Environmental Engineer—B	Textile Engineer—B
Fire Protection Engineer—V	Toxicologist—B/D

Leisure Activities

- Performing lab experiments and doing science projects
- Attending science fairs, exhibits, and demonstrations
- Reading publications related to chemistry or engineering
- Working part time or as a volunteer in a hospital, chemistry lab, engineering firm, science department, or pharmaceutical firm
- Joining a chemistry or engineering club or organization

Skills

- High proficiency in mathematics and physical sciences
- Ability to analyze, organize, and interpret scientific data
- Ability to work well with others
- Ability to make keen observations and sound judgments
- Aptitude for accuracy and detail, spatial perception, and abstract reasoning
- Sensitivity to economic considerations and human needs
- Proficiency in an area of specialization and knowledgeable of current practices and trends
- Ability to conduct and clearly communicate scientific research
- Intellectual capacity to perform well in most undergraduate and graduate college programs
- Proficiency with computers

HELPFUL INFORMATION
*Chemical Engineers
Growth Outlook (2006–2016)

Projected: Grow about as fast as the average (increase 7% to 13%)
Number Employed (2006): 47,000 **(By 2016)** 50,000 (+16%)
Salary Range (2006): $36,200–$145,600
Related Occupations: AIN

	SALARY RANGE:
Materials Engineers	$46,120–$112,140
Petroleum Engineers	$57,960–$145,600
*Electrical Engineers	$49,120–$115,240
*Biomedical Engineers	$44,930–$116,330

*According to the BLS, workers in these occupations are currently in high demand and thus have been designated as "In Demand."

SOURCE CODE(S):
Department of Labor, Bureau of Labor Statistics = BLS
Occupational Outlook Handbook, 2008–2009 = OOH
America's Career InfoNet (Online) = AIN
O*NET (Online) = NET

Values and Attributes

- Creativity
- Achievement
- Knowledge
- Desire to help others live better
- Sensitivity to the health and safety of others
- Desire to see ideas developed into practical use
- Curiosity
- Integrity
- Perseverance
- Responsibility
- Imagination

Resources

- **American Chemical Society**

  1155 16th Street NW

  Washington, DC 20036

  800-227-5558

  http://www.acs.org

  (offers career guidance, counseling, and employment help; see the Career and Jobs link on the Web site)

- **American Institute of Chemical Engineers**

  3 Park Avenue

  New York, NY 10016-5991

  800-242-4363

  http://www.aiche.org

  (offers student membership, internships, career-related information, and related links)

- **Junior Engineering Technical Society**

  1420 King Street, Suite 405

  Alexandria, VA 22314

  703-548-5387

  http://www.jets.org

  (sponsors activities geared to assist students to determine engineering readiness, special outreach to minorities, information about careers, helpful links, etc.)

Chemistry

Chemistry is a major branch of the physical sciences and involves the study of substances and energy. It focuses on their composition, characteristics, changes, reactions, uses, and benefits and dangers to humanity. Major sub-branches within chemistry include inorganic and organic chemistry, analytical chemistry, applied chemistry, biochemistry, and physical chemistry. Chemistry is used to produce food, clothing, furniture, drugs, plastics, glass, paper, and electronic devices. Knowledge of chemistry is crucial to environmental protection efforts and human health and safety.

High School Courses

Algebra	Foods
Calculus	Geometry
Chemistry	Math
Computer Applications	Physical Science
Cooking	Science
Earth Science	Trigonometry

Related Majors

Agriculture	Food Science
Biochemistry	Mathematics
Chemical Engineering	Medicine
Chemistry Education	Pharmacy
Dietetics	Toxicology

Related Occupations

See page 11 for detailed explanation of key.

Agronomist—B/D	Internist—P
Anesthesiologist—B	Laboratory Analyst—B
Biochemist—B/D	Metallurgist—B
Ceramic Engineer—B	Nuclear Scientist—B/D
Chemical Engineer—B	Nutritionist—B
Chemist—B/D	Patent Examiner—B/P
Consumer Protection Specialist—B	Pharmacist—B
Dietitian—B	Pharmacologist—D
Educator—B/M/D	Pharmaceutical Sales Representative—B
Food and Drug Analyst—B	Physicist—B/D
Food Scientist—B	Science Technician—AA
Geneticist—B/D	Technical Writer—B
Geologist—B	Toxicologist—B/D
Industrial Health Engineer—B	Wood Scientist—D

Leisure Activities

- Performing lab experiments and doing science projects
- Attending science fairs, exhibits, and demonstrations
- Reading chemistry and science journals
- Cooking
- Watching scientific TV programs
- Working part time or as a volunteer in a hospital, chemistry lab, or pharmaceutical firm
- Joining a chemistry or science club

Skills

- Good vision and manual dexterity
- Ability to conduct and clearly explain scientific research
- Aptitude for accuracy and detail
- Ability to organize, analyze, and interpret scientific data
- Proficiency in reading, writing, speaking, and memorization
- Ability to make keen observations and appropriate decisions
- Strong mathematical background
- Intellectual capacity to perform well in most undergraduate and graduate college programs
- Proficiency with computers

HELPFUL INFORMATION
*Chemists
Growth Outlook (2006–2016)

Projected: Grow about as fast as the average (increase 7% to 13%)
Number Employed (2006): 47,000   **(By 2016)** 50,000 (+16%)
Salary Range (2006): $36,200–$145,600+
Related Occupations: *AIN*

	SALARY RANGE:
*Chemical Engineers	$50,100–$118,700
Chemistry Teachers	$36,200–$116,900
*Biochemists and Biophysicists	$40,800–$129,500
Food Scientists and Technologists	$29,600–$97,300

*According to the BLS, workers in these occupations are currently in high demand and thus have been designated as "In Demand."

SOURCE CODE(S):
Department of Labor, Bureau of Labor Statistics = *BLS*
Occupational Outlook Handbook, 2008–2009 = *OOH*
America's Career InfoNet (Online) = *AIN*
O*NET (Online) = *NET*

Values and Attributes

- Achievement
- Intellectual growth
- Public recognition
- Desire to help humanity
- Willingness to take risks
- Pleasure in learning new skills
- Sensitivity to the health and safety of others
- Patience
- Curiosity
- Integrity
- Flexibility
- Responsibility

Resources

- **American Chemical Society**

  1155 16th Street NW

  Washington, DC 20036

  800-227-5558

  http://www.acs.org

  (offers career guidance, counseling, and employment help; see the Career Services section of the Web site)

- **American Institute of Chemical Engineers**

  3 Park Avenue

  New York, NY 10016-5991

  800-242-4363

  http://www.aiche.org

  (offers student membership, internships, career-related information, and helpful links)

Civil Engineering

Civil engineering is the practical, economic, and efficient application of mathematical and scientific knowledge, experience, and theory in the use of material and natural resources to design and supervise the building of structures and facilities. Studies include the techniques of constructing bridges, dams, roads, railways, airports, water disposal systems, buildings, pipelines, and more. The four main areas of civil engineering are structures, transportation, sanitation, and soils. Specialties include geotechnical, environmental, transportation, hydraulic, structural, and pipeline engineering.

High School Courses

Algebra	Geometry
Architectural Design	Industrial Arts
Blueprint Reading	Math
Calculus	Physical Science
Chemistry	Physics
Computer Applications	Science
Drafting/Drawing	Trigonometry
Earth Science	

Related Majors

Architecture	Geological Engineering
Architectural Engineering	Mining and Mineral Engineering
Construction Engineering	Petroleum Engineering
Electrical Engineering	Structural Engineering
Engineering Physics	Surveying
Environmental Engineering	Transportation and Material Moving

Related Occupations

See page 11 for detailed explanation of key.

Architect—B/M	Industrial Engineer—B
Architectural Engineer—B	Mechanical Engineer—B
Civil Engineer—B	Mining Engineer—B
Civil Engineering Technician—AA	Petroleum Engineer—B
Construction Engineer—B	Photogrammetrist—B
Consulting Engineer—B/M/D	Pipeline Engineer—B
Ecologist—B	Public Works Engineer—B
Environmental Engineer—B	Research Engineer—B/D
Geological Engineer—B	Safety Engineer—B
Geologist—B	Sanitary Engineer—B

Geotechnical Engineer—B Structural Engineer—B
Highway Engineer—B Transportation Engineer—B
Hydraulics Engineer—B Urban Planner—B/M
Hydrologist—B

Leisure Activities

- Participating in clubs or organizations that require you to make oral presentations and write reports
- Doing jigsaw puzzles and playing games of strategy
- Solving analytic and logic problems
- Reading publications related to civil engineering
- Becoming a member of a student or professional engineering organization
- Attending engineering-related lectures, workshops, or conferences
- Engaging in hobbies related to building and designing structures
- Working part time or as a volunteer with an engineering or construction firm or in a college engineering department

Skills

- Ability to analyze, organize, and interpret scientific data
- Ability to work well with others
- Ability to make appropriate decisions and solve problems
- Ability to make keen observations and sound judgments
- Aptitude for accuracy and detail
- Proficiency in mathematics and science
- Proficiency in spatial perception and abstract reasoning
- Sensitivity to economic considerations and human needs
- Proficiency in an area of specialization and knowledge of current practices and trends
- Proficiency in written and oral communication
- Ability to conduct and clearly communicate scientific research
- Intellectual capacity to perform well in most undergraduate and graduate college programs
- Proficiency with computers

Values and Attributes

- Creativity
- Knowledge
- Desire to help others live better
- Achievement
- Ability to work on a team
- Enjoyment of challenges and the outdoors
- Interest in seeing ideas developed into practical uses
- Interest in moving from place to place
- Curiosity
- Alertness

- Flexibility
- Patience
- Responsibility
- Imagination

Resources

- **American Society of Civil Engineers**
  1801 Alexander Bell Drive
  Reston, VA 20191-4400
  800-548-2723
  http://www.asce.org
  (offers student career development service and student membership, see the Kids & Careers link)
- **Junior Engineering Technical Society**
  1420 King Street, Suite 405
  Alexandria, VA 22314
  703-548-5387
  http://www.jets.org
  (sponsors activities geared to assist students to determine engineering readiness, special outreach to minorities, information about careers, helpful links, etc.)

Communications

Communications is the branch of language arts that focuses on the comprehensive expression of sound and visual, oral, and written symbols. Study in communications is geared toward understanding the many ways human beings develop, collect, disseminate, and transfer information through symbols, particularly via the mass media. Also included are the various ways that communication informs, persuades, entertains, and controls. Communication is involved in almost everything we do and ranges from the simplest nonverbal communication efforts to the complex electronic messages of computers. Major areas of specialization include print and broadcast journalism, film, graphic design, television and radio production, multimedia design, and advertising.

High School Courses

Advertising	Journalism
Computer-Aided Design (CAD)	Speech
Computer Applications	Technical English
Debate	Theater
Drama	Writing
English	

Related Majors

Advertising	Journalism
Art	Photographic Technologies
Broadcast Journalism	Public Relations
Communications Technologies	Radio and Television Broadcasting
Computer Graphics	Speech Communications
English	Telecommunications
Film	Writing

Related Occupations

See page 11 for detailed explanation of key.

Account Executive—B	Lecturer—B
Actor/Actress—V/B	Lobbyist—B
Advertising Manager—B	Media Specialist—V/B
Announcer—AA/B	Marketing Manager—B/M
Arbitrator—B	News Photographer—AA/B
Auctioneer—V	Online Content Developer—B
Broadcast Technician—AA	Producer (Film, TV)—B
Columnist—B	Proofreader—V
Commentator—B	Public Relations Manager—B/M
Copy Editor—B	Publisher—B
Copywriter—B	Reporter—B

Disc Jockey—V　　　　　　　　Research Library Technician—AA
Editor—B　　　　　　　　　　Speech Writer—B
Educator—B/M/D　　　　　　　Technical Writer—B
Foreign Correspondent—B　　　TV Director—B
Journalist—B　　　　　　　　Video Engineer—V/B

Leisure Activities

- Participating in local theater productions
- Attending movies, stage productions, lectures, or readings
- Working part time or as a volunteer for a radio or TV station, printing or publishing firm, department store, or advertising agency
- Participating on a debate or forensic team
- Serving as an editor of a small newspaper, magazine, or newsletter
- Joining a yearbook staff or broadcasting or drama club
- Visiting libraries
- Competing in writing or oratory contests
- Fund-raising
- Reading professional publications
- Participating in election campaigns
- Working as a student assistant in a language arts or communications department
- Freelance writing
- Working or spending a significant amount of time communicating via the computer

Skills

- Ability to analyze, interpret, and appropriately convey physical and social events and behaviors to others
- Ability to meet deadlines and work under pressure
- Ability to read accurately and analytically
- Ability to relate to people of varying backgrounds
- Ability to respond quickly to unexpected circumstances
- Ability to solve problems and make decisions
- Background of general knowledge
- Good listening, clarifying, questioning, and responding skills
- Comprehensive command of grammar
- High proficiency in written and oral communication
- Proficiency in the use of computers

Values and Attributes

- Creativity
- Desire for recognition and to influence others
- Independence
- Intellectual growth
- Poise and composure under close public scrutiny and criticism
- Appreciation for clear and stimulating communication
- Pleasant and friendly attitude
- Imagination
- Integrity
- Self-confidence

- Tactfulness
- Versatility

Resources

- **American Advertising Federation**
  1101 Vermont Avenue NW, Suite 500
  Washington, DC 20005
  (800) 999-2251
  http://www.aaf.org
  (provides information on college chapters, competitions, and internships)
- **Broadcast Education Association**
  1771 N Street NW
  Washington, DC 20036-2891
  202-429-3935
  http://www.beaweb.org
  (provides scholarship information, a list of schools offering degrees in broadcasting, job openings and other useful information)
- **Dow Jones Newspaper Fund**
  PO Box 300
  Princeton, NJ 08543-0300
  609-452-2820
  http://djnewspaperfund.dowjones.com/fund
  (provides information about internships and the newspaper business; see High School and College links)

HELPFUL INFORMATION
Public Relations Manager
Growth Outlook (2006–2016)

Projected: Grow about as fast as the average (increase 7% to 13%)
Number Employed (2006): 50,000   **(By 2016)** 58,000 (+17%)
Salary Range (2006): $43,000–$145,600+
Related Occupations: *AIN*

	SALARY RANGE:
Advertising and Promotion Managers	$36,200–$145,600+
*Marketing Managers	$51,200–$145,600+
Technical Writers	$35,500–$91,700
Broadcast Technicians	$15,700–$64,900

*According to the BLS, workers in these occupations are currently in high demand and thus have been designated as "In Demand."

SOURCE CODE(S):
Department of Labor, Bureau of Labor Statistics = *BLS*
Occupational Outlook Handbook, 2008–2009 = *OOH*
America's Career InfoNet (Online) = *AIN*
O*NET (Online) = NET

Computer Science

Computer study focuses on the design, manufacture, application, and effectiveness of computers, computer materials, and computer equipment. It includes the management, analysis, and dissemination of information via computer. From tiny hand-held electronic devices to huge multiterminal computer networks, computers pervade our culture and affect nearly every aspect of our daily lives.

High School Courses

Algebra	English
Calculus	Geometry
Computer Applications	Statistics
Computer Programming	Trigonometry
Computer Science	Word Processing

Related Majors

Computer Education	Computer Technology
Computer Engineering	Consulting
Computer Graphics	Data Processing
Computer Management	Mathematics
Computer Programming	Software Engineering

Related Occupations

See page 11 for detailed explanation of key.

Chief Information Officer—B	Hardware Service Person—AA/B
Computer-Aided Designer—AA/B	Operations Manager—AA/B
Computer Animator—AA	Robotics Technician—AA
Computer Applications Engineer—B	Software Engineer—B
Computer Hardware Engineer—B	Software Package Developer—B
Computer Programmer—B	Software Package Marketer—B
Computer Science Engineer—B/M/D	Software Salesperson—AA/B
Computer Security Specialist—B	Statistician—B
Computer Support Specialist—AA	Systems Analyst—B
Database Analyst—B	Systems Consultant—B
Database Manager—B	Systems Manager—B
Data-Entry Equipment Operator—AA	Technical Support Technician—V
Data Processing Manager—B	Technical Writer—B
Educator—B/M/D	Webmaster—V
Electronic Data Processing Auditor—B	Word Processor—AA
Hardware Salesperson—AA/B	

Leisure Activities

- Working with a personal computer
- Working part time or as a volunteer in a computer store, computer firm, or computer science department
- Repairing electronic appliances and other mechanical gadgetry
- Writing, score-keeping, or practicing electronics as a hobby
- Doing puzzles and playing games of strategy
- Browsing the Internet
- Solving analytic and logic problems
- Joining a computer club or organization
- Reading computer publications

Skills

- Ability to cope with constant change
- Ability to analyze, make appropriate decisions, and solve problems
- Ability to think logically
- Ability to organize
- Proficiency in writing and speaking
- Aptitude for abstract reasoning, keen observation, and intense concentration
- Ability to work with others
- High proficiency in the understanding and use of computers

HELPFUL INFORMATION
Computer Software Engineers, Applications
Growth Outlook (2006–2016)

Projected: Grow much faster than the average (increase 21% or more)
Number Employed (2006): 507,000 **(By 2016)** 733,000 (+45%)
Salary Range (2006): $49,350–$119,770
Related Occupations: *AIN*

	SALARY RANGE:
*Computer Systems Analysts	$42,800–$106,800
*Computer Hardware Engineers	$53,900–$135,300
*Computer Support Specialists	$25,300–$68,500
*Computer Programmers	$38,500–$106,600

*According to the BLS, workers in these occupations are currently in high demand and thus have been designated as "In Demand."

SOURCE CODE(S):
Department of Labor, Bureau of Labor Statistics = *BLS*
Occupational Outlook Handbook, 2008–2009 = *OOH*
America's Career InfoNet (Online) = *AIN*
O*NET (Online) = *NET*

- Proficiency for accuracy and detail
- Computational ability (using algebra for technician areas and using calculus for computer science areas)
- Ability to work under pressure
- Ability to understand and practically apply information derived from technical manuals and related materials

Values and Attributes

- Achievement
- Continuous intellectual growth
- Curiosity and enthusiasm for gadgetry
- Sense of responsibility
- Sensitivity to multiple perspectives
- Objectivity
- Perseverance
- Creativity
- Patience
- Thoroughness

Resources

- **Association for Computing Machinery**
  2 Penn Plaza, Suite 701
  New York, NY 10121-0701
  800-342-6626
  http://www.acm.org
  (See Career & Job Center link)
- **IEEE Computer Society**
  1828 L Street NW, Suite 1202
  Washington, DC 20036
  202-371-0101
  http://www.computer.org
  (See Career Development & Education link)

Construction

Construction study concentrates on the building trades industry and involves learning about the structural, technical, and finishing aspects of construction, renovation, and maintenance on buildings, highways, industrial structures, systems, and utilities installations. Construction is a vast area and includes many specialties. A few of these are masonry, carpentry, heavy equipment operation, plumbing, electricity, bricklaying, contracting, roofing, painting, and insulation.

High School Courses

Algebra	Health
Applied Math	Industrial Arts
Architectural Drawing	Math
Blueprint Reading	Physical Education
Computer Applications	Triganometry
Drafting	Woodworking
Geometry	

Related Majors

Air Conditioning/Refrigeration	Iron Work
Brick Masonry	Painting
Carpentry	Plastering
Construction Engineering	Plumbing
Construction Technology	Safety Engineering
Electricity	Sheet Metal
Heavy Equipment Operating	Stone Masonry
Insulation Work	Welding

Related Occupations

See page 11 for detailed explanation of key.

Brickmasons—V	Marblesetter—V
Building Manager—AA/V	Operating Engineer—V
Carpenter—V	Painter—V
Carpet Installer—V	Paperhanger—V
Concrete Mason—V	Pipefitter—V
Construction Manager—V/B	Plasterer—V
Drywall Applicator—V	Plumber—V
Electrician—V	Project Manager—V/B
Estimator—AA/B	Rigger—V
General Contractor—B/V	Roofer—V
General Superintendent—B/V	Safety Engineer—B

Glazier—V	Sheet Metal Worker—V
Insulation Worker—V	Stone Mason—V
Ironworker—V	Terrazzo Worker—V
Job Superintendent—V/B	Tilesetter—V

Leisure Activities

- Working part time or as a volunteer worker with a construction firm, land-scape gardening center, on a farm, or in various outdoor physical activities
- Building and repairing items as a hobby
- Reading manuals and books related to construction
- Engaging in outdoor sports and games that involve physical stamina, strength, and endurance
- Renovating and decorating your own home or yard
- Becoming a member of an organization such as the Scouts or 4-H

Skills

- Ability to work in awkward positions and at times in dangerous situations
- Physical stamina and good health, vision, and motor coordination
- Mechanical aptitude
- Manual dexterity
- Aptitude for accuracy and detail
- Proficiency in math

HELPFUL INFORMATION
*Construction Mangers
Growth Outlook (2006–2016)

Projected: Grow much faster than the average (increase 21% or more)
Number Employed (2006): 487,000   **(By 2016)** 564,000 (+16%)
Salary Range (2006): $43,210–$135,780
Related Occupations: *AIN*

	SALARY RANGE:
*Electricians	$26,500–$72,700
Carpenters	$22,600–$63,300
*Brickmasons and Blockmasons	$25,500–$67,500
*Plumbers, Pipefitters, and Steamfitters	$25,600–$72,400

*According to the BLS, workers in these occupations are currently in high demand and thus have been designated as "In Demand."

SOURCE CODE(S):
Department of Labor, Bureau of Labor Statistics = *BLS*
Occupational Outlook Handbook, 2008–2009 = *OOH*
America's Career InfoNet (Online) = *AIN*
O*NET (Online) = *NET*

- Ability to read and interpret blueprints, specifications, diagrams, and schematic drawings
- Ability to meet deadlines
- Ability to make sound judgments, appropriate decisions, and solve problems
- Ability to follow direction and work alone as well as with others
- General knowledge of building trade organizations, practices, and trends
- Thorough knowledge and ability in an area of specialization

Values and Attributes

- Security
- Accomplishment and enjoyment in seeing visual and concrete results of one's work
- Desire to make a contribution to society
- Willingness to work outdoors and in uncomfortable weather
- Ability to adjust to hazardous environments
- Enjoyment of hands-on activities
- Thoroughness
- Patience
- Precision
- Courage
- Resourcefulness
- Carefulness

Resources

- **Associated General Contractors of America**
  2300 Wilson Boulevard, Suite 400
  Alexandria, VA 22201
  703-548-3118
  http://www.agc.org
  (see Career Development link)
- **Mechanical Contractors Association of America**
  1385 Piccard Drive
  Rockville, MD 20850
  301-869-5800
  http://www.mcaa.org
  (provides employment opportunities, sponsors student chapters, internships, and career information)
- **National Association of Home Builders**
  1201 15th Street NW
  Washington, DC 20005
  800-368-5242
  http://www.nahb.com
  (exposes interested students to emerging housing technologies)

Criminal Justice

Criminal justice concerns public safety and law enforcement. Studies include basic criminal justice theories as well as practices, systems, strategies, functions, and problems (particularly crime and its many affects on society). Major criminal justice areas are law enforcement, criminal courts, and corrections. Many disciplines overlap criminal justice, including sociology, psychology, political science, medicine, law, history, philosophy, economics, and computer science. You may elect to specialize in law enforcement, investigations, court administration, criminal law, juvenile and family services, safety and security, forensics, organized crime, corrections, violence, civil disobedience, white-collar crime, applied research, and management.

High School Courses

Civics	Physical Education
Computer Applications	Psychology
Economics	ROTC
Government	Social Studies
Health	Sociology
History	

Related Majors

Computer Science	Psychology
Corrections	Public Administration
Criminology	Social Work
Law	Sociology
Military Science	Urban Studies
Political Science	

Related Occupations

See page 11 for detailed explanation of key.

Academic Teacher—B	Fire Chief—B/M
Attorney—P	Foreign Service Officer—B
Chaplain—V	Forensics Psychologist—P
Child Welfare Worker—B	Fraud Examiner/Investigator—B
CIA Agent—B/M	Judge—P
Corrections Facilities	Loss Prevention Manager—B
Manager—AA/B	Military Officer—B
Coroner—B/M	Police Detective—V
Court Administrator—B/P	Sheriff—B
Criminal Investigator—AA/B	Politician—B
Criminologist—M/D	Sheriff—B
Detective	Secret Service Agent—B

District Attorney—P   Security Guard—V
Drug Enforcement Agent—B   Substance Abuse Counselor—M
FBI Agent—B   Warden—B/M

Leisure Activities

- Working part time or as a volunteer in a law office, as a security guard, or in a courthouse, police station, prison, or juvenile delinquency agency
- Watching police and/or law-related dramas on TV or at the movies
- Reading and/or writing about criminal justice or social issues
- Participating in a related internship or co-op program
- Military experience
- Belonging to a debate or forensic team
- Serving as a leader in a school or community organization

Skills

- Possess good oral and written communication skills
- Sensitivity to and tolerance of people of differing genders, ages, and ethnicities
- Ability to work well under pressure
- Aptitude for leadership
- Good understanding of crime and its affect on society

HELPFUL INFORMATION
*Detectives and Criminal Investigators
Growth Outlook (2006–2016)

Projected: Grow about as fast as the average (increase 7% to 13% or more)
Number Employed (2006): 106,000   **(By 2016)** 125,000 (+17%)
Salary Range (2006): $34,480–$92,590
Related Occupations: *AIN*

	SALARY RANGE:
Judges	$29,500–$145,600+
Forensic Science Technicians	$27,500–$73,100
Attorneys	$50,600–$145,600+
Correction Officers	$23,600–$58,600

*According to the BLS, workers in these occupations are currently in high demand and thus have been designated as "In Demand."

SOURCE CODE(S):
Department of Labor, Bureau of Labor Statistics = *BLS*
Occupational Outlook Handbook, 2008–2009 = *OOH*
America's Career InfoNet (Online) = *AIN*
O*NET (Online) = *NET*

- Ability to conduct scientific research and conduct effective interviewing
- Possess strong ethical and moral values
- Ability to make decisions and solve complex social problems
- Broad background in the liberal arts

Values and Attributes

- Have a knack for scientific inquiry and research
- Analytical and logical thinking
- Place a high priority on safety and protection of citizens
- Genuine desire to help people
- Appreciation for law and order
- Justice
- Integrity
- Trustworthiness

Resources

- **American Bar Association**
  321 North Claim Street
  Chicago, IL 60610
  800-285-2321
  http://www.abanet.org
  (provides general information on law schools and other student services)
- **National Criminal Justice Association**
  720 Seventh Street NW
  Washington, DC 20001
  202-628-8550
  http://www.ncja.org
  (seeks to promote justice systems, enhance public safety, and prevent or
    reduce the harmful effects of crime; offers student membership, internships,
    and a list of related links)
- **Professional Associations in Criminal Justice**
  http://courses.smsu.edu/mkc096f/advisenet/PROFESSIONAL%
    2QASSOCIATIONS/prof.html
  (provides links you may find helpful)

Culinary Arts

Culinary arts include the art, science, and business of cooking, baking, and preparing foods and beverages of all types for public and private institutions, agencies, and eating establishments. It exposes you to the practices and techniques of quantity and fine food preparation as well as presentation, food storage, customer service, budgeting, purchasing, equipment use, recipe/menu development and use, sanitation, employee supervision, management, and governmental regulations. A few of the major specialties are baking, buffet catering, meat cookery, cold meat and seafood preparation, soups and stocks, salads, vegetables, fish and shellfish, and sauces.

High School Courses

Baking	Foods
Chemistry	Health
Computer Applications	Home Economics
Cooking	

Related Majors

Baking and Pastry Arts	Home Economics
Culinary Arts Management	Hospitality
Dietetics	Hotel/Motel Management
Entrepreneurship	Nutrition
Food Science	Restaurant and Resort Management

Related Occupations

See page 11 for detailed explanation of key.

Baker—AA/V	Food Service Supervisor—V/B
Broiler Cook—V	Food Service Manager—V
Butcher—V	Meatcutter—V
Caterer—V	Nutritionist—B
Chef—V	Pastry Chef—V
Coffee Maker—V	Restaurant Owner—V/B
Cook—V	Salad Maker—V
Dietitian—B	Sandwich Maker—V
Executive Chef—V	Sous Chef—V
Food Scientist—B	Technical Writer—B

Leisure Activities

- Attending lectures, clinics, and workshops related to food preparation
- Working part time or as a volunteer in a school or community cafeteria or restaurant
- Baking and/or cooking for church or at home
- Reading publications related to culinary arts
- Joining an organization such as the American Culinary Federation
- Entering baking or food contests
- Attending conventions, trade shows, or fairs that highlight culinary interests

Skills

- Good motor skills, manual dexterity, and eye-hand coordination
- Good health and vision
- Ability to read and interpret recipes and menus
- Ability to meet deadlines and work well under pressure
- Ability to clearly communicate and understand others
- Ability to see and feel differences among shapes, shading, colors, and textures
- Ability to work well alone and with others
- Ability to adapt well to extreme temperature, noise, and odor variations
- Proficiency for accuracy and detail
- Ability to stand or sit in uncomfortable positions for extended periods of time
- Ability to cope with frequent change and variety

HELPFUL INFORMATION
*Chefs and Head Cooks
Growth Outlook (2006–2016)

Projected: Grow faster than the average (increase 14% to 20%)
Number Employed (2006): 115,000   **(By 2016)** 124,000 (+8%)
Salary Range (2006): $20,200–$60,700
Related Occupations: *AIN*

	SALARY RANGE:
Managers of Food Preparation/Servers	$17,300 –$43,800
Cooks, Institutions and Cafeterias	$13,400–$30,800
Bakers	$15,200–$35,400
Food Service Managers	$27,400–$70,800

*According to the BLS, workers in these occupations are currently in high demand and thus have been designated as "In Demand."

SOURCE CODE(S):
Department of Labor, Bureau of Labor Statistics = *BLS*
Occupational Outlook Handbook, 2008–2009 = *OOH*
America's Career InfoNet (Online) = *AIN*
O*NET (Online) = *NET*

- Good mental and emotional well-being
- Keen sense of taste, smell, and touch
- Ability to organize and coordinate activities

Values and Attributes

- Desire for recognition and appreciation from others
- Achievement
- Creativity
- Strong interest in cooking and baking
- Tendency to maintain good health habits
- Willingness to work long and irregular hours and on weekends
- Dedication
- Perseverance
- Resourcefulness
- Flexibility
- Tactfulness
- Cleanliness

Resources

- **American Culinary Federation**
  180 Center Place Way
  St. Augustine, FL 32095
  904-824-4468
  http://www.acfchefs.org
  (sponsors apprenticeship programs, provides information about certification,
  a job bank, and accreditation; see Career Center link)
- **American Institute of Baking**
  PO Box 3999
  Manhattan, KS 66505-3999
  785-537-4750
  http://www.aibonline.org
  (provides information on education and research in the science of baking,
  bakery management, equipment, ingredients, cereal science, nutrition, food
  safety and hygiene, occupational safety, and maintenance engineering)
- **National Restaurant Association Educational Foundation**
  175 West Jackson Boulevard, Suite 1500
  Chicago, IL 60604-2702
  312-715-1010
  http://www.nraef.org
  (offers information about scholarships, career assistance, training, and student
  membership)

Economics

Economics is the study of the production, consumption, and distribution of goods and services. Economics study attempts to clarify how the use of natural, technological, and financial resources affect the lives of human beings. Economic concerns can range from how a poor Appalachian family survives financially to the complex international trade laws between nations. Topics of specialization include the energy costs, business cycles, employment and unemployment, housing, health care, money policies, taxation, labor contracts, agriculture, and international trade.

High School Courses

Accounting	Economics
Algebra	Geometry
Bookkeeping	Math
Business Math	Statistics
Computer Applications	Triganometry
Consumer Math	

Related Majors

Accounting	Insurance
Banking	Market Research
Economic Education	Mathematics
Economic History	Political Science
Finance	Urban Planning
Home Economics	

Related Occupations

See page 11 for detailed explanation of key.

Account Executive—B	Internal Revenue Agent—B
Actuary—B	Labor Relations Specialist—B
Appraiser/Assessor—V	Manpower Director—B
Auditor—B	Market Research Analyst—B
Bank Officer—AA/B	Purchasing Manager—B
Buyer—B	Real Estate Agent—V
Controller—B	Sales Manager—B
Credit and Loan Worker—AA	Sales Representative—AA
Economist—B/D	Securities Analyst—B
Educator—B/M/D	Statistician—B
Financial Analyst—B	Stockbroker—B
Financial Planner—B	Technical Writer—B
Foreign Service Officer—B	Trust Administrator—B
Home Economist—B	Urban Planner—B
Insurance Agent—V/B	

Leisure Activities

- Working as a part time or volunteer cashier, treasurer, pollster, or salesperson
- Joining an international club
- Participating in fund-raising events
- Joining a professional economics organization
- Reading economics-related publications
- Joining an investment club
- Solving budgetary problems
- Bartering
- Writing reports or serving as a research assistant or student aide in an economics department
- Running a part time business
- Joining a financial advisory board

Skills

- Ability to conduct and clearly explain scientific research
- High proficiency in written and oral communication
- Strong background in economic theory and econometrics
- Ability to explain complex concepts and theories to others
- Thorough knowledge of statistical procedures
- Ability to collect and organize data

HELPFUL INFORMATION
Economists
Growth Outlook (2006–2016)

Projected: Grow about as fast as the average (increase 7% to 13%)
Number Employed (2006): 15,000   **(By 2016)** 16,000 (+7%)
Salary Range (2006): $42,280–$236,550
Related Occupations: *AIN*

	SALARY RANGE:
Urban and Regional Planners	$35,600–$86,900
*Financial Analysts	$40,400–$130,100
*Budget Analysts	$40,100–$93,100
Purchasing Managers	$46,600–$132,000

*According to the BLS, workers in these occupations are currently in high demand and thus have been designated as "In Demand."

SOURCE CODE(S):
Department of Labor, Bureau of Labor Statistics = *BLS*
Occupational Outlook Handbook, 2008–2009 = *OOH*
America's Career InfoNet (Online) = *AIN*
O*NET (Online) = *NET*

- Ability for accuracy and detail
- Ability to make keen observations and appropriate decisions
- Ability to solve problems and make sound predictions
- Intellectual capacity to do well in most undergraduate and graduate college programs
- Proficiency with computers

Values and Attributes

- Achievement
- Intellectual growth
- Security
- Ability to adjust to frequent changes
- Fondness for research and detail
- Interest in economic and fiscal trends
- Dependability
- Patience
- Objectivity
- Resourcefulness
- Perseverance
- Curiosity

Resources

- **American Economic Association**
  2014 Broadway, Suite 305
  Nashville, TN 37203
  615-322-2595
  http://www.vanderbilt.edu/AEA
  (offers several journals, publications, and Internet resources for economists)
- **Economic History Association**
  500 El Camino Real
  Santa Clara University
  Santa Clara, CA 95053-0383
  785-864-2847
  http://eh.net/eha/node
  (offers student membership and a newsletter and publishes *Journal of Economic History*)
- **National Association of Business Economists**
  1233 20th Street NW, Suite 505
  Washington, DC 20036
  202-463-6223
  http://www.nabe.com
  (see Careers link)

Education

Education is the study of how human beings teach, learn, and develop values, skills, and character qualities. The survival and success of societies, groups, and individuals hinges on effective education. Education takes place formally or informally from the time you are born until the moment you die. Study in this field is almost unlimited and includes infant care; child psychology and adolescent education; preschool, elementary, and secondary education; adult and parent education; education of the elderly; education of people who have disabilities; education of the disadvantaged; military and employee education; and so on. A few of the major specializations are preschool, elementary, secondary, higher, adult and continuing, and special education; educational administration and supervision, guidance and counseling; testing and evaluation; business, industrial arts, and vocational/technical training.

High School Courses

Computer Applications	Philosophy
Economics	Psychology
English	Public Speaking
History	Religious Studies
Interpersonal Communications	Science
Management	Social Studies
Math	Sociology

Related Majors

Adult Education	Library and Information Science
Art Education	Music Education
Business Education	Physical Education
Educational Administration	Preschool Education
Educational Consulting	Religious Education
Elementary Education	Secondary Education
Guidance and Counseling	Special Education
Health Education	Teacher Education
Higher Education	Vocational Education

Related Occupations

See page 11 for detailed explanation of key.

Adult and Vocational Education Teacher—B	4-H Agent—B
Assistant Principal—M	Librarian—M
Christian Education Worker—B/P	Preschool Teacher—B
	Principal—B

College Dean—D	Registrar—M
College Professor—M/D	School Psychologist—M/D
Counselor—M	School Superintendent—M/D
Director of Admissions—M	Secondary School Teacher—B
Director of Career Placement—M/D	Social Worker—M
Director of Guidance—M/D	Special Education Teacher—B/M
Director of Student Affairs—B	Teacher (ESL)—B
Education Consultant—M/D	Teacher Aide—AA
Elementary School Teacher—B	Tutor—B
Financial Aid Director—M	Vocational Rehabilitation Counselor—M
Personnel Director—B	

Leisure Activities

- Working part time or as a volunteer in a preschool, nursery, elementary, or secondary school
- Participating on a debate or forensic team, in oratory contests, or in a student organization
- Playing team sports or participating in community service organizations
- Serving as a religious school, children's church, or vacation Bible school teacher
- Reading educational publications
- Attending lectures, workshops, or conventions related to education
- Helping to organize and plan social or political events
- Working part time or as a volunteer peer counselor, tutor, 4-H leader, or Scout leader

Skills

- Ability to persuade and influence others
- Proficiency in interpersonal communications
- Intellectual capacity to perform well in most undergraduate and graduate college programs
- Broad background of knowledge
- Ability to organize and maintain accurate records
- Proficiency in one or more specialized areas
- Ability to solve problems and make appropriate decisions
- Aptitude for leadership
- Ability to maintain composure in stressful situations
- Understanding of educational theories and practices
- Ability to communicate ideas, facts, and abstract concepts to others
- Ability to relate to and interact with people of different personalities and backgrounds

Values and Attributes

- Desire to help others to learn and succeed
- Achievement
- Recognition and appreciation from others

- Intellectual growth
- Enjoyment of working and being with people
- Fondness for and dedication to human potential
- Sensitive, warm, friendly attitude
- Thirst for knowledge and understanding
- Patience
- Endurance
- Integrity
- Tactfulness
- Objectivity

Resources

- **American Federation of Teachers, AFL-CIO**
  555 New Jersey Avenue NW
  Washington, DC 20001
  http://www.aft.org
  (provides information about paraprofessionals, preschool, and higher education)
- **National Education Association**
  1201 16th Street NW
  Washington, DC 20056
  202-833-4000
  http://www.nea.org
  (provides information about teachers who work on all levels)

HELPFUL INFORMATION
Secondary School Teachers (except Special and Vocational) Growth Outlook (2006–2016)

Projected: Grow about as fast as the average (increase 7% to 13%)
Number Employed (2006): 1,038,000 **(By 2016)** 1,096,000 (+6%)
Salary Range (2006): $28,590–$876,100
Related Occupations: AIN

	SALARY RANGE:
Special Education Teachers	$31,300–$74,700
Librarians	$30,900–$130,100
Counselors, Educational and Vocational School	$27,200–$75,900
Social Workers	$24,500–$62,500

*According to the BLS, workers in this occupation are currently in high demand and thus has been designated as "In Demand."

SOURCE CODE(S):
Department of Labor, Bureau of Labor Statistics = *BLS*
Occupational Outlook Handbook, 2008–2009 = *OOH*
America's Career InfoNet (Online) = *AIN*
O*NET (Online) = *NET*

Electrical/Electronic Engineering

Electrical/electronic engineering is the practical application of mathematics and science in the production, control, distribution, and uses of electricity as well as the research, design, development, testing, and supervision of the manufacture of electronic equipment. Electrical/electronic engineering is an extremely large branch of engineering and ranges from the design of tiny electrical circuits to the construction of large electrical power plants. The four major branches of electrical engineering are communications, control systems, electronics, and power. Students may concentrate in the area of electronic controls, radio, electromechanics, machine design, or construction.

High School Courses

Algebra	Geometry
Blueprint Reading	Math
Calculus	Physics
Chemistry	Radio/TV Repair
Computer Applications	Science
Computer Science	Statistics
Electricity	Trigonometry
Electronics	

Related Majors

Aeronautical/Aerospace Engineering	Electrician
Biomedical Engineering	Engineering Education
Civil Engineering	Engineering Mechanics
Computer and Information Science	Mathematics
Computer Science Engineering	Nuclear Engineering
Electrical/Electronic Technology	Petroleum Engineering

Related Occupations

See page 11 for detailed explanation of key.

Acoustical Engineer—B/D	Environmental Engineer—B
Aeronautical Engineer—B/D	Field Service Engineer—B
Biomedical Engineer—B/D	Fire Protection Engineer—B
Circuit Engineer—B	Illuminating Engineer—B
Communications Engineer—B	Mechanical Engineer—B
Computer Science Engineer—B	Nuclear Engineer—B
Consulting Engineer—B/M/D	Physicist—B/D

Control Engineer—B
Electrical Engineer—B
Electrical Engineering
 Technician—AA
Electrician—V
Electronics Instructor—B

Radio Engineer—B
Safety Engineer—B
Technical Writer—B
Transmissions Engineer—B
Video Recording Engineer—V

Leisure Activities

- Reading publications related to electricity and engineering
- Attending lectures and conferences related to engineering
- Repairing electrical items around the house
- Developing hobbies and interests related to electronic games and equipment
- Building models
- Belonging to a club or organization related to electrical engineering
- Working part time or as a volunteer in an electronics shop, electrical firm, radio/TV repair shop, or college engineering department
- Participating in clubs or organizations that require you to make oral presentations and write reports

Skills

- Proficiency with computers
- Proficiency in mathematics and physical sciences
- Ability to analyze, organize, and interpret scientific data
- Ability to work well with others
- Ability to make keen observations and sound judgments
- Aptitude for accuracy and detail, spatial perception, and abstract reasoning
- Sensitivity to economic considerations and human needs
- Proficiency in an area of specialization and knowledge of current practices and trends
- Ability to conduct and clearly communicate scientific research
- Intellectual capacity to perform well in most undergraduate and graduate college programs

Values and Attributes

- Achievement
- Creativity
- Knowledge
- Desire to help others live better
- Interest in challenges
- Enthusiasm for developing ideas and concepts in a practical way
- Imagination
- Dependability
- Patience
- Perseverance
- Conscientiousness

Resources

- **Institute of Electrical and Electronic Engineers**
  1828 L Street NW, Suite 1202
  Washington, DC 20036-5104
  202-785-0017
  http://www.ieee.org
  (See Careers link)
- **Junior Engineering Technical Society**
  1420 King Street, Suite 405
  Alexandria, VA 22314
  703-548-5387
  http://www.jets.org
  (sponsors activities to help students determine engineering readiness and
  offers special outreach to minority students and information about careers)
- **National Society of Professional Engineers**
  1420 King Street
  Alexandria, VA 22314
  703-684-2800
  http://www.nspe.org
  (offers career information, student scholarships, job and salary information, etc.)

Electrical/Electronic Technology

Electrical and electronics technology is the application of scientific theories and principles in the design, production, installation, testing, service, use, and control of electrical and electronic parts, equipment, and systems. Study includes theory and history, applied mathematics, testing measurement, circuitry, construction, currents and voltage, safety, pneumatics and electronic instruments, instrumentation, maintenance and repair, and much more. Specialties in this area include instrumentation, construction electricity, robotics, broadcast communications, industrial electronics, radio/TV, radar, automated equipment, and digital technology.

High School Courses

Algebra	Geometry
Applied Math	Math
Blueprint Reading	Physical Science
Computer Applications	Radio/TV Repair
Computer Graphics	Science
Computer Programming	Small Engine Repair
Electricity	Trigonometry
Electronics	

Related Majors

Automotive Technology	Electrical Engineering Technology
Automated Manufacturing Technology	Heating and Air Conditioning
Communications Technology	Industrial Maintenance Technology
Computer Service and Repair	Instrumentation
Data Processing Technology	Machine Tool Technology
Diesel Mechanics	Radio and Television Repair
Electrical Engineering	Robotics

Related Occupations

See page 11 for detailed explanation of key.

Aircraft Electronics Technician—AA	Electronic Systems Tester—AA
Audio and Sound Specialist—AA	Electronics Technician—AA/V
Automated Equipment Technician—AA	Industrial Electronics Maintenance Worker—AA
Biomedical Equipment Technician—AA	Instrumentation Technician—AA
	Marine Electronics Specialist—AA
Broadcast Technician—AA	Photo-Optics Technician—AA

Electrical Appliance Repairer—V   Radar Technician—AA
Electrical Engineering   Radio and Electrical Inspector—B
  Technician—AA   Radio Repairer—V
Electrical Technician—AA   Robotics Technician—AA
Electronic Equipment   Technical Writer—B
  Salesperson—V   TV Technician—AA
Quality Control Technician—AA

Leisure Activities

- Reading publications related to electricity or electronics
- Repairing electrical items around the house
- Developing hobbies and interests involving electronic games and equipment
- Building models
- Belonging to an electronics club or related organization
- Working part time or as a volunteer in an electronics shop, electrical firm, or radio/TV repair shop

Skills

- Ability to understand and apply scientific theories and principles
- Ability to read, interpret, and follow directions, schematic drawings, diagrams, and blueprints
- Eye-hand coordination
- Aptitude for accuracy and detail
- Ability to concentrate intensely and work alone for long periods of time
- Ability to make keen observations and solve problems
- Spatial perception and proficiency in color coordination
- Finger and manual dexterity
- Aptitude for working with electronics and mechanics
- Proficiency in mathematics and physical science
- Ability to analyze, make sound judgments, and make appropriate decisions

Values and Attributes

- Independence
- Wisdom
- Achievement
- Enjoyment of hands-on work related to electrical gadgetry
- Enthusiasm for learning and applying new methods and techniques
- Patience
- Resourcefulness
- Conscientiousness
- Competence
- Thoroughness
- Dependability

Resources

- Serby, Michael. *Careers in Television and Radio*. London, UK: Kogan Page, 2000.
- **Electronics Technicians Association, International**
  ETA-1
  5 Depot Street
  Greencastle, IN 46135
  765-653-8262
  http://www.eta-i.org
  (publishes career brochures and offers student membership, accreditation information, and helpful links)
- **International Society of Certified Electronics Technicians**
  3608 Pershing Avenue
  Fort Worth, TX 76107-4527
  817-921-9101
  http://www.iscet.org
  (offers training and testing programs for certified electronics technicians)
- **Junior Engineering Technical Society**
  1420 King Street, Suite 405
  Alexandria, VA 22314
  703-548-5387
  http://www.jets.org
  (sponsors activities to help students determine engineering readiness and offers special outreach to minority students and information about careers)

HELPFUL INFORMATION
*Electrical/Electronic Engineering Technicians
Growth Outlook (2006–2016)

Projected: Grow about as fast as the average (increase 7% to 13%)
Number Employed (2006): 170,000   **(By 2016)** 177,000 (+4%)
Salary Range (2006): $30,120–$73,200
Related Occupations: *AIN*

	SALARY RANGE:
*Electrical and Electronic Repairers (Commercial and Industrial Equipment)	$27,900–$64,300
*Electronic Drafters	$29,300–$74,500
*Electrical Powerline Installers/Repairers	$29,000–$71,100
*Computer Support Specialists	$25,300–$68,500

*According to the BLS, workers in these occupations are currently in high demand and thus have been designated as "In Demand."

SOURCE CODE(S):
Department of Labor, Bureau of Labor Statistics = *BLS*
Occupational Outlook Handbook, 2008–2009 = *OOH*
America's Career InfoNet (Online) = *AIN*
O*NET (Online) = *NET*

English

English is a major branch of the language arts and its main focus is on the written word. However, a broader, more commonly accepted definition would include the study of literature, speech, and writing in all forms. The study of English orients you to the discipline of thinking. You learn to critically evaluate your own speaking and writing, as well as the speaking and writing of others, and to express your thoughts and feelings coherently. You also learn how to edit your work and write for different audiences. The appropriate use and understanding of English is considered basic to everyday life and reflects a person's level of educational achievement. A few of the specialized areas within English are writing, literature, reading, and speech.

High School Courses

Business English	Poetry
Computer Applications	Public Speaking
Debate	Speech
Drama	Speed Reading
English	Technical English
Forensics	Writing
Literature	

Related Majors

American Literature	Journalism
Communications	Linguistics
Comparative Literature	Publishing
Creative Writing	Speech
English Language	Technical and Business English
English Literature	Theater Arts
Foreign Language	

Related Occupations

See page 11 for detailed explanation of key.

Actor/Actress—B/V	Library Technical Assistant—AA
Author—B	Linguist—M
Bibliographer—B	Lobbyist—B
Book Store Manager—B	Media Specialist—B
Broadcast News Analyst—V	Playwright——V/B
Columnist—B	Proofreader—V
Copy Editor—B	Publisher—B
Editor—B	Reading Specialist/Consultant—B
Educator—B/M/D	Reporter—B

Freelance Writer—V   Secretary—AA
Interpreter/Translator—B   Speech Writer—B
Journalist—B   Technical Writer—B
Librarian—M

Leisure Activities

- Participating in local theater productions
- Attending movies, plays, lectures, or readings
- Freelance writing
- Providing a typing, tutoring, resume, or editing service
- Writing reports, papers, or poems
- Conversing with others
- Participating on a debate or forensics team or in practical politics
- Editing or reporting for a small newspaper or newsletter
- Joining a yearbook staff
- Participating in a book club
- Visiting libraries
- Working part time or as a volunteer for a high school or college radio or TV station
- Competing in writing or oratory contests
- Reading essays, articles, novels, short stories, plays, poetry, and professional journals

Skills

- Background of general knowledge
- High proficiency in reading, writing, and speaking
- Comprehensive command of grammar and vocabulary
- Good listening, clarifying, questioning, and responding skills
- Ability to conduct and clearly explain research results
- Ability to read analytically
- Capacity to work well under pressure
- Ability to make keen observations and appropriate decisions
- Ability to concentrate for long periods of time

Values and Attributes

- Intellectual growth
- Independence
- Creativity
- Desire for recognition and to influence others
- Willingness to work toward a deadline
- Fondness for writing and/or speaking
- Self-discipline
- Tactfulness
- Integrity
- Imagination

Resources

- **Association of American Publishers (AAP)**
  71 Fifth Avenue
  New York, NY 10003-3004
  212-255-0200
  http://www.publishers.org
  (has general information about the book publishing and marketing business)
- **Dow Jones Newspaper Fund**
  PO Box 300
  Princeton, NJ 08543-0300
  609-452-2820
  http://djnewspaperfund.dowjones.com/fund
  (sponsors various internships and job placement assistance)
- **Magazine Publishers of America**
  810 Seventh Avenue, 24th Floor
  New York, NY 10019
  212-872-3700
  http://www.magazine.org
  (See Careers link)

Food and Beverage Management/Service

Food and beverage management/service is the art and business of managing and providing food services of all types for public and private institutions, agencies, and eating establishments. It includes the study of food-service techniques in hospitality, hotel and restaurant maintenance, facilities, food purchasing and cost, food preparation and service, and front office operations. Other areas of focus are marketing, sanitation and safety, menu and nutrition, catering, and financial record keeping.

High School Courses

Bookkeeping	Health
Business Management	Home Economics
Computer Applications	Psychology
Cooking	Sales
Food Service	Sociology
Foods	Speech

Related Majors

Bookkeeping	Hotel/Motel Management
Culinary Arts	Marketing and Tourism Management
Customer and Personal Services	Nutrition
Food Service	Pastry Arts
Home Economics	Restaurant Management
Hospitality Management	Senior Services Management

Related Occupations

See page 11 for detailed explanation of key.

Assistant Restaurant Manager—AA/V	Food Service Manager—V/B
Banquet Manager—AA/V	Home Economist—B
Cafeteria Manager—AA/V	Host/Hostess—V
Chef—AA/V	Hotel/Motel Manager—B
Dietitian—B	Maitre d'Hotel—V
Dining Room Attendant—V	Merchandising Supervisor—V
Director of Recipe—V	Nutritionist—B
Executive Housekeeper—B	Purchasing Agent—B
Fast Food Worker—V	Restaurant Manager—AA/B
Food and Beverage Director—V	Sanitation/Maintenance Worker—AA
Food Production Manager—V	Steward/Stewardess—V
	Storeroom Supervisor—V

Leisure Activities

- Working part time or as a volunteer in a restaurant or hotel
- Planning or organizing community events that involve eating and/or serving
- Engaging in your own part-time food business endeavor
- Helping to organize, plan, and implement church or school picnics
- Reading publications related to food service or management
- Working part time as a store cashier or manager
- Attending workshops, lectures, or conferences related to food service
- Hosting social events

Skills

- Ability to solve problems and make appropriate decisions
- Aptitude for accuracy and detail
- Ability to follow directions and read and interpret menus
- Ability to work under pressure, maintain composure, and react spontaneously
- Ability to organize and coordinate activities
- Proficiency in interpersonal communication
- Ability to accept public scrutiny and criticism
- Ability to interact with people of different backgrounds and personalities

---

HELPFUL INFORMATION
*Food Service Managers
Growth Outlook (2006–2016)

Projected: Grow more slowly than the average (increase 3% to 6%)
Number Employed (2006): 350,000 **(By 2016)** 368,000 (+5%)
Salary Range (2006): $27,400–$70,810
Related Occupations: *AIN*

	SALARY RANGE:
*Lodging Managers	$25,120–$82,510
*Chefs and Head Cooks	$20,160–$60,730
*Dietitians and Nutritionists	$29,860–$68,330
Supervisors, Sales Workers, Retail	$21,470–$59,710

*According to the BLS, workers in these occupations are currently in high demand and thus have been designated as "In Demand."

SOURCE CODE(S):
Department of Labor, Bureau of Labor Statistics = *BLS*
Occupational Outlook Handbook, 2008–2009 = *OOH*
America's Career InfoNet (Online) = *AIN*
O*NET (Online) = *NET*

- Good health and vision
- Ability to work well with others
- Good motor skills, manual dexterity, and eye-hand coordination
- Familiarity with laws related to alcoholic beverages and minors

Values and Attributes

- Recognition and appreciation from others
- Desire to help others
- Creativity
- Achievement
- Pleasant and friendly personality
- Desire to serve and please others
- Willingness to work long and irregular hours and on weekends
- Sensitivity, poise, and integrity
- Persuasiveness
- Neatness
- Diplomacy
- Cleanliness
- Leadership
- Industriousness

Resources

- **American Culinary Federation**
  180 Center Place Way
  St. Augustine, FL 32095
  904-824-4468
  http://www.acfchefs.org
  (sponsors an apprenticeship program and provides information about certification and accreditation, which includes how to become a certified chef; see Career Center link)
- **International Council on Hotel, Restaurant and Institutional Education**
  2810 North Parham, Suite 230
  Richmond, VA 23294
  804-346-4800
  http://chrie.org
  (has a list of schools with programs in hotel and restaurant management, food service management, and the culinary arts; see Just for Students link)
- **National Restaurant Association Educational Foundation**
  175 West Jackson Boulevard, Suite 1500
  Chicago, IL 60604-2702
  312-715-1010
  http://www.edfound.org
  (offers information about scholarships, career assistance, training, and student membership; see Careers and Education link)

Foreign Language

Foreign language is a branch of the language arts that involves the study of languages other than your native tongue. Studies in a foreign language improve your ability to communicate, help you to develop cultural awareness and sensitivity, and expand your general knowledge. Proficiency in more than one language has become a valuable asset and enhances your occupational possibilities as well as enjoyment of overseas travel. Foreign language courses are offered in most schools, colleges, and universities in the United States.

High School Courses

Anthropology	Literature
English	Sociology
Foreign Language	Speech
History	World History
Latin	

Related Majors

Anthropology	Humanities
Arabic	International Relations
Chinese	International Studies
Classics	Italian
English	Japanese
French	Linguistics
German	Portuguese
Greek	Russian
Hebrew	Spanish

Related Occupations

See page 11 for detailed explanation of key.

Actor/Actress—V/B	Hotel Information Clerk—V
Announcer—B	Hotel Manager—AA/B
Anthropologist—B/D	Import/Export Clerk—V
Bilingual Educator—B/M	Interpreter/Translator—B
Civil Service Worker—B	Journalist—B
Copy Editor—B	Linguist—M
Customs Inspector—AA	Maitre d'Hotel—AA/V
Diplomat—B/M	Missionary—B
FBI/CIA Agent—B/D	Proofreader—V
Film Editor—AA	Speech Pathologist—B/M
Flight Attendant—AA	Technical Writer—B
Foreign Correspondent—B	Translator—B

Foreign Service Officer—B   Peace Corps/VISTA Volunteer—B
Historian—B/D   Travel Agent—AA

Leisure Activities

- Traveling abroad
- Attending movies or participating in stage productions
- Visiting libraries
- Attending lectures and readings
- Working part time or as a volunteer for Peace Corps, VISTA, or Red Cross International
- Joining a foreign language club
- Participating in oratory contests, student exchanges, or pen-pal experiences
- Working part time or as a volunteer news announcer for a local radio or TV station, in a foreign language department, or in an ethnic restaurant
- Joining an international service organization such as the American Friends

Skills

- Ability to make analogies
- Ability to adjust to new environments
- Ability to organize and memorize detailed information
- Background of general knowledge

HELPFUL INFORMATION
Interpreters and Translators
Growth Outlook (2006–2016)

Projected: Grow faster than the average (increase 14% to 20%)
Number Employed (2006): 41,000 **(By 2016)** 1,000 (+24%)
Salary Range (2006): $29,600–$64,300
Related Occupations: *AIN*

	SALARY RANGE:
Travel Guides	$17,000–$48,600
Reporters and Correspondents	$19,200–$73,900
Anthropologists	$29,000–$81,500
Historians	$23,500–$89,900

*According to the BLS, workers in these occupations are currently in high demand and thus have been designated as "In Demand."

SOURCE CODE(S):
Department of Labor, Bureau of Labor Statistics = *BLS*
Occupational Outlook Handbook, 2008–2009 = *OOH*
America's Career InfoNet (Online) = *AIN*
O*NET (Online) = *NET*

- Comprehensive command of grammar and vocabulary
- Good listening, clarifying, and responding skills
- High proficiency in reading, speaking, and writing
- Proficiency in phonetics and ability to imitate sounds
- Tendency toward logical thinking

Values and Attributes

- Intellectual growth
- Appreciation for the culture and lifestyles of others
- Desire for peace and harmony
- Linguistic ability
- Adaptability
- Alertness
- Creativity
- Patience
- Self-discipline

Resources

- **American Institute for Foreign Study**
  River Plaza, 9 West Broad Street
  Stamford, CT 06902-3788
  866-906-2437
  http://www.aifs.com
  (sponsors exchange and study-abroad programs, internships, and scholarships
  and seeks to promote international understanding)
- **American Translators Association**
  225 Reinekers Lane, Suite 590
  Alexandria, VA 22314
  703-683-6100
  http://www.atanet.org
  (has information on the translating and interpreting professions)
- **Modern Language Association**
  26 Broadway, 3rd Floor
  New York, NY 10004-1789
  646-576-5000
  http://www.mla.org
  (promotes study and teaching of language and literature, offers job placement
  assistance, and provides career information)

Forestry

Forestry is concerned with the management, development, and use of forests and related areas. It involves the application of scientific methods as well as creative imagination. Forestry covers a broad spectrum and includes the care and maintenance of rangelands, grasslands, and brushlands. Study in this field includes wood science, forestry management, economics, conservation, fire protection and disease control, scaling, surveying, recreational use, research, and a number of other areas. Forestry overlaps with several fields including biology, physics, chemistry, and engineering. Among the many specializations are tree planting/harvesting, watershed management, wildlife management, forestry management, public recreation, fire control, disease and pest control, conservation, and wood science.

High School Courses

Algebra	Math
Biology	Physical Science
Chemistry	Physics
Computer Applications	Science
Earth Science	Trigonometry
Geometry	

Related Majors

Agriculture	Forestry Engineering
Biology	Horticulture
Botany	Natural Resources
Conservation	Rangeland Ecology and Management
Fire Protection/Safety Technology	Recreation Parks and Tourism
Forest Resource Management	Management
Forestry Education	Wildlife and Fisheries Resources

Related Occupations

See page 11 for detailed explanation of key.

Agricultural Extension Worker—B	Park Ranger—B
Agronomist—B	Plant Geneticist—B
Biological Technician—AA	Rancher—V
Botanist—B	Range Manager—AA/B
Conservation Scientist—B/D	Smoke Jumper—V
Ecologist—B	Soil Conservationist—B
Educator—B/M/D	Surveyor—AA
Farm/Ranch Manager—B/V	Taxonomist—B
Fish and Game Warden—V	Tree Nursery Manager—V
Forester—B	Tree Surgeon—V

Forestry Technician—AA   Virologist—B
Mycologist—D   Wildlife Manager—B
Naturalist—B   Wood Technologist—B
Park Police—AA/B

Leisure Activities

- Visiting nature centers, botanical gardens, state and national parks, conservatories, camps, and museums
- Hiking, exploring, camping, sightseeing, backpacking, and collecting items related to nature
- Joining a professional organization such as the Society of American Foresters
- Subscribing to a science publication such as the *Journal of Forestry*
- Joining a forestry club or conservation group
- Supporting or participating in natural resource preservation efforts
- Undertaking nature studies or rural expeditions
- Working part time as a park aide, forest aide, nursery worker, or nature tour guide

Skills

- Physical stamina, good vision, and manual dexterity
- Ability to work alone and with little supervision
- Ability to conduct and clearly explain scientific research
- Ability to communicate well with others
- Proficiency in reading, writing, speaking, and memorization
- Ability to supervise and manage people and activities
- Intellectual ability to perform well in most undergraduate and graduate college programs
- Thorough knowledge of forestry and related areas
- Proficiency in problem solving and decision making

Values and Attributes

- Independence
- Aesthetic awareness
- Desire to help humanity
- Intellectual growth
- Creativity
- Fondness for outdoor activities
- Desire to conserve and protect the natural environment
- Ability to endure sometimes challenging physical conditions
- Appreciation of nature
- Perseverance
- Desire for challenges
- Curiosity
- Responsibility

Resources

- **American Forests**
  PO Box 2000
  Washington, DC 20013
  202-737-1944
  http://www.americanforests.org
  (promotes conservation and publishes *American Forests* magazine; has information on a wide variety of forest-related activities)

- **Society of American Foresters**
  5400 Grosvenor Lane
  Bethesda, MD 20814-2198
  301-897-8720
  http://www.safnet.org/index.shtml
  (provides forestry facts and information; see Career and Students links)

- **USDA Forest Service**
  1400 Independence Avenue SW
  Washington, DC 20250-1355
  800-832-1355
  http://www.fs.fed.us
  (has information about government careers in forestry as well as information on national forests across the country)

HELPFUL INFORMATION
Foresters and Conservation Scientists
Growth Outlook (2006–2016)

Projected: Grow more slowly than the average (increase 3% to 6%)
Number Employed (2006): 20,000 **(By 2016)** 21,000 (+5%)
Salary Range (2006): $33,490–$74,570
Related Occupations: *AIN*

	SALARY RANGE:
*Forest and Conservation Technicians	$22,400–$49,400
*Biological Technicians	$23,700–$57,900
Fish and Game Wardens	$28,300–$62,300
Conservation Scientists	$29,900–$80,300

*According to the BLS, workers in these occupations are currently in high demand and thus have been designated as "In Demand."

SOURCE CODE(S):
Department of Labor, Bureau of Labor Statistics = *BLS*
Occupational Outlook Handbook, 2008–2009 = *OOH*
America's Career InfoNet (Online) = *AIN*
O*NET (Online) = *NET*

Geography

Geography is the study of the interrelationships between the earth and its people. It is considered both a social and natural science. Geography focuses on climate, land, water, space, mineral resources, population density, changes in environment, and how people adapt to them. Geographical study encompasses human geography, economic geography, physical geography, political geography, medical geography, regional geography, and educational geography.

High School Courses

Civics	Government
Computer Applications	Physical Geography
Computer Programming	Social Studies
Earth Science	Sociology
Economics	World History
Geography	

Related Majors

Anthropology	Geology
Archaeology	Global Studies
Cartography	History
Economic Geography	Human Geography
Economics	Physical Geography
Educational Geography	Sociology
Environmental Studies	Urban Planning

Related Occupations

See page 11 for detailed explanation of key.

Anthropologist—D	Mapping Technician—AA
Cartographer—B	Market Research Analyst—B
Cartographic Technician—AA	Meteorologist—B
Climatologist—B	Oceanographer—B
Ecologist—B	Petrologist—B
Educator—B/M/D	Photogrammetric Technician—AA
Environmental Scientist—B	Photogrammetrist—B
Environmental Technician—AA	Photographer—B
Geographer—B/D	Research Assistant—B/M
Geologist—B	Seismologist—B
Geomorphologist—B/D	Sociologist—D
Geophysicist—B/D	Soil Conservationist—B

Historian—B/D Surveyor—AA/V
International Economist—B Urban Planner—M/D

Leisure Activities

- Visiting natural science museums
- Involvement in outdoor activities
- Attending geographical seminars and conferences
- Watching TV shows related to the natural habitat
- Exploring and traveling
- Hiking, camping, and backpacking
- Reading or subscribing to professional publications
- Solving analytical and logical problems
- Joining organizations such as the American Geographical Society
- Working part time or as a volunteer in an architectural firm, school geography department, or at an archaeological site

Skills

- Proficiency in the use of computers
- Ability to understand and interpret maps, graphs, and charts
- Acute spatial and form perception
- Good vision and finger dexterity
- Thorough understanding of geographical principles and statistical techniques
- Proficiency in reading, writing, and speaking
- Ability to analyze, make appropriate decisions, and solve quantitative problems
- Ability to conduct and clearly explain scientific research
- Aptitude for accuracy and detail
- Intellectual capacity to perform well in most undergraduate and graduate college programs

Values and Attributes

- Achievement
- Intellectual growth
- Independence
- Desire to help and influence humanity
- Desire to help people understand and adapt to their environment
- Keen interest in both the natural and social sciences
- Spirit of scientific inquiry
- Curiosity
- Patience
- Persistence
- Resourcefulness

Resources

- **American Geographical Society**
  120 Wall Street, Suite 100
  New York, NY 10005-3904
  212-422-5456
  http://www.amergeog.org
  (provides information about college programs and career pathways; offers scholarships and internships)

- **Association of American Geographers**
  1710 16th Street NW
  Washington, DC 20009-3198
  202-234-1450
  http://www.aag.org
  (see Jobs/Careers link)

- **National Geographic Society**
  PO Box 98199
  Washington, DC 20090-8199
  800-647-5463
  http://www.nationalgeographic.com/main.html
  (provides a wealth of information for geography lovers and publishes an outstanding periodical)

HELPFUL INFORMATION
Geographers
Growth Outlook (2006–2016)

Projected: Grow more slowly than the average (increase 3% to 6%)
Number Employed (2006): 1,100   **(By 2016)** 1,200 (+6%)
Salary Range (2006): $37,500–$93,900
Related Occupations: *AIN*

	SALARY RANGE:
*Cartographers and Photogrammetrists	$30,900–$80,500
*Hydrologists	$42,100–$98,300
*Mapping Technicians	$20,000–$53,300
*Urban and Regional Planners	$35,600–$86,900

*According to the BLS, workers in these occupations are currently in high demand and thus have been designated as "In Demand."

SOURCE CODE(S):
Department of Labor, Bureau of Labor Statistics = *BLS*
Occupational Outlook Handbook, 2008–2009 = *OOH*
America's Career InfoNet (Online) = *AIN*
O*NET (Online) = *NET*

Geology

Geology is a major branch of the physical sciences that involves the study of the earth. Geology is divided into two main fields: physical geology (the study of earth matter and influencing forces) and historical geology (the history of the earth). Geology includes the study of rocks, soils, mountains, rivers, oceans, and caves. Study in geology also encompasses the exploration and production of mineral and energy resources. Subbranches of geology include meteorology, climatology, oceanography, geophysics, petrology, sedimentology, stratigraphy, paleontology, mineralogy, and geochemistry.

High School Courses

Algebra	Math
Chemistry	Physical Science
Computer Applications	Physics
Earth Science	Science
Geography	Trigonometry
Geometry	

Related Majors

Astronomy	Geophysical Engineering
Astrophysics	Geophysics and Seismology
Earth and Planetary Science	Hydrology
Environmental Science	Metallurgy
Geography	Meteorology
Geochemistry	Mineralogy
Geological Engineering	Oceanography

Related Occupations

See page 11 for detailed explanation of key.

Astronomer—D	Metallurgist—B
Cartographer—B	Meteorological Technician—AA
Chemist—B	Mining Engineer—B
Environmental Scientist—B	Mineralogist—B/D
Geodesist—B	Mining Engineer—B
Geodetic Surveyor—B	Nuclear Engineer—B/D
Geographer—B/D	Oceanographer—B/D
Geologist—B	Paleontologist—B/D
Geophysicist—B/D	Petroleum Engineer—B
Geospatial Information	Petrologist—B
Scientist—B/D	Pharmacist—B
Geospatial Information Systems	Photogrammetrist—B
Technicians—AA	Physicist—B/D

Hydrographer—B	Seismologist—B
Hydrologist—B	Stratigrapher—B
Laboratory Technician—AA	Surveyor—AA
Metallurgical Engineer—B	Technical Writer—B

Leisure Activities

- Visiting science museums
- Participating in outdoor activities
- Attending science fairs and exhibits
- Watching TV shows related to the natural habitat
- Exploring and traveling
- Hiking, mountain climbing, camping, and backpacking
- Doing jigsaw puzzles and playing games of strategy
- Joining a geology or archeological club
- Developing hobbies and collections related to soils, rocks, coins, jewelry, or other artifacts
- Reading science magazines

Skills

- Intellectual capacity to perform well in most undergraduate and graduate college programs
- Ability to work with people of varied backgrounds

HELPFUL INFORMATION
Geoscientists
Growth Outlook (2006–2016)

Projected: Grow much faster than the average (increase 21% or more)
Number Employed (2006): 31,000 **(By 2016)** 38,000 (+22%)
Salary Range (2006): $39,740–$135,950
Related Occupations: *AIN*

	SALARY RANGE:
Mining and Geological Engineers	$42,000–$128,400
Hydrologists	$42,100–$98,300
Petroleum Engineers	$57,900–$145,600+
Physicists	$52,100–$143,600

*According to the BLS, workers in these occupations are currently in high demand and thus have been designated as "In Demand."

SOURCE CODE(S):
Department of Labor, Bureau of Labor Statistics = *BLS*
Occupational Outlook Handbook, 2008–2009 = *OOH*
America's Career InfoNet (Online) = *AIN*
O*NET (Online) = *NET*

- Acute spatial and form perception
- Ability to make appropriate decisions and to solve quantitative problems
- Aptitude for accuracy and detail
- Proficiency in reading, writing, speaking, and memorization
- Ability to conduct and clearly explain scientific research
- Physical stamina, good vision, and manual dexterity
- Thorough knowledge of geological principles and mathematics
- Proficiency with computers

Values and Attributes

- Independence
- Intellectual growth
- Achievement
- Enthusiasm for exploration, travel, and outdoor work
- Spirit of scientific inquiry
- Resourcefulness
- Imagination
- Patience
- Determination
- Dedication

Resources

- **American Geological Institute**
  4220 King Street
  Alexandria, VA 22302-1502
  703-379-2480
  http://www.agiweb.org
  (provides information about scholarships and careers, including career statistics and much more)
- **The Geological Society of America**
  PO Box 9140
  3300 Penrose Place
  Boulder, CO 80301-9140
  303-357-1000
  http://www.geosociety.org
  (distributes information about careers in geoscience and offers employment service, internships, and a helpful list of links)
- **Society of Exploration Geophysicists**
  8801 South Yale
  Tulsa, OK 74137
  918-497-5500
  http://www.seg.org
  (provides useful information for students)

Health Administration, Management, and Related Services

Health administration, management, and related services are concerned with the effective and efficient delivery of health care services to community residents. It involves the coordination and management of public and private hospitals, nursing homes, assisted-living facilities, medical centers, clinics, mental health organizations, community health programs, and more. Study in this area concentrates on the business practices, leadership skills, and support services employed by health care administrators and managers in their effort to identify, treat, prevent, and control disease, sickness, and injury. Students are exposed to the various strategies used to ensure a high quality of patient care service in a cost-effective manner. A few of the concentrations within this field are patient care, publicity, budget and finance, maintenance, housekeeping, personnel, food service and nutrition, employee relations, facilities and equipment, governmental regulations, benefits, and record keeping.

High School Courses

Accounting

Bookkeeping

Business Management

Business Math

Computer Science

Consumer Math

Economics

Health

Psychology

Sociology

Speech

Related Majors

Business

Business Administration

Business Economics

Business Education

Marketing Management

Public Administration

Public Health

Public Relations

Related Occupations

See page 11 for detailed explanation of key.

Activities Supervisor—B

Chief Dietitian—B

Hospital Personnel Director—B

Hospital Records Administrator—B

Coordinator of Rehabilitation Services—B/M

Director of Volunteer Services—B

Emergency Medical Services Coordinator—B

Executive Housekeeper—B

Health Consultant—B/D

Health Information Specialist—B

Health Services Administrator—M

Hospital Comptroller—B

Hospital Food Service Manager—B

Information Specialist—B/M

Medical Engineer—B

Medical Records Administrator—B

Nursing Home Director—M

Occupational Safety and Health Inspector—B

Psychiatric Social Worker—M

Public Health Educator—B

Public Health Service Officer—B

Public Health Statistician—B

Public Relations Specialist—B

Leisure Activities

- Reading publications related to health care services and management
- Attending lectures, workshops, and conferences related to health concerns
- Belonging to a health club or professional health organization
- Working part time or as a volunteer in a hospital or nursing home, health agency, or business establishment
- Actively supporting health endeavors
- Joining a health advisory board
- Serving as a club or program officer

Skills

- Ability to clearly communicate ideas and concepts to others
- Ability to inspire productivity and exact loyalty from others
- Aptitude for leadership
- Proficiency in interpersonal communications
- Proficiency in reading, writing, and speaking
- Knowledge of health care services, policies, and trends
- Intellectual capacity to perform well in most undergraduate and graduate college programs
- Ability to solve problems and make appropriate decisions
- Proficiency in organizing, planning, coordinating, and directing activities
- Ability to meet deadlines and work well under pressure
- Proficiency in the use of computers

Values and Attributes

- Desire to help others and make a contribution to humanity
- Health
- Achievement
- Prestige
- Willingness to work beyond expectations
- Strong interest in health care services
- Initiative
- Resourcefulness

- Decisiveness
- Diplomacy
- Integrity
- Responsibility

Resources

- **American College of Health Care Administrators**
  300 North Lee Street, Suite 301
  Alexandria, VA 22314
  703-739-7900
  http://www.achca.org
  (offers student membership and college chapters)
- **American College of Healthcare Executives**
  One North Franklin Street, Suite 1700
  Chicago, IL 60606-3521
  312-424-2800
  http://www.ache.org
  (offers scholarships, student workshops and membership, career information, minority student internships, and publishes a number of career-related books)

History

History is the study of major social, political, cultural, and economic events of the past. Applying the results of historical study is important for the preservation and future growth of nations and institutions. Knowledge of the past enables people to develop pride and appreciation for the accomplishments of others. In addition, a thorough understanding of past problems and the strategies used to resolve them can help people to plan their present and future lives more effectively. Historical study is usually divided into ancient, medieval, and modern periods.

High School Courses

Anthropology

Civics

Government

History

Social Studies

Sociology

World History

Related Majors

African American History

Anthropology

Archaeology

Art History

Genealogy

History Education

Humanities

Library and Information Science

Music History

Political Science

Related Occupations

See page 11 for detailed explanation of key.

Anthropologist—D

Archaeologist—D

Archivist—B

Curator—B

Economist—B

Educator—B/M/D

FBI/CIA Agent—B

Foreign Correspondent—B

Foreign Service Officer—B/M

Freelance Writer—B

Genealogist—B/D

Gerontologist—B

Historian—B/D

Lawyer—P

Librarian—M

Market Research Analyst—B

News Reporter—B

Peace Corps/VISTA Volunteer—B

Political Scientist—B/D

Public Administrator—B

Research Assistant—B

Technical Writer—B

Writer—V

Leisure Activities

- Traveling
- Visiting libraries and museums

- Collecting relics, stamps, antiques, or coins
- Working part time or as a volunteer in a library, museum, historical society, or history department
- Maintaining a diary
- Viewing historical dramas or documentaries on TV or at a theater
- Joining a historical association or supporting historical preservation efforts
- Visiting book stores, antique shops, or flea markets
- Reading history-related publications
- Attending auctions or antique shows
- Participating in activities that involve research

Skills

- Ability to accurately identify and evaluate records of past events, ideas, and facts
- Intellectual capacity to perform well in most undergraduate and graduate college programs
- Proficiency in reading comprehension, writing, and speaking
- Ability to conduct and clearly explain scientific research
- Ability to collect and organize important historical data
- Ability to concentrate for long periods of time
- Broad background of general knowledge

- Ability to make keen observations, solve problems, and make appropriate decisions
- Proficiency for accuracy and detail

Values and Attributes

- Appreciation for past events and accomplishments
- Independence
- Intellectual growth
- Recognition
- Strong interest in reading and writing
- Continuous desire to study and research the past
- Analytical mind
- Objectivity
- Curiosity
- Resourcefulness
- Reflective nature
- Integrity
- Patience

Resources

- **American Historical Association**
  400 A Street SE
  Washington, DC 20003-3889
  202-544-2422
  http://www.historians.org
  (offers job placement assistance and online career-related articles; see Jobs and Careers link)
- **Society of American Archivists**
  527 South Wells, 5th Floor
  Chicago, IL 60607
  312-922-0140
  http://www.archivists.org
  (sponsors student chapters; offers career information and a list of helpful related associations)

Home Economics

Home economics is concerned with the quality and efficiency of family life and home care. Study in this area covers a broad spectrum and overlaps with a number of related fields. The four major divisions of home economics are food and nutrition; family life and child care; clothing and textiles; and home management, decorating, and equipment. Key areas of concentration include consumer management, budget, education, recreation, housing, health, nutrition, and transportation.

High School Courses

Child Care	Food Service
Clothing Design	Foods
Consumer Math	Health
Cooking	Home Economics
Family Living	Sewing

Related Majors

Child Care	Home Economics Education
Clothing, Apparel, and Textile Studies	Home Furnishing
Family/Community Studies	Individual and Family Development
Family Resource Management Studies	Interior Design
Food and Nutrition Studies	Vocational Home Economics
Health Education	

Related Occupations

See page 11 for detailed explanation of key.

Buyer—B	Food Scientist—B
Child Care Worker—AA	Food Service Manager—V/B
Child Welfare Worker—B	Home Economics Teacher—B
Clothing Designer—B	Home Health Aide—V/C
Cook/Chef—AA/V	Hotel/Motel Manager—B
Cooperative Extension Worker—B	Interior Decorator—B
Day Care Director—AA/B	Market Researcher—B
Dietitian—B	Merchandise Displayer—B
Director of Food Service—B	Nutritionist—B
Dressmaker—V	Purchasing Agent—B
Economist—B	Sales Manager—B
Executive Housekeeper—B	Social Service Aide—AA
Fashion Designer—B	Social Worker—B/M
Food and Drug Inspector—B	Tailor—V

Leisure Activities

- Participating in charitable outreach endeavors
- Working part time or as a volunteer in a day care center, hotel, hospital, or community service agency
- Reading publications related to homemaking
- Joining an organization such as 4-H
- Attending lectures, workshops, or conferences related to home economics
- Cooking
- Sewing
- Working part time in a food, clothing, furniture, appliance, or hardware store
- Working as a student aide in a home economics department

Skills

- Ability to organize, conduct, and clearly explain scientific research
- Ability to persuade and influence others
- Knowledge of community resources
- Proficiency in interpersonal communications
- Ability to communicate and interact with people of different backgrounds and personalities
- General knowledge in many areas

HELPFUL INFORMATION
Child Care Workers
Growth Outlook (2006–2016)

Projected: Grow faster than the average (increase 14% to 20%)
Number Employed (2006): 1,388,000 **(By 2016)** 1,636,000 (+18%)
Salary Range (2006): $12,900–$27,050
Related Occupations: *AIN*

	SALARY RANGE:
Economists	$42,300–$136,600
Interior Designers	$24,300–$70,700
*Nutritionists and Dietitians	$29,900–$68,300
Education Administrators, Preschool and Child Care/Primary	$24,500–$70,400

*According to the BLS, workers in these occupations are currently in high demand and thus have been designated as "In Demand."

SOURCE CODE(S):
Department of Labor, Bureau of Labor Statistics = *BLS*
Occupational Outlook Handbook, 2008–2009 = *OOH*
America's Career InfoNet (Online) = *AIN*
O*NET (Online) = *NET*

- Proficiency in speaking, writing, and listening
- Ability to analyze and think practically
- Ability to make keen observations, evaluations, and appropriate decisions
- A good understanding of human nature
- Ability to solve problems

Values and Attributes

- Helpfulness
- Achievement
- Creativity
- Desire to work closely with people
- Strong interest in improving the quality of home life
- Sensitivity to the practical needs of people
- Resourcefulness
- Dependability
- Organization
- Patience
- Tactfulness

Resources

- **American Association of Family and Consumer Sciences**
  400 North Columbus Street, Suite 202
  Alexandria, VA 22314
  703-706-4600
  http://www.aafcs.org
  (offers student membership, mentorships, networking opportunities, information about accreditation, a job bank, and an extensive list of helpful resource links)
- **American Dietetic Association**
  120 South Riverside Plaza, Suite 200
  Chicago, IL 60606-6995
  800-877-1600
  http://www.eatright.org
  (see Careers and Students link)
- **National Child Care Association**
  2025 M Street NW, Suite 800
  Washington, DC 20036-3309
  202-367-1133
  http://www.nccanet.org
  (provides information regarding quality child care; offers student membership and helpful related links)

Horticulture

Horticulture is the branch of agriculture that involves the production and use of fruits, vegetables, and ornamental plants. It includes the study of trees, flowers, shrubs, vines, and grasses. Horticulture sites, such as greenhouses, garden centers, and nurseries, play an important role in home gardening and landscaping pursuits. Specialties include fruits, vegetables, flowers; food handling, processing, and storage; landscaping, arboriculture, turf and range management, nursery management, and plant breeding.

High School Courses

Biology	Gardening
Chemistry	Landscape Gardening
Computer Applications	Physiology
Earth Science	Science
Floral Arranging	

Related Majors

Agriculture	Forestry
Agronomy	Greenhouse Technology
Biology	Land Management
Botany	Landscape Design
Floriculture	Plant Sciences
Food Science	Turf Management

Related Occupations

See page 11 for detailed explanation of key.

Agronomist—B	Greenhouse Manager—V
Biochemist—B	Landscape Architect—B
Botanist—B	Landscape Gardener—V
Dietitian—B	Nutritionist—B
Educator—B/M/D	Park Ranger—V
Entomologist—B	Plant Breeder—B
Florist—V	Plant Geneticist—B/D
Food Scientist—B	Seed Analyst—B
Forester—B	Silviculturist—B
Grounds Manager—V	Soil Conservationist—B
Horticultural Therapist—B	Technical Writer—B
Farmer—V	Tree Surgeon—V

Leisure Activities

- Working part time in a garden center, nursery, fruit orchard, or greenhouse
- Reading publications related to horticulture
- Visiting botanical gardens, state and national parks, conservatories, and arboretums
- Attending flower shows and state fairs
- Gardening, canning, and freezing fruits and vegetables
- Developing hobbies and collections around flowers, leaves, house plants, or floral design
- Joining a science club, 4-H club, orchid club, or a conservation group
- Supporting or participating in natural resource preservation efforts
- Belonging to a professional organization such as the American Society for Horticultural Science
- Attending clinics, lectures, and workshops related to horticulture
- Working as a student aide in a high school or college greenhouse

Skills

- A good understanding of and familiarity with all types of plants
- Physical stamina, good vision, and manual dexterity
- Ability to recognize differences in shapes, shading, and color
- Ability to work alone as well as with others
- Ability to make keen observations and sound judgments
- Proficiency in reading and writing
- General knowledge of horticulture supplies, equipment, services, and business/marketing practices
- Proficiency for accuracy and detail
- Ability to manage and supervise others
- Ability to apply scientific methods to horticultural concerns

Values and Attributes

- Creativity
- Aesthetic awareness
- Desire to help humanity
- Independence
- Green thumb
- Strong interest in plants
- Fondness for outdoor activities
- Perseverance
- Industriousness
- Curiosity
- Imagination
- Cooperation
- Friendliness

Resources

■ **American Horticultural Society**
7931 East Boulevard Drive
Alexandria, VA 22308
703-768-5700
http://www.ahs.org
(offers information about Master Gardeners programs and membership)

■ **American Society for Horticultural Science**
113 South West Street, Suite 200
Alexandria, VA 22314-2851
703-836-4606
http://www.ashs.org
(see Careers link)

■ **Botanical Society of America**
P.O. Box 299
St. Louis, MO 63166-0299
314-577-9566
http://www.botany.org
(see Careers/Jobs link)

Hotel/Motel Management

Hotel/motel management is concerned with the efficient, profitable management and operation of hotels, motels, and other hospitality-oriented institutions. Study in this area focuses on customer service, public relations, marketing, sales, maintenance, housekeeping, supervision, hotel and restaurant management and service, sanitation and safety, budgeting, conventions, and personnel. Specializations include executive housekeeping, maintenance engineering, front office operations, food and beverage management, budget, sales, advertising, recreation, purchasing, accounting, personnel training, conventions, restaurant management, reservations, sanitation and safety, and security.

High School Courses

Accounting	Foods
Business	Math
Business Management	Psychology
Computer Applications	Sociology
Economics	Speech
Food Service	

Related Majors

Business Management	Recreation and Leisure
Hospitality and Restaurant Management	Resort and Condominium Management
	Senior Services Management
Professional Golf Management	Tourism/Travel Management

Related Occupations

See page 11 for detailed explanation of key.

Airport Manager—B	Front Office Manager—V
Assistant Housekeeper—V	General Manager—B
Assistant Manager—AA	Mall Manager—B
Building Engineer—AA/V	Managing Director—B
Building Manager—V	Marketing Manager—B
Cafeteria Manager—AA/V	Office Manager—AA
Club Manager—B	Personnel Director—B
Director of Sales—V/B	Purchasing Agent—B
Executive Housekeeper—B	Tour Planner—V
Food and Beverage Director—AA/V	Resident Manager—B

Food Production Manager—V   Resort Manager—B
Food Service Manager—V   YMCA/YWCA Director—B

Leisure Activities

- Working part time as a bellhop, desk clerk, or hotel restaurant employee
- Organizing get-togethers, parties, or community events
- Leading a student group
- Participating on a debate or forensic team
- Participating in writing or oratory contests
- Reading publications related to management
- Attending lectures, workshops, and conferences related to hotel/motel management
- Joining a related professional organization
- Managing or helping others to manage apartments on a part-time basis

Skills

- Proficiency in interpersonal communication
- Proficiency in reading, writing, and speaking
- Ability to solve problems and make appropriate decisions
- Ability to interact with people of different backgrounds and personalities
- Aptitude for accuracy and detail
- Ability to maintain composure under pressure and react spontaneously
- Good physical stamina, vision, and health
- Ability to accept public scrutiny and criticism
- Ability to supervise and coordinate the activities of others
- General knowledge of the hospitality industry
- Familiarity with business, finance, and marketing techniques
- Ability to persuade and influence others

Values and Attributes

- Recognition and appreciation from others
- Skill with people
- Achievement
- Desire to help others
- Willingness to go the extra mile
- Desire to work with and please others
- Willingness to work long and irregular hours and on weekends
- Pleasant and friendly personality
- Diplomacy
- Helpfulness
- Ability to adapt to frequent relocation
- Attentiveness
- Leadership
- Imagination
- Knowledge

Resources

- **American Hotel and Lodging Association**
  Human Resources Department
  1201 New York Avenue NW, Suite 600
  Washington, DC 20005-3931
  202-289-3100
  http://www.ahla.com
  (offers joh-hunting and scholarship services)

- **International Council on Hotel, Restaurant and Institutional Education**
  2810 North Parham Road, Suite 230
  Richmond, VA 23294
  804-346-4800
  http://chrie.org
  (publishes a career self-development magazine, *HOSTEU,* as well as *Guide to College Programs in Hospitality and Tourism;* see Just for Students link)

Industrial Engineering

Industrial engineering uses the principles of science, mathematics, and engineering to efficiently and economically integrate people, machines, equipment, materials, and energy in order to maximize production. In this major you learn techniques for efficient production, time-and-motion study, data processing design, management control, quality control, plant layout, safety procedures and conditions, and environmental control. Specialties include operations research, management, ergonomics, environmental controls, plant layout and design, production planning and control, and computer processing.

High School Courses

Algebra

Blueprint Reading

Business Management

Calculus

Chemistry

Computer Applications

Drafting

Economics

Geometry

Industrial Arts

Math

Mechanical Drawing

Physical Science

Trigonometry

Related Majors

Computer Engineering

Computer Systems Analysis

Electrical/Electronics Engineering

Engineering Technology

Environmental Health Engineering

Industrial Production Technology

Materials Engineering

Mechanical/Manufacturing Engineering

Quality Control/Safety Technology

Welding Engineering

Related Occupations

See page 11 for detailed explanation of key.

Automotive Engineer—B

Consulting Engineer—B/M

Electrical Engineer—B

Educator—M/D

Electrical Engineer—B

Environmental Engineer—B

Fire Protection Engineer—B

Industrial Engineer—B

Manufacturing Engineer—B

Materials Handling Engineer—B

Mechanical Engineer—B

Operating Engineer—B

Plant Engineer—B

Plastics Engineer—B

Process Engineer—B

Quality Control Engineer—B

Research Engineer—B/D

Safety Engineer—B

Systems Analyst—B

Systems Engineer—B

Leisure Activities

- Participating in fund-raising or social events that involve organization and planning
- Working part time or as a volunteer in a supervisory position in a factory or a school industrial arts department
- Solving analytic, logic, and budgetary problems
- Reading publications related to engineering
- Attending engineering-related lectures and workshops
- Participating in clubs or organizations that require you to make oral presentations and write reports
- Working part time as a research assistant

Skills

- Ability to synthesize and integrate various factors of production
- Proficiency in mathematics and science
- Ability to make keen observations and sound judgments
- Proficiency in written and oral communication
- Ability to conduct and clearly communicate scientific research
- Knowledge of work measurements and standards
- Intellectual capacity to perform well in most undergraduate and graduate college programs
- Aptitude for leadership

HELPFUL INFORMATION
*Industrial Engineers
Growth Outlook (2006–2016)

Projected: Grow faster than the average (increase 14% to 20%)
Number Employed (2006): 227,000   **(By 2016)** 270,000 (+19%)
Salary Range (2006): $44,790–$100,980
Related Occupations: AIN

	SALARY RANGE:
*Mechanical Engineers	$45,170–$104,900
Petroleum Engineers	$57,960–$145,600+
*Electrical Engineers	$49,120–$115,240
*Aerospace Engineers	$59,610–$124,550

*According to the BLS, workers in these occupations are currently in high demand and thus have been designated as "In Demand."

SOURCE CODE(S):
Department of Labor, Bureau of Labor Statistics = BLS
Occupational Outlook Handbook, 2008–2009 = OOH
America's Career InfoNet (Online) = AIN
O*NET (Online) = NET

- Ability to analyze, organize, and interpret scientific data
- Knowledge of basic manufacturing and assembly processes
- Good interpersonal skills and ability to work effectively with others

Values and Attributes

- Creativity
- Knowledge
- Achievement
- Desire to help others live better
- Enjoyment of challenges
- Interest in seeing ideas developed into practical use
- Initiative
- Perseverance
- Flexibility
- Organization
- Imagination
- Curiosity

Resources

- **The Institute of Industrial Engineers**
  3577 Parkway Lane, Suite 200
  Norcross, GA 30092
  770-449-0460
  http://www.iienet.org
  (provides job placement service and offers student membership; see the Web
  site's Career Center section)
- **Junior Engineering Technical Society**
  1420 King Street, Suite 405
  Alexandria, VA 22314
  703-548-5387
  http://www.jets.org
  (sponsors activities to help students determine engineering readiness, has special outreach to minority students, and offers information about careers)
- **National Society of Professional Engineers**
  1420 King Street
  Alexandria, VA 22314
  703-684-2800
  http://www.nspe.org
  (offers career information, scholarships, etc.)

Industrial and Precision Production/Technology

Industrial and precision production/technology is the study of the design and production of tools and machines as well as consumer products. This area is usually referred to as the machine trades field. Students are exposed to intricate and precise techniques of machine and product development. Areas of focus include blueprint reading, machine function and operation, precision and accuracy, applied mathematics, production, materials applications, installation, repair, and service. Specialties include tool-and-die, machines, job setting, toolmaking, machine operating, moldmaking, diemaking, inspection, instrument making, computer-aided design (CAD), and computer-aided manufacturing (CAM).

High School Courses

Algebra	Drafting
Applied Math	Geometry
Blueprint Reading	Graphic Arts
Computer Applications	Industrial Arts
Computer-Aided Design (CAD)	Machine/Metal Shop
Computer-Aided	Mechanical Drawing
Manufacturing (CAM)	Trigonometry

Related Majors

Data Processing Technology	Environmental Control Technology
Design Technology	Machine Technology
Electrical/Electronics Technology	Mechanical Technology
Engineering Technology	Quality Control/Statistics Technology
Electromechanical Instrumentation	
and Maintenance Technology	

Related Occupations

See page 11 for detailed explanation of key.

Blacksmith—V	Machine Repairer—V
Boilermaker—V	Machine Tool Operator—V
Butcher—V	Machine Tool Setter—V
Cabinetmaker—V	Machinist—V
CAD/CAM Operator—V	Millwright—V
Compositor—V	Photoengraver—V

Gunsmith—V

Hand Molder—V

Instrument Maker—V

Jeweler—V

Layout Worker—V

Lithographer—V

Locksmith—V

Machine Operator—V

Printing Press Operator—V

Set Up Worker—V

Shoe Repairer—V

Tool and Die Maker—V

Tool Programmer—V

Upholsterer—V

Welder—V

Leisure Activities

- Working part time or as a volunteer worker in a machine shop, school industrial arts or metal shop
- Fixing and repairing mechanical items such as household appliances
- Overhauling car engines or building race cars, go-carts, dune buggies, or other mechanical vehicles as a pastime
- Reading mechanically related manuals and books

Skills

- Aptitude for mathematics and mechanics
- Aptitude for spatial perception, precision, accuracy, and detail
- Good vision, motor coordination, and manual and finger dexterity

---

HELPFUL INFORMATION
Machinists
Growth Outlook (2006–2016)

Projected: Expected to decline slowly to moderately (decrease 3% to 9%)

Number Employed (2006): 397,000   **(By 2016)** 384,000 (-3%)

Salary Range (2006): $21,400–$52,600

Related Occupations: *AIN*

	SALARY RANGE:
Numerical Tool and Process Programmers	$27,300–$66,200
Tool and Die Makers	$28,800–$67,400
*Multimachine Tool Setters and Related Workers	$19,100–$49,900
*Welders and Related Workers	$21,000–$46,800

*According to the BLS, workers in these occupations are currently in high demand and thus have been designated as "In Demand."

SOURCE CODE(S):

Department of Labor, Bureau of Labor Statistics = *BLS*

Occupational Outlook Handbook, 2008–2009 = *OOH*

America's Career InfoNet (Online) = *AIN*

O*NET (Online) = *NET*

- Knowledge of machine operations and industrial practices and trends
- Ability to read and interpret blueprints, diagrams, and schematic drawings
- Ability to follow directions and work alone as well as with others
- Ability to meet deadlines
- Thorough knowledge and ability in an area of specialization
- Ability to make sound judgments and appropriate decisions and solve problems
- Proficiency with computerized equipment

Values and Attributes

- Achievement
- Security
- Desire to be exact and to the point
- Ability to adapt to awkward and uncomfortable positions
- Enjoyment of hands-on activities
- Thoroughness
- Patience
- Precision
- Carefulness

Resources

- **Association for Computing Machinery**
  2 Penn Station, Suite 701
  New York, NY 10121-0701
  800-342-6626
  http://www.acm.org
  (offers student membership, curriculum recommendations, accreditation information, and a career and job center link)
- **Precision Machined Products Association**
  6700 West Snowville Road
  Brecksville, OH 44141
  440-526-5803
  http://www.pmpa.org
  (offers career information)
- **Tooling and Manufacturing Association**
  1177 South Dee Road
  Park Ridge, IL 60068
  847-825-1120
  http://www.tmanet.com
  (provides information about careers, school activities, training programs, and an extensive list of related links)

Law

Law is the study of the rules and guidelines by which a society maintains order and cooperation. The effective development, implementation, interpretation, and modification of rules and guidelines is a requirement for transmitting societal values and expectations. Study in law exposes the student to civil and constitutional law, contracts, property, legal methods, research and writing, torts, criminal law and taxation, lawyer and client theory, law history, and many other areas. Specialties include civil, criminal, or labor law; real estate, corporate, or patent law; tort, taxation, or international law; entertainment, trust, or admiralty law; bankruptcy; and environmental law.

High School Courses

Civics	Government
Computer Applications	Psychology
Creative Writing	Public Speaking
Debate	Sociology
English	Speech
Forensics	

Related Majors

Bankruptcy Law	Foreign and International Law
Constitutional Law	Labor Law
Corporate Law	Law Education
Criminal Law	Paralegal/Legal Assisting
English	Political Science
Entertainment Law	Real Estate Law
Environmental Law	Tort and Insurance Law
Family Law	

Related Occupations

See page 11 for detailed explanation of key.

Adjudicator—P	Insurance Attorney—P
Appeals Referee—P	Judge—P
Appellate Court Judge—P	Paralegal—AA
Bankruptcy Attorney—P	Lawyer—P
Bar Examiner—P	Parole/Probation Officer—B
Corporation Lawyer—P	Patent Agent—B
Court Reporter—AA	Patent Lawyer—P
Criminal Lawyer—P	Real Estate Buyer—B
District Attorney—P	Tax Attorney—P
District Court Judge—P	Title Attorney—P

Employment Lawyer—P   Traffic Court Magistrate—P
Environmental Lawyer—P   Trial Court Judge—P
Escrow Officer—B

Leisure Activities

- Participating in activities that involve research
- Visiting libraries and attending court sessions
- Reading law publications
- Viewing dramas or documentaries about law on TV or at a theater
- Attending lectures or conferences related to law
- Working part time or as a volunteer in a law office or department
- Joining a student government or newspaper staff
- Freelance or technical writing
- Participating in a community association
- Joining a debate or forensics team
- Competing in oratory contests
- Conversing with others

Skills

- Ability to speak articulately, read comprehensively, and write well
- Ability to persuade and influence others
- Broad background of general knowledge
- Ability to make keen observations and sound judgments
- Ability to research, collect, organize, and clearly present information to others
- Familiarity with legal practices, policies, and trends
- Intellectual capacity to perform well in most undergraduate and graduate college programs
- Ability to analyze and evaluate data, make appropriate decisions, and solve problems
- Ability to communicate abstract ideas to others
- Aptitude for accuracy and detail
- Aptitude for leadership

Values and Attributes

- Intellectual growth
- Power
- Prestige
- Desire for recognition and appreciation from others
- Ability to work under pressure, meet deadlines, and accept close public scrutiny and criticism
- High regard for and appreciation of the law and an orderly society
- Sensitivity to the needs of human beings
- Persistence
- Integrity

- Resourcefulness
- Persuasiveness
- Analytical mind
- Trustworthiness

Resources

- **American Bar Association**
  321 North Clark Street
  Chicago, IL 60610
  800-285-2221
  http://www.abanet.org
  (provides information about accredited law schools, exam preparation, an array of career publications, and student membership)

- **Law School Admission Council**
  661 Penn Street
  Newtown, PA 18940
  215-968-1001
  http://www.lsac.org
  (provides information on how to prepare for various law school exams, choosing a law school, and financial aid)

Legal and Protective Services

Legal and protective services is the study of several related fields that focus on the effective implementation of law and legal procedures, as well as the relationship of laws to the safety and protection of life and property. Legal services involves research and support related to the understanding and interpretation of law, legal procedures, and practices. Study in protective services concentrates on the implementation of laws aimed at ensuring the peaceful cooperation, security, and safety of human lives and property. Some specialties are legal assisting, criminal justice, public safety, corrections and rehabilitation, and law enforcement.

High School Courses

Civics

Computer Applications

Government

Health

Physical Education

Psychology

ROTC

Social Studies

Sociology

Related Majors

Corrections

Court Reporting

Criminal Justice

Fire Protection/Safety Technology

Fire Science

Law Enforcement/Police Science

Military Science

Military Technology

Paralegal/Legal Assisting

Physical Education

Safety and Security Technology

Related Occupations

See page 11 for detailed explanation of key.

Administrative Examiner—P

Bailiff—V

Border Patrol Officer—AA

Case Worker—B

Corrections Officer—AA

Criminal Investigator—AA

Deputy Sheriff—AA

Detective—AA

District Attorney—P

Drug Enforcement Officer—AA

Military Officer—B

Paralegal—AA/B

Parole/Probation Officer—B

Penologist—B

Police Commissioner—B

Police Officer—AA

Polygraph Examiner—AA/B

Private Investigator—V

Public Safety Captain—AA

Security Guard—V

Firefighter—AA   Security Guard—V

Fish and Game Warden—AA/B   Special Agent—B

Lifeguard—V/AA

Leisure Activities

- Working part time or as a volunteer in a fire or police station, law office, or insurance firm
- Participating in individual or team sports
- Being involved in activities that require investigation and research
- Viewing law-related dramas and documentaries on TV
- Visiting libraries
- Reading publications related to legal or protective services
- Working as a security guard
- Writing reports
- Participating in student government
- Belonging to a debate or forensics team
- Serving in the armed forces

Skills

- Background of legal knowledge
- Ability to react spontaneously and maintain composure under pressure

---

HELPFUL INFORMATION
*Police and Sheriff's Patrol Officers
Growth Outlook (2006–2016)

Projected: Grow about as fast as the average (increase 7% to 13%)

Number Employed (2006): 654,000   **(By 2016)** 724,000 (+11%)

Salary Range (2006): $27,310–$95,590

Related Occupations: *AIN*

	SALARY RANGE:
*Detectives and Criminal Investigators	$34,500–$92,600
*Security Guards	$15,000–$35,800
*Police, Fire, and Ambulance Dispatchers	$20,000–$47,200
Correctional Officers and Jailers	$23,600–$58,600

*According to the BLS, workers in these occupations are currently in high demand and thus have been designated as "In Demand."

SOURCE CODE(S):

Department of Labor, Bureau of Labor Statistics = *BLS*

Occupational Outlook Handbook, 2008–2009 = *OOH*

America's Career InfoNet (Online) = *AIN*

O*NET (Online) = NET

- Proficiency in reading, writing, and speaking
- Ability to make appropriate decisions and sound judgments
- Ability to interact with people of different personalities and backgrounds
- Ability to solve problems and meet deadlines
- Proficiency in interpersonal communication
- Aptitude for accuracy and detail
- Ability to persuade and influence others
- Ability to conduct and clearly explain scientific research
- Good vision, health, physical stamina, and manual dexterity

Values and Attributes

- Security
- Wisdom
- Desire to help others
- Appreciation for order and thoroughness
- Analytical and logical thinking
- Interest in investigating and exploring for factual detail
- Integrity
- Persistence
- Alertness
- Trustworthiness
- Desire for challenges

Resources

- **American Correctional Association**
  206 North Washington Street, Suite 200
  Alexandria, VA 22314
  800-222-5646
  http://www.aca.org
  (offers employment assistance, information about accreditation, and a helpful list of links to other resources)
- **American Jail Association**
  1135 Professional Court
  Hagerstown, MD 21740
  301-790-3930
  http://www.corrections.com/aja
  (provides certification opportunities and informative online publications)
- **International Association of Chiefs of Police**
  515 North Washington Street
  Alexandria, VA 22314-2357
  703-836-6767
  http://www.theiacp.org
  (has information about careers in law enforcement)

Library and Information Science

Library and information science is concerned with how information of all kinds is stored, organized, classified, and made available for use by others. Study in this area exposes you to the intricate logistics of acquiring, circulating, and maintaining massive amounts of information and materials. You also learn various ways to access information and techniques of promotion. Major concentrations in this field include materials for children and young adults, reference materials, audiovisual materials, school and college services, special library services, cataloging, special collections, material acquisitions, adult materials, community outreach, information systems, and administration.

High School Courses

Anthropology	Literature
Computer Science	Management
English	Social Studies
History	Sociology
Introduction to Computers	Speed Reading
Language Arts	World History

Related Majors

History	Library Science Education
Information Science	Linguistics
Information Management	Museum Studies
Law Librarianship	

Related Occupations

See page 11 for detailed explanation of key.

Academic Librarian—M	Librarian—M
Acquisitions Librarian—M	Library Assistant—V
Archivist—M	Library Consultant—M/D
Bibliographer—M	Library Director—M/D
Book Conservator—M	Library Technician—C/AA
Cataloger—M	Media Center Manager—M
Children's Librarian—M	Medical Public Librarian—M
Classifier—M	Reference Librarian—M
Community Outreach Librarian—M	Special Collections Librarian—M
Information Scientist—M/D	Systems Analyst—M

Leisure Activities

- Reading
- Freelance writing
- Attending book fairs, used book sales, and book stores
- Visiting libraries and museums
- Belonging to a book club, literary society, or professional organization, such as the American Library Association
- Attending lectures, workshops, and conferences related to library and information sciences
- Working part time or as a volunteer in a library, bookstore, law office, or research firm
- Participating in activities that involve research
- Subscribing to a professional library publication
- Collecting items such as stamps or rare books

Skills

- Knowledge in an area of specialization as well as a background of general knowledge
- Proficiency in reading and grammar and having an extensive vocabulary
- Ability to organize, collect, classify, arrange, and coordinate materials of all kinds
- Ability to critically evaluate, make sound judgments and appropriate decisions, and solve problems
- Good vision and physical stamina
- Proficiency in interpersonal communication
- Ability to work with others as well as work quietly alone for long periods of time
- Ability to conduct and clearly explain scientific research
- Intellectual ability to perform well in most undergraduate and graduate college programs
- Aptitude for accuracy, detail, and memorization
- Proficiency with computers

Values and Attributes

- Intellectual growth
- Wisdom
- Desire to help others learn
- Love of reading and exploring for information
- Willingness to engage in lifelong learning
- Flexibility
- Resourcefulness
- Analytical mind
- Intellectual curiosity
- Perseverance
- Alertness

Resources

- **American Library Association**
  50 East Huron Street
  Chicago, IL 60611
  800-545-2433
  http://www.ala.org
  (offers student membership, provides employment assistance, and scholarship
  information, as well as a list of accredited programs; see Education
  and Careers link)

- **American Society for Information Science and Technology**
  1320 Fenwick Lane, Suite 510
  Silver Spring, MD 20910
  301-495-0900
  http://www.asis.org
  (offers career information and a list of schools that have information science
  programs)

- **Special Libraries Association**
  331 South Patrick Street
  Alexandria, VA 22314
  703-647-4900
  http://www.sla.org
  (see Careers link)

HELPFUL INFORMATION
*Marketing Research Analysts
Growth Outlook (2006–2016)

Projected: Grow faster than the average (increase 14% to 20%)
Number Employed (2006): 234,000 **(By 2016)** 281,000 (+20%)
Salary Range (2006): $32,250–$112,510
Related Occupations: *AIN*

	SALARY RANGE:
*Marketing Managers	$51,200–$145,600+
*Customer Service Representatives	$18,100–$46,000
*Sales Representatives, Wholesale	$26,000–$101,000+
*Sales Managers	$45,100–$145,600+

*According to the BLS, workers in these occupations are currently in high
demand and thus have been designated as "In Demand."

SOURCE CODE(S):
Department of Labor, Bureau of Labor Statistics = *BLS*
Occupational Outlook Handbook, 2008–2009 = *OOH*
America's Career InfoNet (Online) = *AIN*
O*NET (Online) = *NET*

Marketing and Distribution

Marketing and distribution is a major field of business administration that involves the study of consumer needs and desires for products and services, consumers' willingness and ability to pay for those needs/desires, and consumer demographics. A strong focus is on the various strategies used to attract and motivate people to buy or subscribe to a product or service and the numerous methods of distribution. Specializations in this area include sales, advertising, sales promotion, retail management, brand management, and marketing research.

High School Courses

Advertising	Fashion Merchandising
Business	Forensics
Computer Applications	Psychology
Debate	Sales
Economics	Speech

Related Majors

Advertising	Fashion Merchandising
Business	Marketing Education
Business Marketing	Marketing Research
Economics	Retail Management

Related Occupations

See page 11 for detailed explanation of key.

Advertising Account Executive—B	Online Marketer—V/B
Advertising Manager—B	Package Designer—B
Advertising Salesperson—AA	Pharmaceutical Sales Representative—B
Buyer—B	Product Manager—B
Customer Service Representative—V	Purchasing Agent—B
Direct Salesperson—AA	Real Estate Agent—AA
Director of Marketing—V	Sales Manager—B
Economist—B	Sales Representative—B
Fashion Model—V	Sales Supervisor—B
Field Representative—AA	Securities Sales Agent—B
Human Resources Manager—B/M	Store Controller—B
Insurance Agent—V/B	Store Manager—B
Manufacturer Sales Workers—AA	Survey Researcher—B
Market Research Analyst—B	Wireless Sales Worker—V
Merchandise Manager—B	

Leisure Activities

- Working part time in a department store, advertising firm, warehouse, or wholesale/retail establishment
- Belonging to a Junior Achievement Club, the DECA (an association of marketing students), or professional organization, such as the American Marketing Association
- Participating in oratory contests
- Participating on a debate or forensics team
- Attending auctions, political rallies, or sales lectures
- Participating in a civic fund-raising event or in student government
- Writing promotional materials
- Reading publications related to marketing and distribution
- Attending sales and marketing workshops and conferences
- Serving as a student aide in a school or college distributive education or marketing department
- Selling products or services on a part-time basis

Skills

- Ability to work well with people of different personalities and backgrounds
- Ability to make appropriate decisions and sound judgments
- Ability to persuade and influence others
- A good vocabulary
- Articulacy
- Good knowledge of marketing techniques and consumer products and needs
- Ability to solve problems
- Physical stamina and emotional well-being
- Ability to conduct and apply the results of consumer research
- Aptitude for selling

Values and Attributes

- Achievement
- Prestige
- Wealth
- Desire for recognition and appreciation from others
- Creativity
- Outgoing, polite, and friendly attitude
- Desire to serve and please others
- Tendency to be alert and ambitious
- Competitiveness and flexibility
- Energy
- Patience
- Poise
- Neatness
- Self-confidence

Resources

- **American Marketing Association**

  311 South Wacker Drive, Suite 5800

  Chicago, IL 60606

  312-542-9000

  http://www.marketingpower.com

  (offers student membership and publishes a variety of marketing materials)

- **National DECA**

  1908 Association Drive

  Reston, VA 20191

  703-860-5000

  http://deca.org

  (an association of marketing students; sponsors high school and college chapters and offers scholarships)

- **Sales and Marketing Executives International**

  PO Box 1390

  Sumas, WA 98295-1390

  312-893-0751

  http://www.smei.org

  (provides information on sales/marketing careers in the form of career documents and career videos, and certification)

HELPFUL INFORMATION
*Marketing Research Analysts
Growth Outlook (2006–2016)

Projected: Grow faster than the average (increase 14% to 20%)

Number Employed (2006): 234,000   **(By 2016)** 281,000 (+20%)

Salary Range (2006): $32,250–$112,510

Related Occupations: *AIN*

	SALARY RANGE:
*Marketing Managers	$51,200–$145,600+
*Customer Service Representatives	$18,100–$46,000
*Sales Representatives, Wholesale	$26,000–$101,000+
*Sales Managers	$45,100–$145,600+

*According to the BLS, workers in these occupations are currently in high demand and thus have been designated as "In Demand."

SOURCE CODE(S):

Department of Labor, Bureau of Labor Statistics = *BLS*

Occupational Outlook Handbook, 2008–2009 = *OOH*

America's Career InfoNet (Online) = *AIN*

O*NET (Online) = *NET*

Mathematics

Mathematics is the study of quantitative relationships expressed in numbers and symbols. It focuses on mathematical concepts and theories and involves their formulation, testing, interpretation, and practical application. Mathematics is usually referred to as either pure (theoretical and abstract) or applied (practical and result-oriented). Mathematics is used by just about everyone in some manner. A minimal understanding and use of mathematics is considered basic to daily life. Major branches include arithmetic, algebra, geometry, trigonometry, calculus, probability, and statistics.

High School Courses

Accounting
Algebra
Calculus
Computer Applications
Geometry
Math
Physics
Statistics
Trigonometry

Related Majors

Accounting
Actuarial Science
Applied and Industrial Mathematics
Auditing
Banking
Computer Science
Economics
Engineering
Finance
Mathematical Education
Mathematical Statistics
Physics

Related Occupations

See page 11 for detailed explanation of key.

Accountant—B
Actuary—B/M
Aerospace Engineer—B
Appraiser—B
Astronomer—D
Bank Officer—AA/B
Bookkeeper—AA
Cartographer—B
Computer Programmer—B
Credit Manager—AA/B
Educator—B/M/D
Financial Planner—B
Market Research Analyst—B
Mathematician—B/D
Nuclear Scientist—B/D
Physicist—B/D
Radar Technician—AA
Statistician—B
Surveyor—AA
Systems Analyst—B
Tool and Die Maker— V

Leisure Activities

- Doing jigsaw puzzles and playing games of strategy
- Participating in tournaments, quiz bowls, and other competitive events
- Solving problems involving analytical and logical processes
- Joining a math club, science organization, or investment group
- Serving as a committee or church treasurer or as a financial officer for a civic or social agency
- Working as a part-time or volunteer sports statistician
- Reading math or science publications
- Trouble-shooting computer problems

Skills

- Ability to make sound judgments and decisions and to solve quantitative problems
- Ability to concentrate for long periods of time
- Proficiency in writing, speaking, and memorization
- Proficiency for accuracy and detail
- Ability to understand both concrete and abstract mathematical concepts
- Ability to organize, analyze, and interpret numerical data
- Ability to make keen observations
- Ability to conduct and clearly explain scientific research
- Proficiency in use of scientific calculator

Values and Attributes

- Independence
- Intellectual growth
- Achievement
- Security
- Ability to frame inquiry and respond objectively
- Tendency toward analytical and logical thinking
- Capacity for precision and detail
- Desire for challenges
- Thoroughness
- Imagination
- Patience
- Persistence
- Self-discipline

Resources

- **American Mathematical Society**
  201 Charles Street
  Providence, RI 02904-2294
  800-321-4267
  http://www.ams.org
  (provides an excellent Careers and Employment link as well as interesting
  career profiles)
- **Mathematical Association of America**
  1529 18th Street NW
  Washington, DC 20036-1358
  800-741-9415
  http://www.maa.org
  (see Information for Undergraduate Students)

Mechanical Engineering

Mechanical engineering focuses on the practical application of science, mathematics, and energy in the design and development of machines and related mechanical equipment that produce and use power as well as those used in manufacturing products. Internal combustion engines, motors of all types, nuclear reactors, refrigerators, elevators, robots, and a variety of medical equipment are some of the visible results of mechanical engineering. Specialties in this field include automotive, air-conditioning/refrigeration and heating, research, nuclear power, and aircraft.

High School Courses

Algebra	Mechanical Drawing
Blueprint Reading	Mechanics
Calculus	Physical Science
Computer Applications	Physics
Geometry	Small Engine Repair
Industrial Arts	Trigonometry
Math	

Related Majors

Aerospace Engineering	Industrial Engineering
Automotive Engineering	Industrial Production Technology
Computer Engineering	Materials Engineering
Electrical/Electronics Engineering	Mechanical Design Technology
Heating, Refrigeration, and Air-Conditioning Engineering	Mechanical Engineering Technology

Related Occupations

See page 11 for detailed explanation of key.

Aerospace Engineer—B/D	Materials Handling Engineer—B
Astronaut—B/M	Mechanical Drafter—AA
Automotive Engineer—B	Mechanical Engineer—B
Biomedical Engineer—B	Mechanical Engineering Technician—AA
Computer Science Engineer—B	Mechatronics—B
Consulting Engineer—B/M	Millwright—V
Electrical Engineer—B	Packaging Engineer—B
Engineer—B	Plastics Engineer—B
Engineering Mechanic—AA	Research Engineer—B/D

Engineering Technician—AA

Heating and Air-Conditioning
Engineer—B

Industrial Engineer—B

Safety Engineer—B

Systems Analyst—B

Systems Engineer—B

Test Engineer—B

Leisure Activities

- Tinkering with electrical appliances or other mechanical devices
- Participating in a club or organization that requires you to make oral presentations and write reports
- Developing hobbies related to radios, stereos, building go-carts, fixing cars, and similar activities
- Reading publications related to mechanics or engineering
- Belonging to a student or professional engineering organization
- Working part time or as a volunteer in an engineering firm, mechanics shop, or engineering department
- Attending lectures, workshops, and classes related to mechanical engineering

Skills

- Ability to make keen observations and sound judgments
- Proficiency in mathematics and science
- Ability to synthesize and integrate various factors of production
- Proficiency in written and oral communication
- Ability to conduct and clearly communicate scientific research
- Intellectual capacity to perform well in most undergraduate and graduate college programs
- Ability to work well with others
- Ability to solve problems and make appropriate decisions
- Aptitude for accuracy and detail, spatial perception, and abstract reasoning
- Manual dexterity and understanding of mechanics
- Proficiency with computers
- Proficiency in an area of specialization and knowledge of current practices and trends
- Sensitivity to economic considerations and human needs

Values and Attributes

- Creativity
- Achievement
- Knowledge
- Desire to help others live better
- Interest in seeing ideas developed into practical use
- Desire for challenges
- Imagination
- Flexibility
- Persuasiveness
- Curiosity

Resources

- **American Society of Mechanical Engineers**
  Three Park Avenue
  New York, NY 10016-5990
  800-843-2763
  http://www.asme.org
  (see Career Center link)

- **Junior Engineering Technical Society**
  1420 King Street, Suite 405
  Alexandria, VA 22314
  703-548-5387
  http://www.jets.org
  (sponsors activities geared to assist students to determine engineering readiness, has special outreach to minority students, and offers information about careers)

- **National Society of Professional Engineers**
  1420 King Street
  Alexandria, VA 22314-2794
  703-684-2800
  http://www.nspe.org
  (offers career information, scholarships, and internships)

Mechanics and Related Services

Mechanics involves the study of machine design, building, operation, repair, and service. Mechanics covers a broad range and includes appliances, communications and computer equipment, industrial machinery, and office machines as well as vehicle and mobile mechanics. Among the specialties within this area are automotive, aircraft, diesel, farm equipment, appliances, office machines, radio/TV, air-conditioning, refrigeration, and heating.

High School Courses

Algebra

Applied Math

Automotive Mechanics

Computer Applications

Electronics

Mechanical Drawing

Small Engine Repair

Related Majors

Air Conditioning, Refrigeration, and Maintenance Technology

Data Processing Technology

Diesel Mechanics

Electrical/Electronics Technology

Electromechanical Instrumentation and Heating Mechanics

Mechanical Engineering Technology

Quality Control and Safety Technology

Related Occupations

See page 11 for detailed explanation of key.

Air-Conditioning, Refrigeration, and Heating Mechanic—AA

Aircraft Mechanic—AA

Automotive Body Repairer—V

Automotive Mechanic—V

Bicycle Repairer—V

Cable Splicer—V

Commercial/Industrial Electronic Equipment Repairer—V

Computer Service Technician—AA

Diesel Mechanic—V

Electronic Home Equipment Repairer—V

Engine Specialist—V

Farm Equipment Mechanic—V

General Maintenance Mechanic—V

Gunsmith—V

Industrial Machine Repairer—V

Instrument Mechanic—V

Instrument Repairer—V

Instrumentation Technician—AA/V

Line Installer—V

Locksmith—V

Millwright—V

Motorcycle Mechanic—V

Musical Instrument Repairer—V

Office Machine Servicer—V

Telephone Installer/Repairer—V

Vending Machine Servicer—V

Watchmaker—V

Leisure Activities

- Working part time or as a volunteer mechanic in a service station or bicycle repair or small engine shop
- Repairing electric appliances or other mechanical gadgetry
- Reading manuals and books related to auto mechanics
- Developing hobbies and collections related to cars, model kits, or racing
- Doing your own car repair
- Building and/or repairing go-carts, mini-bikes, lawn mowers, or scooters
- Attending auto shows
- Racing

Skills

- Good health, vision, hearing, and coordination
- Aptitude for mechanics and computer instrumentation
- Ability to read and understand technical and service manuals and diagrams
- Good listening skills
- Ability to work alone as well as with others
- Ability to meet deadlines
- Ability to interact with people with different personalities and backgrounds
- Proficiency in spatial perception and mechanical dexterity

HELPFUL INFORMATION
*Automotive Technicians
Growth Outlook (2006–2016)

Projected: Grow faster than the average (increase 14% to 20%)
Number Employed (2006): 773,000   **(By 2016)** 883,000 (+14%)
Salary Range (2006): $19,100–$56,600
Related Occupations: *AIN*

	SALARY RANGE:
*Heating, Air-Conditioning and Refrigeration Mechanics	$23,700–$59,400
*Mobile/Heavy Equipment Mechanics	$26,300–$58,600
*Industrial Machinery Mechanics	$26,700–$62,100
*Aircraft Mechanics and Service Technicians	$31,100–$71,800

*According to the BLS, workers in these occupations are currently in high demand and thus have been designated as "In Demand."

SOURCE CODE(S):
Department of Labor, Bureau of Labor Statistics = *BLS*
Occupational Outlook Handbook, 2008–2009 = *OOH*
America's Career InfoNet (Online) = *AIN*
O*NET (Online) = *NET*

- Ability to make sound judgments and appropriate decisions and solve problems
- Proficiency in an area of mechanical specialization

Values and Attributes

- Skill
- Accomplishment
- Security
- Willingness to work with dirty, greasy materials and sometimes in awkward and hazardous positions
- Enjoyment of hands-on activities
- Willingness to continue training and education throughout life
- Dependability
- Precision
- Trustworthiness
- Carefulness
- Thoroughness

Resources

- **National Automotive Technicians Education Foundation**
  101 Blue Seal Drive SE, Suite 101
  Leesburg, VA 20175
  703-669-6650
  http://www.natef.org
  (offers information about certification and careers)
- **National Institute for Automotive Service Excellence**
  101 Blue Seal Drive SE, Suite 101
  Leesburg, VA 20175
  703-669-6600
  http://www.asecert.org
  (publishes *ASE Blue Seal Tech News* as well as preparation guides and sample test questions; promotes high standards of automotive service)

Medicine

Medicine, a branch of the health sciences, addresses the application of medicine and medical techniques in the treatment, care, and prevention of disease, illness, and injury in both humans and animals. The study of medicine focuses on procedures, drugs, and technology that help minimize pain and preserve health. Among the numerous specialties are anesthesiology, colon and rectal surgery, dermatology, family practice, internal medicine, neurology, obstetrics and gynecology, pediatrics, urology, gastroenterology, surgery, dentistry, psychiatry, and veterinary medicine.

High School Courses

Algebra	Health
Biology	Physical Education
Chemistry	Physiology
Computer Applications	Science
First Aid	Trigonometry
Geometry	

Related Majors

Athletic Training	Physician Assisting
Dermatology	Pre-Dentistry
Family Medicine	Pre-Optometry
Gynecology	Pre-Veterinary Medicine
Health Services	Psychiatry
Medical Technology	Psychology
Neurology	Sports Medicine
Pharmacy	Urology

Related Occupations

See page 11 for detailed explanation of key.

Allergist—P	Orthodontist—P
Anesthesiologist—P	Osteopath—P
Cardiologist—P	Pathologist—P
Chiropractor—P	Pediatrician—P
Dentist—P	Pharmacologist—P
Dermatologist—P	Physician—P
Endocrinologist—P	Physician Assistant—B
Gastroenterologist—P	Plastic Surgeon—P
Geriatrician—P	Podiatrist—P
Gynecologist—P	Psychiatrist—P
Immunologist—P	Radiologist—P
Internist—P	Reproductive Endocrinologist—P
Naturopathic Physicians—P	Sports Medicine Physicians—P

Neurologist—P   Surgeon—P
Obstetrician—P   Urologist—P
Ophthalmologist—P   Veterinarian—P
Optometrist—P

Leisure Activities

- Attending medical science fairs and exhibits and visiting science museums
- Reading medically related publications
- Joining a health club
- Doing lab experiments and researching medically related topics
- Belonging to a medical science club or related professional organization
- Working part time or as a volunteer in a local hospital, nursing home, or community health agency
- Actively participating in or financially supporting medical research efforts
- Attending lectures and conferences related to medicine

Skills

- High proficiency for accuracy and detail
- Ability to react quickly and maintain emotional and physical composure in stressful situations
- Proficiency in interpersonal communication
- Ability to work well and concentrate under pressure
- Proficiency in critical thinking, analyzing, and problem solving
- Physical stamina, good vision, and manual dexterity
- Intellectual capacity to perform well in most undergraduate and graduate college programs
- Thorough knowledge of medical theories and practices
- Ability to conduct and clearly explain scientific research
- Ability to make keen observations and appropriate decisions
- Aptitude for applied science
- Proficiency in reading and memorization

Values and Attributes

- Prestige
- Health
- Wisdom
- Achievement
- Desire to help others and make a contribution to humanity
- Interest in challenges
- Willingness to work long and irregular hours
- Desire to alleviate the pain and suffering of others
- Scientific inquiry
- Analytical mind
- Perseverance
- Dedication
- Imagination
- Alertness

Resources

- **American Dental Association**
  211 East Chicago Avenue
  Chicago, IL 60611-2678
  312-440-2500
  http://www.ada.org
  (offers information on dentistry careers, education requirements, and memberships for dentistry students)
- **American Medical Association**
  515 North State Street
  Chicago, IL 60610
  800-621-8335
  http://www.ama-assn.org
  (offers student membership and information on how to become a medical doctor)
- **American Osteopathic Association**
  142 East Ontario Street
  Chicago, IL 60611
  800-621-1773
  http://www.osteopathic.org
  (provides information about accreditation and publishes informative brochures)
- **Association for Chiropractic Colleges**
  4424 Montgomery Avenue, Suite 102
  Bethesda, MD 20814
  http://www.chirocolleges.org
  (provides list of chiropractic colleges)

HELPFUL INFORMATION
*Physicians and Surgeons
Growth Outlook (2006–2016)

Projected: Grow faster than the average (increase 14% to 20%)
Number Employed (2006): 663,000   **(By 2016)** 723,000 (+14%)
Salary Range (2006): $45,200–$145,600+
Related Occupations: *AIN*

	SALARY RANGE:
*Physician Assistants	$43,100–$102,200
*Dentists	$69,000–$145,600+
*Psychiatrists	$60,900–$145,600+
*Pharmacists	$67,900–$119,500

*According to the BLS, workers in these occupations are currently in high demand and thus have been designated as "In Demand."

SOURCE CODE(S):
Department of Labor, Bureau of Labor Statistics = BLS
Occupational Outlook Handbook, 2008–2009 = OOH
America's Career InfoNet (Online) = AIN
O*NET (Online) = NET

Metallurgical and Mining Engineering

Metallurgical and mining engineering is the practical application of science, mathematics, and energy in the extraction, treatment, and processing of metals, coal, and other nonmetallic resources from the earth. It involves the research and refinement of these natural materials as well as the discovery of new ways to use them in the development of new products. You may elect to concentrate in research, extractive engineering, processing, applications, management, or other areas.

High School Courses

Algebra	Industrial Arts
Blueprint Reading	Math
Calculus	Mechanical Drawing
Chemistry	Physical Science
Computer Applications	Science
Earth Science	Trigonometry
Geometry	

Related Majors

Chemical Engineering	Geological Engineering
Civil Engineering	Geophysical Engineering
Electrical/Electronics Engineering	Materials Engineering
Engineering Science	Mathematics
Engineering Technology	Petroleum Engineering
Environmental Engineering	Safety Engineering

Related Occupations

See page 11 for detailed explanation of key.

Ceramic Engineer—B	Materials Handling Engineer—B
Chemical Engineer—B	Metallurgical Engineering Technician—AA
Civil Engineer—B	Mining Engineer—B
Construction Engineer—B	Nuclear Engineer—B
Consulting Engineer—B/M	Petroleum Engineer—B
Electrical Engineer—B	Pipeline Engineer—B
Energy Engineer—B	Plastics Engineer—B
Environmental Engineer—B	Research Engineer—B
Geological Engineer—B	Safety Engineer—B
Geologist—B	Sanitary Engineer—B
Geophysical Engineer—B	Surveyor—B
Geophysicist—B	Systems Engineer—B

Leisure Activities

- Developing hobbies and interests related to building items out of metal or other materials, collecting rocks and minerals, and mechanics
- Reading publications about engineering or metallurgy
- Attending related lectures and workshops
- Doing experiments to see how materials react
- Working part time with a mining company, in a foundry, or in a college engineering department
- Belonging to a student or professional engineering organization
- Solving analytic and logic problems
- Participating in clubs or organizations that require you to make oral presentations and write reports

Skills

- Ability to analyze, organize, and interpret scientific data
- Ability to work well with others
- Ability to make appropriate decisions and solve problems
- Ability to make keen observations and sound judgments
- Aptitude for accuracy and detail, spatial perception, and abstract reasoning
- Sensitivity to economic considerations and human needs
- Proficiency in an area of specialization and knowledgeable of current practices and trends

HELPFUL INFORMATION
Mining and Geological Engineers
Growth Outlook (2006–2016)

Projected: Grow about as fast as the average (increase 7% to 13%)
Number Employed (2006): 7,100   **(By 2016)** 7,800 (+10%)
Salary Range (2006): $42,040–$128,410
Related Occupations: *AIN*

	SALARY RANGE:
Materials Engineers	$46,120–$112,140
Petroleum Engineers	$57,960–$145,600+
*Mechanical Engineers	$45,170–$104,900
*Civil Engineers	$44,810–$104,420

*According to the BLS, workers in these occupations are currently in high demand and thus have been designated as "In Demand."

SOURCE CODE(S):
Department of Labor, Bureau of Labor Statistics = *BLS*
Occupational Outlook Handbook, 2008–2009 = *OOH*
America's Career InfoNet (Online) = *AIN*
O*NET (Online) = NET

- Proficiency in written and oral communication
- Ability to conduct and clearly communicate scientific research
- Intellectual capacity to perform well in most undergraduate and graduate college programs
- Proficiency with computers

Values and Attributes

- Creativity
- Achievement
- Desire to help others live better
- Desire for challenges
- Interest in seeing ideas developed into practical use
- Curiosity
- Imagination
- Perseverance
- Flexibility
- Alertness

Resources

- **ASM International**
  9639 Kinsman Road
  Materials Park, OH 44073-0002
  440-338-5151
  http://www.asm-intl.org
  (offers student membership, college chapters, and networking opportunities)
- **Junior Engineering Technical Society**
  1420 King Street, Suite 405
  Alexandria, VA 22314
  703-548-5387
  http://www.jets.org
  (sponsors activities geared to assist students to determine engineering readiness, has special outreach to minority students, and offers information about careers)
- **The Minerals, Metals, & Materials Society**
  184 Thorn Hill Road
  Warrendale, PA 15086-7514
  800-759-4867
  http://www.tms.org
  (Career Center contains lots of helpful information)
- **National Mining Association**
  101 Constitution Avenue NW, Suite 500 East
  Washington, DC 20001-2133
  202-463-2600
  http://www.nma.org
  (publishes educational brochures and sponsors mine tours)

Military Science

Military science is the study of the philosophies, theories, and practices of military leadership and warfare. Effective implementation of the principles of military science is considered vital to the protection of a country's citizens. Military science exposes you to military history, the nature of war, leadership and management skills, organization, customs and traditions, first aid, lifesaving and survival techniques, weaponry, marksmanship, equipment use and design, methods of combat, offensive and defensive strategies, and communications. The five major concentrations within military science are communications, engineering, logistics, strategy, and tactics. Keep in mind that some of the occupations listed below are limited to simulated or actual war environments. However, many of the skills developed in preparation for them (particularly leadership, administration, and management skills) are transferable to civilian occupations such as engineering, clerical, maintenance, and mechanics.

High School Courses

Civics	Psychology
Computer Applications	Social Studies
Government	Sociology
History	ROTC
Law	World History
Physical Education	

Related Majors

Business Administration	Mechanical Engineering
Communications	Military Technologies
Corrections	Physical Education
Criminal Justice	Political Science
Geography	Psychology
Law Enforcement/Police Science	ROTC

Related Occupations

See page 11 for detailed explanation of key.

Airplane Engineer—V/B	Journalist—AA/B
Airplane Pilot—V/B	Medical Lab Technician—AA
Air Traffic Controller—V	Military Officer—B
Career Counselor—B/M	Military Warrant Officer—B
Cartographer—AA/V	Musician—V/B
Computer Programmer—AA	Public Information Specialist—AA/B
Diver—V	Radio Equipment Technician—AA/V
Educator—B/M	Recruiter—AA/B

Electronics Technician—AA/V	ROTC Instructor—B
Enlisted Soldier—B 5	Ship's Pilot—B
Graphic Designer—AA	Systems Analyst—B
Intelligence Specialist—B/D	Topographic Engineer—B
Interpreter/Translator—B	Trainer—AA/B

Leisure Activities

- Participating in an ROTC program
- Belonging to a national guard unit
- Playing games of logic, strategy, and warfare
- Serving in a branch of the armed forces
- Reading publications related to the military
- Attending military-related lectures and conferences
- Viewing war-related TV programs and movies
- Working part time or as a volunteer in a police station or as a security guard
- Visiting military exhibits
- Participating in competitive team and individual sports

Skills

- Intellectual capacity to do well in most undergraduate and graduate college programs
- Aptitude for leadership
- Proficiency for analytical and logical reasoning
- Ability to react instantly and maintain composure in stressful situations
- Proficiency in reading and understanding directions
- Ability to make sound judgments and appropriate decisions
- Ability to interact with people of different personalities and backgrounds
- Good vision and health
- Physical stamina, good motor coordination, and manual dexterity
- Ability to clearly communicate ideas and concepts to others
- Ability to motivate and extract loyalty from others
- Background in military history, principles, and procedures
- Be in excellent physical condition

Values and Attributes

- Loyalty
- Independence
- Security
- Achievement
- Willingness to follow orders and take risks
- Courage
- Ability to respond well in emergencies
- Order and discipline
- Perseverance
- Analytical mind
- Competitive drive
- Spontaneity

- Responsibility
- Determination

Resources

- **Air Force Web Site**
  http://www.af.mil
- **Army Web Site**
  http://www.army.mil
- **Coast Guard Web Site**
  http://www.uscg.mil
- **Marine Corps Web Site**
  http://www.usmc.mil
- **Navy Web Site**
  http://www.navy.mil
- **Association of Military Colleges and Schools of the United States**
  Dr. Rudolph H. Ehrenberg Jr.
  3604 Glenbrook Road
  Fairfax, VA 22031-3211
  703-279-8406
  http://www.amcsus.org

HELPFUL INFORMATION
Military Workers, including Officers
Growth Outlook (2006–2016)

Projected: Prospects expected to be excellent in most areas
Number Employed (2006): See sources below **(By 2016)** See sources below
Salary Range (2006): See sources below
Related Occupations: *AIN*
SALARY RANGE:

For specific information, contact the branch of your interest online or at your local recruiting office

Air Force: http://www.af.mil
Army: http://www.army.mil
Navy: http://www.navy.mil
Marines: http://www.usmc.mil
Coast Guard: http://www.uscg.mil

For more detailed information about a variety of positions, salary, outlook and much more see the Occupational Outlook Handbook, 2008–2009 (Look under Job Opportunities in the Armed Forces)

SOURCE CODE(S):
Department of Labor, Bureau of Labor Statistics = *BLS*
Occupational Outlook Handbook, 2008–2009 = *OOH*
America's Career InfoNet (Online) = *AIN*
O*NET (Online) = *NET*

Nursing and Related Services

Nursing and related services is the study of the direct personal care, support, and condition monitoring (usually accompanied by frequent hands-on activities) of those who are sick, injured, disabled, or elderly. You learn the day-to-day skills and practices involved in quality patient care. Study includes human anatomical and physiological processes; human growth, development, and behavior; teamwork, observation, and referral; responding to emergencies; health care facility operations, philosophy, and management; and diet and nutrition. Some of the specialties of nursing and related services are midwifery, occupational nursing, public health nursing, physical therapy, occupational therapy, school nursing, private duty nursing, and family practice nursing.

High School Courses

Algebra	First Aid
Applied Math	Geometry
Biology	Health
Chemistry	Physiology
Computer Applications	Science

Related Majors

Family Practice Nursing	Physical Therapy
Nursing Administration	Practical Nursing
Nursing Anesthetist	Psychiatric/Mental Health Nursing
Nursing Education	Public Health Nursing
Nursing Midwifery	Registered Nursing
Occupational Therapy	

Related Occupations

See page 11 for detailed explanation of key.

Acute Care Nurse—B	Nurse-Midwife—M
Art Therapist—B	Nurse Practitioner—M
Athletic Trainer—B	Nurse Supervisor—B
Critical Care Nurse—B	Occupational Therapist—B
General Duty Nurse—AA/B	Physical Therapist—B
Head Nurse—B/M	Private Duty Nurse—AA/B
Licensed Practical Nurse—C	Recreational Therapist—B
Music Therapist—B	Registered Nurse—AA/B

Nurse Anesthetist—M   Respiratory Therapist—AA

Nurse Clinician—M   School Nurse—B

Nurse Instructor—B

Leisure Activities

- Attending lectures, workshops, and conferences related to nursing
- Belonging to a health guild, club, or advisory board
- Watching TV programs or movies related to hospitals, nursing, or medicine
- Reading nursing publications
- Belonging to a professional organization such as the National League for Nursing or American Nurses Association
- Working part time or as a volunteer in a hospital, nursing home, health agency, or college nursing department
- Actively supporting health care and charitable efforts

Skills

- Aptitude for applied science
- Ability to make keen observations, sound judgments, and appropriate decisions
- Thorough knowledge of nursing and/or related practices and techniques
- Proficiency for accuracy and detail
- Physical stamina, good vision, and manual dexterity

HELPFUL INFORMATION
*Registered Nurses
Growth Outlook (2006–2016)

Projected: Grow much faster than the average (increase 21% or more)

Number Employed (2006): 2,505,000   **(By 2016)** 3,092,000

Salary Range (2006): $40,250–$83,440

Related Occupations: *AIN*

	SALARY RANGE:
*Licensed Practical Nurses	$26,400–$50,000
Nursing Instructors and Teachers, Postsecondary	$34,100–$88,600
*Occupational Therapists	$40,900–$89,400
*Physical Therapists	$46,500–$94,800

*According to the BLS, workers in these occupations are currently in high demand and thus have been designated as "In Demand."

SOURCE CODE(S):

Department of Labor, Bureau of Labor Statistics = *BLS*

Occupational Outlook Handbook, 2008–2009 = *OOH*

America's Career InfoNet (Online) = *AIN*

O*NET (Online) = *NET*

- Ability to solve problems
- Proficiency in reading, writing, and following directions
- Understanding of normal human behavior, growth, and development
- Ability to react spontaneously and maintain emotional and physical composure in stressful situations
- Ability to work cooperatively with people of different backgrounds and personalities

Values and Attributes

- Health
- Wisdom
- Desire to work directly with people and to help others
- Warm, understanding, and friendly attitude
- Sensitivity to the needs and pain of others
- Willingness to work irregular hours and on weekends
- Patience
- Self-confidence
- Poise
- Responsibility
- Capability

Resources

- **American Nurses Association**
  2515 Georgia Avenue, Suite 400
  Silver Spring, MD 20910
  800-274-4ANA
  http://nursingworld.org
  (see Considering Nursing? link)
- **National League for Nursing**
  61 Broadway
  New York, NY 10006
  800-669-1656
  http://www.nln.org
  (information on nursing education programs)
- **National Student Nurses Association**
  45 Main Street, Suite 606
  Brooklyn, NY 11201
  718-210-0705
  http://www.nsna.org
  (offers scholarships, career advice, and much more)

Performing Arts

Study in the performing arts offers exposure to creative, dramatic expression, primarily in front of live audiences. It involves all types of artistic performance in theaters, in educational institutions, on TV, in movies, and outdoors. All major aspects of performance preparation are studied, including music, dance, acting, set design, stage setup, scenery, decorations, light and sound production, costumes, and makeup. Speaking techniques and developing stage presence are also taught. Major specializations include acting, singing, playing musical instruments, comedy, and dance.

High School Courses

Arts	Forensics
Band	Orchestra
Choir	Physical Education
Dance	Public Speaking
Debate	Speech
Drama	Theater

Related Majors

Cinematography and Production	Film/Video Making
Dance	Music
Dance Therapy	Music Therapy
Design and Applied Art	Physical Education
Drama and Dance Education	Speech
Dramatic/Theater Arts and Stagecraft	

Related Occupations

See page 11 for detailed explanation of key.

Actor/Actress—AA/B	Magician—V
Announcer (Radio, TV)—AA/B	Merchandise Displayer—AA
Choreographer—B	Motion Picture Photographer—B
Circus Performer—V	Music Director—B
Comedian—V	Music Teacher—B/M
Composer—B	Musician—B
Costumer—V	Orchestra Conductor—B/V
Dance Instructor—B/V	Producer—B
Dancer—V	Public Relations Specialist—B
Drama Coach—B/M	Puppeteer—V
Educator—B/M/D	Set Designer—B
Fashion Model—V	Singer—B
Film Director—B	Stage Manager—B

Leisure Activities

- Participating in local theater productions
- Attending plays, concerts, lectures, and movies
- Working part time or as a volunteer for a radio or TV station
- Joining a choir, glee club, marching band, orchestra, cheerleading team, or popular music group
- Practicing aerobics, modeling, or sports
- Participating in a talent or variety show, skit, or play
- Joining the student council or a debate team
- Serving as an assistant in a theater arts or communications department
- Running for political office or competing in an oratory contest
- Reading publications related to the performing arts

Skills

- Ability to concentrate and practice intensely for long periods of time
- Ability to speak articulately, listen introspectively, and make keen observations
- Good health, physical stamina, and body coordination
- Ability to work well under pressure and meet deadlines
- Ability to maintain composure when faced with the unexpected
- Ability to communicate emotions and ideas creatively
- Ability to relate to people of varying backgrounds
- Proficiency in memorization
- Ability to attract the attention of others
- Ability to analyze and interpret the emotions and motives of others

Values and Attributes

- Aesthetic awareness
- Independence
- Self-expression and fulfillment
- Desire for recognition and influence
- Creativity
- Ability to withstand close scrutiny and criticism
- Ability to adjust to ups and downs
- Sense of drama and showmanship
- Physical stamina
- Patience
- Determination
- Imagination
- Self-discipline
- Analytical mind
- Dedication
- Poise

Resources

- **American Federation of Musicians of the United States and Canada**
  Paramount Building
  1501 Broadway, Suite 600
  New York, NY 10036
  212-869-1330
  http://www.afm.org
  (see Career Corner link)
- **Dance USA**
  1111 16th Street NW, Suite 300
  Washington, DC 20036
  202-833-1717
  http://www.danceusa.org
  (provides advice for young dancers)
- **Screen Actors Guild**
  5757 Wilshire Boulevard, 7th Floor
  Los Angeles, CA 90036-3600
  323-954-1600
  http://www.sag.com
  (provides a list of FAQs and information about careers)

HELPFUL INFORMATION
Musicians and Singers
Growth Outlook (2006–2016)

Projected: Grow about as fast as average (increase 7% to 13%)
Number Employed (2006): 196,000   **(By 2016)** 216,000
Salary Range (2006): $7.08 per hour–$57.37 per hour
Related Occupations: *AIN*

	SALARY RANGE:
Actors/Actresses	$7.31 per hour–$51.02 per hour
Models	$16,000–$38,900
Dancers	$6.62 per hour–$25.75 per hour
Choreographers	$15,700–$64,100

*According to the BLS, workers in these occupations are currently in high demand and thus have been designated as "In Demand."

SOURCE CODE(S):
Department of Labor, Bureau of Labor Statistics = *BLS*
Occupational Outlook Handbook, 2008–2009 = *OOH*
America's Career InfoNet (Online) = *AIN*
O*NET (Online) = *NET*

Philosophy

Philosophy is a branch of the language arts and involves the study of the truths or principles underlying all knowledge. Philosophical study involves the analysis, interpretation, and logical explanation of what people believe, value, and do. While the Related Occupations below are generally only indirectly linked to the study of philosophy, a number of other disciplines, avocations, and leisure activities offer additional pursuits for interested students. Among the major subbranches are metaphysics (the study of reality and being), epistemology (the study of knowledge), logic (the study of the formal principles of reasoning), and ethics (the study of values and morals).

High School Courses

Anthropology
Computer Applications
Debate
English
Forensics
Government
History

Language Arts
Literature
Psychology
Religion
Social Studies
Sociology

Related Majors

Anthropology
English
History
Humanities
Liberal Arts

Literature
Psychology
Religion
Sociology
Theology

Related Occupations

See page 11 for detailed explanation of key.

Anthropologist—D
College Administrator—B/D
College Instructor—M/D
Diplomat—B
Film Editor—AA
Foreign Correspondent—B
Freelance Writer—B
Historian—B/D
Journalist—B
Judge—P

Lawyer—P
Lecturer—B/M
Librarian—M
Market Research Analyst—B
Political Scientist—B/D
Psychologist—D
Public Administrator—B
Publisher—B
Research Assistant—B
Social Worker—B/M

Leisure Activities

- Participating on a debate or forensics team
- Writing
- Playing word games and games of strategy
- Participating in oratory contests
- Joining an organization such as the American Philosophical Association
- Subscribing to professional publications related to philosophy
- Visiting libraries
- Working part time or as a volunteer research assistant or in a philosophy department
- Attending lectures
- Listening to radio talk shows
- Participating in political campaigns
- Joining a student government or student association group

Skills

- Ability to formulate and defend positions
- Ability to make keen observations, evaluations, and appropriate decisions
- Ability to summarize complicated materials and solve problems
- Ability to concentrate for long periods of time
- Ability to speak articulately
- Objectivity

HELPFUL INFORMATION
Philosophy and Religious Teachers, Postsecondary
Growth Outlook (2006–2016)

Projected: Unknown (See Postsecondary Teachers in OOH)
Number Employed (2006): 25,000
Salary Range (2006): $31,700–$96,600
Related Occupations: *AIN*

	SALARY RANGE:
Sociology Teachers, Postsecondary	$30,900–$104,800
Historians	$23,500–$89,900
Sociologists	$36,800–$115,800
Anthropologists	$29,100–$81,500

*According to the BLS, workers in these occupations are currently in high demand and thus have been designated as "In Demand."

SOURCE CODE(S):
Department of Labor, Bureau of Labor Statistics = *BLS*
Occupational Outlook Handbook, 2008–2009 = *OOH*
America's Career InfoNet (Online) = *AIN*
O*NET (Online) = *NET*

- Ability to organize, conduct, and clearly explain research
- Proficiency in analytical reasoning
- Ability to synthesize information
- Broad background of general knowledge
- Comprehensive command of grammar and vocabulary

Values and Attributes

- Intellectual growth
- Logical thought and self-expression
- Desire for recognition and to influence others
- Independence
- Tendency to question and seek answers
- Tendency to support beliefs with facts and logic
- Thoughtfulness
- Persuasiveness
- Objectivity
- Imagination

Resources

- **American Philosophical Association**
  31 Amstel Avenue
  University of Delaware
  Newark, DE 19716-4797
  302-831-1112
  http://www.udel.edu/apa
- **EpistemeLinks.com**
  http://www.epistemelinks.com/Main/MainOrgs.asp
  (philosophy resources on the Internet)
- **Society of Christian Philosophers**
  Calvin College
  Department of Philosophy
  Grand Rapids, MI 49546-4388
  http://www.siu.edu/departments/cola/philos/SCP
  (provides forum for discussion of Christian and philosophical issues)

Physics

Physics is a major branch of the physical sciences and involves the study of matter and energy. It attempts to find out how and why physical matter and energy interact, as well as how to describe force, motion, and gravity. Physics is considered to be the foundation of science and technology. It is closely related to astronomy, engineering, chemistry, mathematics, geology, and biology.

High School Courses

Algebra	Math
Biology	Physical Science
Calculus	Physics
Chemistry	Science
Computer Science	Statistics
Earth Science	Trigonometry
Geometry	

Related Majors

Astronomy	Geophysics
Astrophysics	Geophysical Engineering
Biophysics	Mathematics
Chemistry	Nuclear Engineering
Geology	Physics Education

Related Occupations

See page 11 for detailed explanation of key.

Aerodynamist—B/D	Geoscientist—B/D
Aeronautical Engineer—B	Laboratory Technician—AA
Aerospace Engineer—B/D	Mathematician—B/D
Airplane Pilot—AA/B	Metallurgical Engineer—B
Astronomer—B/D	Metallurgist—B
Astrophysicist—B/D	Meteorologist—B
Biophysicist—B	Nuclear Engineer—B/D
Civil Engineer—B	Nuclear Medicine Technologist—AA
Computer Programmer—B	Nuclear Technician—AA
Educator—B/M/D	Optical Technician—AA
Electrical Engineer—B	Physicist—B/D
Environmental Engineer—B	Seismologist—B

Leisure Activities

- Joining a science club, the American Physical Society, the Society of Physics Students, or another physics club
- Reading physics or science publications

- Computer programming
- Operating a ham radio
- Repairing radios, TVs, or stereos
- Playing board games and doing puzzles
- Performing lab experiments
- Solving analytic and logic problems

Skills

- Ability to organize, analyze, and interpret scientific data
- Intellectual capacity to perform well in most undergraduate and graduate college programs
- Ability to make keen observations and appropriate decisions
- Ability to conduct and clearly explain scientific research
- Proficiency with computers
- Aptitude for accuracy and detail
- Proficiency in questioning and problem solving
- Proficiency in reading, writing, memorization, and speaking
- Strong background in mathematics
- Good vision and manual dexterity

Values and Attributes

- Achievement
- Independence

HELPFUL INFORMATION
Physicists
Growth Outlook (2006–2016)

Projected: Grow about as fast as the average (increase 7% to 13%)
Number Employed (2006): 17,000 **(By 2016)** 18,000
Salary Range (2006): $52,070–$145,600
Related Occupations: *AIN*

	SALARY RANGE:
Astronomers	$44,600–$145,600+
Geoscientists	$39,700–$135,900
Hydrologists	$42,100–$98,300
Physics Teachers, Postsecondary	$39,700–$96,700

*According to the BLS, workers in these occupations are currently in high demand and thus have been designated as "In Demand."

SOURCE CODE(S):
Department of Labor, Bureau of Labor Statistics = *BLS*
Occupational Outlook Handbook, 2008–2009 = *OOH*
America's Career InfoNet (Online) = *AIN*
O*NET (Online) = *NET*

- Intellectual growth
- Recognition
- Strong desire to know why and how things work
- Fondness for mathematics and science
- Analytical mind
- Curiosity
- Dedication
- Imagination
- Perseverance

Resources

- **American Institute of Physics**
  One Physics Ellipse
  College Park, MD 20740-3843
  301-209-3100
  http://www.aip.org
  (offers an outstanding career information link; see Physics Education link)
- **American Physical Society**
  One Physics Ellipse
  College Park, MD 20740-3844
  301-209-3200
  http://www.aps.org
  (offers student membership and provides career information which includes
  a special focus on minorities and women)
- **Society of Physics Students**
  One Physics Ellipse
  College Park, MD 20740
  301-209-3007
  http://www.spsnational.org/education
  (offers scholarships, internships, networking opportunities, publications, and
  career information)

Physiology

Physiology is a branch of the biological sciences that involves the study of life processes and functions. This study requires the close observation, recording, and analysis of cellular and subcellular constructions, tissues, and organs to understand how they function and why. Research into the way these systems respond within and between organisms and to environmental influences is important to physiological study. Major branches of this discipline include plant physiology and animal physiology. Physiology also overlaps with chemistry, physics, and mathematics.

High School Courses

Algebra
Biology
Chemistry
Computer Applications
First Aid
Geometry
Health
Physics
Physiology
Science
Trigonometry

Related Majors

Animal Physiology
Biochemistry
Biology
Botany
Chemistry
Genetics
Health
Mathematics
Medicine
Microbiology
Nutritional Science
Pharmacology
Physics
Physiology Education
Veterinary Science
Zoology

Related Occupations

See page 11 for detailed explanation of key.

Anatomist—B
Anesthesiologist—P
Biochemist—B
Biophysicist—B/D
Botanist—B
Cardiologist—P
Chemist—B/D
Dietitian—B
Funeral Director—AA/B
Geneticist—D
Gynecologist—P
Nutritionist—V
Osteopath—P
Pathologist—P
Pediatrician—P
Pharmacist—P
Pharmacologist—D/P
Physiologist—B/D
Psychiatrist—P
Respiratory Therapist—AA
Surgeon—P
Toxicologist—B/D

Internist—P Urologist—P

Medical Assistant—AA Veterinarian—P

Microbiologist—B/D

Leisure Activities

- Attending science fairs or exhibits
- Visiting museums or zoos
- Reading science journals, magazines, and books
- Joining a health club
- Doing lab experiments and researching science topics
- Volunteering for the American Red Cross, American Cancer Society, or a local mental health association, hospital, or nursing home
- Owning or caring for pets
- Watching medical shows on TV or at a theater
- Actively or financially supporting blood donor drives or medical research efforts

Skills

- Ability to concentrate for long periods of time
- Ability to conduct and clearly explain scientific research
- Ability to make keen observations and appropriate decisions
- Ability to work under pressure
- Good understanding of mathematical principles and basic knowledge of chemistry and physics
- Proficiency in reading, writing, speaking, and memorizing
- Intellectual capacity to perform well in most undergraduate and graduate college programs
- Thorough knowledge of basic biological theories and practices
- Proficiency in critical thinking, analysis, and problem solving
- Physical stamina, good vision, and manual dexterity

Values and Attributes

- Achievement
- Creativity
- Helpful attitude
- Independence
- Intellectual growth
- Prestige
- Desire to help improve our world
- Interest in public health and safety
- Strong interest in how and why living organisms function
- Curiosity
- Empathy
- Endurance
- Patience

- Persistence
- Self-discipline
- Thoroughness

Resources

- **American Physiological Society**
  9650 Rockville Pike
  Bethesda, MD 20814-3991
  301-634-7164
  http://www.the-aps.org
  (offers student membership and provides career information)
- **American Society for Microbiology**
  1752 N Street NW
  Washington, DC 20036
  202-737-3600
  http://www.asm.org
  (provides information about women and minorities in microbiology, certification, career and employment, and much more)

Political Science

Political science is the study of government and focuses on its structure and function and the need for social order. Political science study provides you with a better understanding of political parties, interest groups, international relationships, public law, public administration, liberty, freedom, justice, and power. Major subbranches include political theory and philosophy, comparative government, American government and politics, public administration, international relations, and political behavior.

High School Courses

Civics	History
Computer Applications	Psychology
Debate	Public Speaking
English	Social Studies
Forensics	Sociology
Government Economics	Speech

Related Majors

Criminal Justice	Political Science Education
Economics	Psychology
History	Public Administration
International Relations	Public Health
Law	Public Relations
Military Science	Sociology
Philosophy	Urban Studies

Related Occupations

See page 11 for detailed explanation of key.

Announcer—B	Mayor—V
Campaign Worker—V	Military Officer—B
Chamber of Commerce Manager—B	News Reporter—B
Chief Executive—B	Parole/Probation Officer—B
City Manager—B	Penologist—B
Diplomat—B/M	Political Consultant—B
Educator—B/M/D	Political Scientist—B/D
FBI/CIA Agent—B/M	Politician—B
Foreign Service Officer—B/M	Public Health Official—B
Geographer—B/D	Public Recreation Director—B
Judge—P	Research Assistant—B
Labor Relations Specialist—B	School Administrator—B
Lawyer—P	Urban Planner—B
Lobbyist—B	

Leisure Activities

- Attending political rallies or lectures
- Serving as a part-time worker or volunteer precinct clerk, party worker, poll watcher, or intern
- Running for or serving in a public school or municipal office
- Joining a debate or forensics team
- Participating in fund-raising or writing promotional materials for a political campaign
- Participating in student government
- Chairing a public panel discussion
- Working part time or as a volunteer news broadcaster for a school radio or TV station
- Joining a school newspaper staff
- Participating in a neighborhood association
- Freelance writing
- Reading political publications
- Joining a professional group such as the American Political Science Association

Skills

- Ability to conduct and clearly explain research clearly
- Ability to effectively communicate ideas to others
- Intellectual capacity to perform well in most undergraduate and graduate college programs
- Ability to relate to people from varying backgrounds
- Ability to speak articulately, read comprehensively, and write well
- Charisma and public appeal
- Aptitude for leadership
- Ability to organize and interpret social, economic, and political data
- Understanding of and sensitivity to community needs
- Broad background of general knowledge
- Ability to effectively evaluate problems and make appropriate decisions

Values and Attributes

- Achievement
- Desire for recognition and to influence others
- Prestige
- Tendency to be ambitious and outgoing
- Desire to render public service
- Willingness to take risks
- Poise
- Tactfulness
- Patience
- Perseverance
- Flexibility
- Competitive drive

Resources

- **American Political Science Association**
  1527 New Hampshire Avenue NW
  Washington, DC 20036-1206
  202-483-2512
  http://www.apsa.com
  (publishes *Careers and the Study of Political Science* as well as the video, *Career Encounters: Political Science*)
- **National Association of Schools of Public Affairs and Administration**
  1029 Vermont Avenue, NW, Suite 1100
  Washington, DC 20005
  202-628-8965
  http://www.naspaa.org
  (provides information about accreditation; see For Students link)

Psychology

Psychology is the study of human and animal behavior. It seeks to understand and explain both normal and abnormal behavior, mental ability, perception, development, and differences in individuals. Psychological study also explores human emotions, thoughts, and motives. Among the major subbranches within this field are educational psychology, social psychology, psychometrics, developmental psychology, comparative psychology, psychology of the personality, abnormal psychology, applied psychology, differential psychology, statistics, and child psychology.

High School Courses

Computer Applications	Psychology
Economics	Religion
Government	Social Studies
Health	Sociology
History	Statistics

Related Majors

Anthropology	Political Science
Criminal Justice	Psychiatry
Economics	Psychology Education
Guidance Counseling	Religion
History	Social Work
Philosophy	Sociology

Related Occupations

See page 11 for detailed explanation of key.

Advertising Manager—B	Outplacement Specialist—B/D
Educator—B/M/D	Penologist—B
Employee Assistance	Police Officer—AA
Administrator—B	Probation Officer—B
Employment Counselor—B	Psychiatric Nurse—B
Guidance Counselor—M	Psychiatric Social Worker—M
Human Resource Manager—B	Psychiatrist—P
Industrial Psychologist—M/D	Psychologist—D
Job Analyst—B	Psychometrist—B/M
Market Research Analyst—B	Public Relations Specialist—B
Mental Health Worker—B	Speech Pathologist—M
Minister—P/V	Vocational Rehabilitation
Occupational Therapist—B	Counselor—B/M

Leisure Activities

- Serving as a peer advisor
- Working part time or as a volunteer in a mental health agency, psychology department, or senior citizens' home
- Assisting with college recruitment efforts
- Serving on a student council or as a tutor
- Participating in Junior Achievement
- Serving as a leader or chairperson in a community or school organization
- Working part time or as a volunteer in an advertising firm, sales department, special education class, or day care center
- Serving as a camp counselor or hotline assistant
- Freelance writing
- Reading psychology-related publications.

Skills

- Ability to interpret and clearly explain psychological research and tests of all types
- Proficiency in reading comprehension, writing, and speaking
- Understanding of human development and behavior
- Ability to observe and analyze introspectively
- Sensitivity to and understanding of the needs and emotions of others
- Ability to evaluate personal problems and make appropriate decisions

- Intellectual capacity to do well in most undergraduate or graduate college programs
- Proficiency in interpersonal communication

Values and Attributes

- Intellectual understanding
- Helpfulness
- Mental and emotional well-being
- Sensitivity to the inconsistencies of human behavior
- Desire to continue learning throughout life
- Warm and personable character
- Tactfulness
- Inquisitiveness
- Integrity
- Patience

Resources

- **American Psychological Association**
  750 First Street NE
  Washington, DC 20002-4242
  202-336-5510
  http://www.apa.org
  (provides information about psychology careers, and much more)
- **National Association of School Psychologists**
  4340 East West Highway, Suite 402
  Bethesda, MD 20814
  301-657-0270
  http://www.nasponline.org/index2.html
  (offers scholarships and career information)

Recreation and Leisure

Recreation and leisure focuses on the design, management, implementation, supervision, expansion of, and need for recreational and leisure activities among individuals and groups of all ages and backgrounds. The recreation and leisure field encompasses a broad range of events and activities related to camping, natural resources, outdoor activities, tourism, amusement parks, sporting events, and community recreation programs. A few of the many specialties within this growing field are gerontology, youth organizations, parks and forestry, public recreation, tourism, commercial enterprise, therapeutic recreation, professional sports, resource management, and recreation and parks administration.

High School Courses

Arts	Psychology
First Aid	Social Studies
Health	Sociology
Physical Education	Theater

Related Majors

Dance	Psychology
Forest Management	Recreation/Leisure Facilities
Gerontology	Management
Health	Recreation Therapy
Music	Sociology
Natural Resources	Theater Arts/Drama
Physical Education	Travel/Tourism Management

Related Occupations

See page 11 for detailed explanation of key.

Armed Forces Recreation Leader—AA	Municipal Recreation Director—B
Athletic Trainer—B	Music Therapist—B
Camp Director—B	Park Ranger—B
Church Recreation Director—V	Physical Education Instructor—B
Circus Performer—V	Playground Leader—AA
Coach—V	Prison Recreation Specialist—B
College Recreation Instructor—B/M	Professional Athlete—V
Community Center Director—AA/B	Recreation Facility Manager—B
Concert Promoter—B/V	Recreational Worker—V/B
	Recreational Therapist—B

Dance Instructor—B/V	Resort Manager—B
Dance Therapist—B	Ski Instructor—V
Exercise Physiologist—B	Spa Manager—B
Fitness Instructor/Specialist—B	Sports Marketer—B
Game Official—B	Sports Reporter—B
Lifeguard—V/AA	

Leisure Activities

- Playing or participating in sports
- Working as a camp counselor or at a fitness club, playground, or other recreational facility
- Engaging in physical and outdoor activities
- Serving as a part-time coach, official, or scorer
- Reading publications related to recreation, sports, health, and fitness
- Organizing and participating in community recreational activities
- Attending lectures and workshops related to recreation and leisure
- Serving as an aide in a school physical education or recreation department

Skills

- Ability to relate to and interact with people of varying ages and backgrounds
- Ability to lead, supervise, and direct others

HELPFUL INFORMATION
Recreation Workers
Growth Outlook (2006–2016)

Projected: Grow about as fast as the average (increase 7% to 13%)
Number Employed (2006): 320,000   **(By 2016)** 360,000 (+13%)
Salary Range (2006): $14,150–$35,780
Related Occupations: *AIN*

	SALARY RANGE:
Recreational Therapists	$20,900–$55,500
Lifeguards, Ski Patrols and Related Occupations	$12,800–$24,000
Fitness Trainers and Related Occupations	$14,960–$56,800
Recreation and Fitness Studies Teachers, Postsecondary	$25,100–$90,800

*According to the BLS, workers in these occupations are currently in high demand and thus have been designated as "In Demand."

SOURCE CODE(S):
Department of Labor, Bureau of Labor Statistics = *BLS*
Occupational Outlook Handbook, 2008–2009 = *OOH*
America's Career InfoNet (Online) = *AIN*
O*NET (Online) = *NET*

- Ability to react spontaneously and maintain emotional composure in stressful situations
- Understanding of human nature
- Good health, vision, and physical stamina
- Ability to solve problems and make appropriate decisions
- Proficiency in written and oral communication
- Ability to organize and coordinate activities
- General knowledge of recreational and leisure theories and practices
- A high level of athletic ability (for a career as a fitness instructor or athlete)

Values and Attributes

- Health
- Achievement
- Emotional well-being
- Sensitivity to the human need for recreation and balance
- A good sense of humor and fondness for being around people
- Friendliness
- Tactfulness
- Dedication
- Patience
- Outgoing personality

Resources

- **American Alliance for Health, Physical Education, Recreation, and Dance**
  1900 Association Drive
  Reston, VA 20191-1598
  800-213-7193
  http://www.aahperd.org
  (offers scholarships, student membership, and career information; publishes a student newsletter)
- **American Therapeutic Recreation Association**
  1414 Prince Street, Suite 204
  Alexandria, VA 22314
  703-683-9420
  http://www.atra-tr.org
  (offers career information and resources)
- **National Recreation and Park Association**
  22377 Belmont Ridge Road
  Ashburn, VA 20148-4501
  703-858-0784
  http://www.nrpa.org
  (provides information about accreditation, certification, and more; see Career Center link)

Rehabilitation Therapy and Related Services

Rehabilitation therapy is the study of the history, theories, practices, and medical issues related to rehabilitation and disability. It includes a careful look at how rehabilitation efforts impact individual evaluation, case management activities, and society at large. A primary focus is on the rehabilitative needs of individuals and how to deliver these services. Students learn about a variety of supportive programs as well as the special needs of clients seen regularly by rehabilitation specialists. Clients served usually have one or more physical, mental, or emotional disabilities.

High School Courses

Algebra

Biology

Chemistry

Economics

First Aid

Geometry

Health

Math

Physical Education

Psychology

Social Studies

Sociology

Related Majors

Art Therapy

Athletic Training

Horticultural Therapy

Medicine

Music Therapy

Nursing

Occupational Therapy

Pharmacy

Physical Therapy

Recreational Therapy

Rehabilitative Counseling

Special Education

Speech Therapy

Related Occupations

See page 11 for detailed explanation of key.

Art Therapist—B

Athletic Trainer—B

Audiologist/Speech Pathologist—M

Consultant—M/D

Dance Therapist—B

Educator—M/D

Exercise Physiologist—B

Nurse—AA/B

Occupational Therapist—B

Orthotics/Prosthetics Technician—AA

Pharmacist—B/M

Physical Therapist—B

Recreational Therapist—B

Respiratory Therapist—B

Horticultural Therapist—B   Special Education Teacher—B
Music Therapist—B   Vocational Rehabilitation Counselor—M

Leisure Activities

- Attending lectures, workshops, conferences, and other events related to rehabilitation and/or individuals with special needs
- Working part time or volunteering at an assisted living center, nursing home, veteran's or children's hospital
- Reading biographies, periodicals, and other publications about people with special needs
- Belonging to an organization such as the National Rehabilitation Association
- Regular observation/attendance at Special Olympic events, wheelchair basketball, or arts programs for people with disabilities

Skills

- High proficiency in a therapeutic area of expertise (art, music, occupational, physical, etc.)
- Aptitude for applied science
- Thorough knowledge of the theories, practices, and techniques of a rehabilitation or therapeutic specialty
- Ability to make keen observations, sound judgments, and appropriate decisions

- Ability to think outside of the box, go beyond, and be innovative
- Ability to work with people of differing backgrounds and personalities
- Understanding of normal human behavior, growth, and development

Values and Attributes

- Sensitivity and compassion, particularly for those with special needs
- Empathy
- Patience
- Self-confidence
- Being responsible
- Creativity
- Health

Resources

- **The American Occupational Therapy Association**
  4720 Montgomery Lane
  PO Box 31220
  Bethesda, MD 20824-1220
  301-652-2682
  http://www.aota.org
  (see For Prospective Students Link)
- **American Physical Therapy Association**
  1111 North Fairfax Street
  Alexandria, VA 22314-1488
  703-684-2782
  http://www.apta.org
  (publishes student e-newsletter, career and scholarship information, etc.)
- **American Speech-Language Hearing Association**
  10801 Rockville Pike
  Rockville, MD 20852
  800-638-8255
  http://www.asha.org
  (offers job placement and career information)
- **National Rehabilitation Association**
  633 South Washington Street
  Alexandria, VA 22314
  703-836-0850
  http://www.nationalrehab.org
  (offers student membership and job placement information)

Religion and Theology

Religion and theology is the study of human beliefs, practices, and worship activities related to a supreme power or deity. Study includes religious history, doctrine, theological concepts, and worship practices as well as issues related to faith, virtue, and morality. Focus may be on a particular denomination or faith or in a specialization such as youth work, religious education, mission work, clerical studies, administration and leadership, evangelism, or outreach.

High School Courses

Anthropology	Religion
Computer Applications	Religious History
Government	Social Studies
History	Sociology
Philosophy	

Related Majors

Biblical Languages/Literature	Philosophy
Biblical Studies	Religious Education
History	Social Work
Missionary Studies	Sociology
Pastoral Counseling	

Related Occupations

See page 11 for detailed explanation of key.

Campus Minister—B	Rabbi—P
Campus Religious Coordinator—D	Religious Brother—V/B
Chaplain—P	Religious EducationTeacher—B
Church Camp Director—B	Religious Educational Administrator—V/B
Director of Religious Education—B	Religious Researcher—B
Evangelist—V/P	Religious Sister—V/B
Minister of Music—B	Religious Writer—V/B
Missionary—V/B	Salvation Army Officer—V/B
Clergy/Pastor—V/P	Social Worker—B/M
Priest—P	Youth Minister—V

Leisure Activities

- Regularly participating in church or synagogue activities
- Working part time or as a volunteer in a religious institution or bookstore
- Attending religious retreats, conferences, revivals, or workshops

- Listening to religious lectures, tapes, and music
- Participating in and financially contributing to religious and charitable endeavors
- Visiting shut-ins or those who are sick or in jail
- Belonging to a religious club or fellowship group
- Attending Bible study
- Reading publications related to religion or theology
- Viewing religious programs on TV
- Engaging in activities that help others

Skills

- Knowledge and proficiency in some area of personal ministry
- Ability to interact with people of varying ages and backgrounds
- General knowledge of the practices, procedures, guidelines, and doctrine of your faith
- Ability to persuade and influence others
- Ability to carry out and integrate occupational responsibilities with religious faith
- Proficiency in reading, writing, and oral communication
- Proficiency in interpersonal communication
- Understanding of human spiritual and social needs
- Sensitivity to and compassion for others
- Ability to make appropriate decisions and solve problems

Values and Attributes

- Religious faith
- Desire to do God's will and love others
- Wisdom
- Morality
- Willingness to continue learning throughout life
- An inner spiritual conviction or calling to serve in a religious capacity
- Sensitivity and concern for the spiritual welfare of others
- Dedication
- Perseverance
- Integrity
- Determination

Resources

- **Intercristo**
  19303 Fremont Avenue North
  Seattle, WA 98133
  206-546-7200
  http://www.jobleads.org
  (offers Christian employment assistance and career development services)
- **National Council of Churches**
  475 Riverside Drive, Suite 880
  New York, NY 10115

212-870-2228

http://ncccusa.org

(represents 45 million members and 100,000 local congregations)

■ **National Religious Vocation Conference**

5401 South Cornell Avenue, Suite 207

Chicago, IL 60615

773-363-5454

http://www.nrvc.net

(offers various materials on religious vocations within the Roman Catholic
   Church, including the annual *Vision Guide* in print and online)

■ **JewishCareers.com**

1046 Park Avenue, Suite 700

Baltimore, MD 21701

410-752-3504

http://www.jewishcareers.com

(provides career coaching assistance and a variety of job opportunities in
   Jewish communities including faith-based positions)

Secretarial (Management and Administrative) Services

Secretarial services include administrative, clerical, information management, and human relations activities associated with and necessary for the efficient operation of an office or workplace. You learn keyboarding, filing, stenography, and word processing and other computer programs. You are also introduced to methods of information management, organization, schedule coordination, problem solving, decision making, accounting, and communication as well as general office procedures. Specialties in this area are legal, medical, executive, technical, and education.

High School Courses

Accounting	English/Writing
Bookkeeping	Math
Business	Office Operations/Practices
Business Machines	Psychology
Computer Applications	Speech
Computer Programming	Word Processing

Related Majors

Accounting	Legal Administrative Assistant
Business Data Processing	Medical Assisting
Business Education	Office Management
Court Reporting	Paralegal Assistant
Dental Assisting	

Related Occupations

See page 11 for detailed explanation of key.

Accounting Clerk—V	Legal Secretary—AA
Administrative Assistant—AA	Medical Assistant—C/AA
Bank Teller—V	Medical Secretary—C/AA
Cashier—V	Office Clerk—AA/B
Court Reporter—AA/B	Office Manager—AA/B
Data Input Operator—V	Paralegal—AA
Dental Assistant—AA	Receptionist—V
Educational Secretary—C/AA	Records Manager—AA
Educator—V/B	Secretary—V
Executive Secretary—AA/B	Stenographer—AA

File Clerk—V   Typist—AA
Foreign Service Secretary—AA   Word Processor—V

Leisure Activities

- Working as a part-time or volunteer student aide, secretarial assistant, or office clerk
- Reading materials on administrative and secretarial careers
- Volunteering as an office helper for a local church, neighborhood association, club, or community agency
- Belonging to a student or professional office personnel organization
- Writing reports and making oral presentations
- Working on a school newspaper
- Providing a word processing, résumé-writing, or editing service
- Organizing social events

Skills

- Good vision and health
- Proficiency for memorization, accuracy, and detail
- Ability to work independently as well as interact effectively with people of different backgrounds
- Ability to work quickly, with distractions, and under tight deadlines
- Ability to take the initiative, make sound judgments and appropriate decisions, and solve problems
- Proficiency with computers
- Strong office skills, including proficiency in operating electronic office equipment, such as scanners, fax machines, and copiers
- Knowledge of practices and trends in office procedures
- Ability to understand and interpret written and oral communication
- Proficiency in spelling, grammar, punctuation, and editing
- Ability to maintain emotional composure under stressful circumstances

Values and Attributes

- Security
- Recognition
- Achievement
- Neatness and flexibility
- Pleasant, positive, and friendly attitude
- Fairness
- Sense of professionalism
- Willingness to perform tasks that may be repetitive or tedious
- Organization
- Self-confidence
- Dependability

Resources

- **American Association for Medical Transcription**
  20 North Wacker Drive, Suite 1575
  Chicago, IL 60606
  312-899-1500

http://www.aamt.org

(provides online resources, including suggestions on how to prepare for a career in medical transcription, a career overview, and tips for students)

■ **Association of Executive and Administrative Professionals**

900 South Washington Street, Suite G-B

Falls Church, VA 22046

703-237-8016

http://www.theap.com

(provides a salary survey, career advancement information, a newsletter, and much more)

■ **International Assistants Association of Administrative Professionals**

10502 Northwest Ambassador Drive

PO Box 20404

Kansas City, MO 64195-0404

816-891-6600

http://www.iaap-hq.org

(runs job placement service for administrative support personnel, publishes free career booklets)

■ **National Association of Legal Secretaries**

8159 East 41st Street

Tulsa, OK 74145

918-582-5188

http://www.nals.org

(offers tips on education, certification, accreditation, etc.)

HELPFUL INFORMATION
Executive Secretaries and Administrative Assistants
Growth Outlook (2006–2016)

Projected: Grow about as fast as the average (increase 7% to 13%)
Number Employed (2006): 1,618,000   **(By 2016)** 1,857,000 (+15%)
Salary Range (2006): $25,190–$56,740
Related Occupations: *AIN*

	SALARY RANGE:
*Medical Secretaries	$19,800–$40,000
Legal Secretaries	$23,900–$58,800
Supervisors/Managers of Office/Administrative Support Workers	$26,500–$71,300
*Medical Records and Health Information Technicians	$19,100–$45,300

*According to the BLS, workers in these occupations are currently in high demand and thus have been designated as "In Demand."

SOURCE CODE(S):
Department of Labor, Bureau of Labor Statistics = *BLS*
Occupational Outlook Handbook, 2008–2009 = *OOH*
America's Career InfoNet (Online) = *AIN*
O*NET (Online) = *NET*

Social Work

Social work is the study of the processes that assist people who are unable to cope with serious personal and social problems. Study is aimed at helping the needy and disadvantaged in such areas as child abuse, substance abuse, juvenile delinquency and crime, hunger, financial budgeting, unemployment, health care, mental illness, disability education, parenting, family problems, and homelessness. Some areas of specialization are health care and mental health, education, family services, child welfare, drug abuse, gerontology, clinical practice, and occupational counseling.

High School Courses

Civics

Computer Applications

Economics

Government

Health

History

Psychology

Social Studies

Sociology

Related Majors

Community Services

Criminal Justice

Demography

Economics

Education

Gerontology

History

Political Science

Protective Services

Psychology

Public Affairs

Sociology

Urban Studies

Related Occupations

See page 11 for detailed explanation of key.

Child Welfare Worker—B

Community Service
   Agency Director—B

Cooperative Extension Worker—B

Drug Rehabilitation Counselor—B

Educator—M/D

Employee-Assistance
   Administrator—M

Family Services Social Worker—B

Geriatric Case Worker—M

Gerontologist—B/D

Group Home Director—AA/B

Peace Corps/VISTA Volunteer—B

Probation Officer—B

Psychiatric Social Worker—M

Psychologist—D

Residential Counselor—AA

Rehabilitation Counselor—M

School Counselor—M

School Psychologist—D

Social Service Aide—AA

Social Service Director—M

Social Worker—B/M

Sociologist—D

Home Economist—B

Human Services Worker—B

Minister—P

Substance Abuse and Behavior
Disorder Counselor—M

Technical Writer—B

Vocational Rehabilitation Counselor—M

Leisure Activities

- Working part time or as a volunteer in a community social agency
- Participating in charitable outreach endeavors and church activities
- Serving as a peer counselor, tutor, or hotline assistant
- Donating money to social concerns
- Reading publications that focus on social problems and issues
- Belonging to a professional organization such as the National Association of Social Workers, Inc.
- Attending lectures and conferences related to social work
- Participating in a Big Brother/Big Sister program

Skills

- Understanding of human behavior and familiarity with community services
- Familiarity with social work theories, practices, and trends
- Ability to interact with people of different backgrounds in a variety of situations
- Proficiency in interpersonal communication
- Intellectual capacity to do well in most undergraduate and graduate college programs
- Proficiency in reading comprehension, writing, and speaking
- Ability to respond spontaneously and maintain composure in stressful situations
- Ability to keenly observe, evaluate, and solve problems
- Ability to conduct and clearly explain social research
- Ability to make appropriate decisions and sound judgments

Values and Attributes

- Achievement
- Desire for recognition and appreciation from others
- Desire to work directly with those challenged by social problems
- Sensitivity to the needs and pains of others
- Ability to work under unpleasant and stressful conditions
- Patience
- Resourcefulness
- Empathy
- Tactfulness
- Integrity
- Discretion

Resources

- **American Association of State Social Work Boards**
  400 South Ridge Parkway, Suite B
  Culpepper, VA 22701
  540-829-6880
  http://www.aswb.org
  (provides information about licensure and certification standards as well as examination study guides and registration materials)
- **Council on Social Work Education**
  1725 Duke Street, Suite 500
  Alexandria, VA 22314
  703-683-8080
  http://www.cswe.org
  (Provides information on social work careers and educational programs)
- **National Association of Social Workers, Inc.**
  750 First Street NE, Suite 700
  Washington, DC 20002-4241
  202-408-8600
  http://www.socialworkers.org
  (reported to be the largest social work organization in the United States with more than 150,000 members; provides information about accredited schools, licensure, and social work careers)

HELPFUL INFORMATION
Social Workers
Growth Outlook (2006–2016)

Projected: Grow much faster than the average (increase 21% or more)
Number Employed (2006): 66,000 **(By 2016)** 78,000 (+18%)
Salary Range (2006): $28,540–$68,500
Related Occupations: *AIN*

	SALARY RANGE:
*Substance Abuse and Behavior Disorder Counselors	$22,600–$52,300
*Rehabilitation Counselors	$19,300–$53,200
*Child, Family and School Social Workers	$24,500–$62,500
*Mental Health Counselors	$21,900–$59,700

*According to the BLS, workers in these occupations are currently in high demand and thus have been designated as "In Demand."

SOURCE CODE(S):
Department of Labor, Bureau of Labor Statistics = *BLS*
Occupational Outlook Handbook, 2008–2009 = *OOH*
America's Career InfoNet (Online) = *AIN*
O*NET (Online) = *NET*

Sociology

Sociology is the study of social life and social behavior. It focuses on the interaction between population groups and institutions and their influences on each other. Sociology ranges from the study of relationships in family units in the most primitive cultures to the research of large bureaucratic institutions in major industrialized nations. Among the specialties within sociology are criminology, demography, cultural traditions, family relations, social psychology, gerontology, social welfare, race relations, education, social status, and social change.

High School Courses

Anthropology
Civics
Computer Applications
Economics
Government
Health
History
Psychology
Religion
Social Studies
Sociology

Related Majors

Anthropology
Criminology
Demography
Economics
Education
Gerontology
History
Political Science
Psychology
Religion
Urban Affairs

Related Occupations

See page 11 for detailed explanation of key.

Anthropologist—M/D
Case Worker—AA
City Manager—B
Consultant—D
Counselor—M
Criminologist—B
Demographer—B
Educator—B/M/D
Foreign Service Worker—V
Gerontologist—B
Historian—M/D
Human Services Worker—V/B
Labor Relations Specialist—B
Minister—V/P
Peace Corps/VISTA Volunteer—B
Political Scientist—B/D
Probation Officer—B
Psychologist—D
Public Administrator—B
Public Relations Manager—B
Research Assistant—B
Social Worker—B/M
Sociologist—D
Surveying Technician—AA/B
Urban Planner—B

Leisure Activities

- Participating in charitable outreach endeavors
- Joining church activities
- Donating money toward social concerns
- Working as a part-time or volunteer in a day care center or community service agency
- Organizing games, parties, or get-togethers
- Joining a professional organization such as the American Sociological Association
- Serving as a camp counselor, on a school board, or as a social research aide
- Freelance writing
- Reading social-issue publications
- Joining a school or community club

Skills

- Proficiency in interpersonal communication
- Intellectual capacity to do well in most undergraduate and graduate college programs
- Ability to conduct and clearly explain sociological research
- Ability to interact with people of different backgrounds in various situations
- Knowledge of community resources
- Ability to maintain composure in stressful situations

HELPFUL INFORMATION
Sociologists
Growth Outlook (2006–2016)

Projected: Grow about as fast as the average (increase 7% to 13%)
Number Employed (2006): 3,700   **(By 2016)** 4,100 (+11%)
Salary Range (2006): $36,800–$115,800
Related Occupations: *AIN*

	SALARY RANGE:
Historians	$23,500–$89,900
Anthropologists	$29,000–$81,500
Geographers	$37,500–$93,900
Political Scientists	$36,700–$133,100

*According to the BLS, workers in these occupations are currently in high demand and thus have been designated as "In Demand."

SOURCE CODE(S):
Department of Labor, Bureau of Labor Statistics = *BLS*
Occupational Outlook Handbook, 2008–2009 = *OOH*
America's Career InfoNet (Online) = *AIN*
O*NET (Online) = *NET*

- Proficiency in reading comprehension, writing, and speaking
- Ability to evaluate problems and make appropriate decisions
- Proficiency with computers

Values and Attributes

- Desire for recognition and appreciation from others
- Desire to help humanity
- Intellectual growth
- Strong interest in human problems and events
- Sensitivity to and understanding of social problems
- Desire to solve social problems
- Curiosity
- Resourcefulness
- Empathy
- Tactfulness
- Integrity
- Independence

Resources

- **American Sociological Association**
  1307 New York Avenue NW, Suite 700
  Washington, DC 20005
  202-383-9005
  http://www.asanet.org
  (offers student membership and an excellent source of career information)
- **Society for the Study of Social Problems**
  901 McChung Tower
  University of Tennessee
  Knoxville, TN 37996-0490
  865-974-7076
  http://www.ssspl.org
  (provides information about scholarships and employment opportunities)

Transportation

The field of transportation that focuses on the movement of people, materials, and equipment from one place to another. The logistics required for the numerous methods of transportation in an industrialized society are complex. Study in transportation concentrates on how automobiles, buses, trucks, trains, waterways, airplanes, pipelines, and industrial equipment are scientifically, technologically, and creatively manipulated to effectively meet the location needs and deadlines of materials and people. Transportation students specialize in such areas as trucking, automobiles, busing, railroads, waterways, construction machine operation, industrial machine operation, and aircraft.

High School Courses

Business	Health
Computer Applications	Mathematics
Computer Programming	Physical Education
Driver's Education	Statistics
Economics	

Related Majors

Air Transportation	Electrical/Electronics Technology
Business	Engineering Mechanics
Computer Engineering	Marketing and Distribution
Construction Trades	Quality Control and Safety Technologies
Diesel Mechanics	Water Transportation

Related Occupations

See page 11 for detailed explanation of key.

Air Traffic Controller—AA	Logistics Engineer—B
Airline Pilot—AA/B	Logistics Manager—B
Ambulance Driver—V	Merchant Mariner—AA/B
Bus Driver—V	Motorboat Operator—V
Chauffeur—V	Oil Pumper—V
Coal Pipeline Operator—V	Operating Engineer—V
Deep Submergence Vehicle	Storage and Distribution Manager—B
Operator—AA	Service Station Worker—V
Dispatcher—AA	Taxi Driver—V
Driving Instructor—V	Traffic Manager—B
Educator—B/M/D	Train Conductor—V
Ferryboat Operator—V	Transportation Manager—B
Industrial Truck Operator—V	Truck Driver—V
Locomotive Engineer—V	

Leisure Activities

- Working part time in a service station, parking garage, or at a truck, bus, or airport terminal
- Engaging in activities that involve moving, hauling, or driving
- Reading publications related to transportation
- Developing hobbies, collections, and interests related to model cars, trains, aircraft, or other vehicles
- Participating in or visiting racing events or car, truck, or boat shows or exhibits
- Operating farm equipment

Skills

- Ability to clearly understand and apply instructions for operating vehicular or mobile equipment
- Manual dexterity and mechanical aptitude
- Aptitude for accuracy and detail
- Knowledge of transportation and safety codes and regulations in an area of specialization
- Good health and physical stamina
- Good vision, color perception, and eye-hand-foot coordination
- Ability to give and understand directions
- Ability to make keen observations, sound judgments, and appropriate decisions
- Ability to react quickly, work under pressure, and meet deadlines
- Good understanding of computerized instrumentation

Values and Attributes

- Power
- Sense of adventure
- Achievement
- Ability to work in stressful situations and awkward positions
- Enjoyment and appreciation of the importance of moving people, materials, or equipment and/or maintaining vehicles and equipment
- Enjoyment of challenges
- Patience
- Responsibility
- Dependability
- Competence
- Endurance
- Alertness

Resources

- **Air Transport Association of America**
  1301 Pennsylvania Avenue NW, Suite 1100
  Washington, DC 20004

202-626-4000

http://www.airlines.org

(organization of airlines that transport people and goods; provides job listings
and helpful hints)

■ **American Public Transportation Association**

1666 K Street NW

Washington, DC 20006

202-496-4800

http://www.apta.com

(see Services and Programs link)

■ **American Trucking Association**

950 North Glebe Road, Suite 210

Arlington, VA 22203-4181

703-838-1938

http://www.trucking.com

(provides information on trends in transportation, publishes job listings, and
offers resume posting service; see the Web site's Career Center section)

■ **U.S. Department of Transportation**

1200 New Jersey Avenue SE

Washington, DC 20590

202-366-4000

http://www.dot.gov

Zoology

Zoology is a major branch of the biological sciences and involves the study of animals. Zoology ranges from the subatomic and cellular level of the smallest organism to the largest mammal. Zoological study focuses on embryonic development, body structure and function of parts, habitat, and ecological interactions with other living organisms. Specializations within this subject include embryology, cytology, ecology, entomology, ornithology, anatomy, physiology, paleontology, genetics, herpetology, parasitology, mammalogy, marine biology, and wildlife fisheries biology.

High School Courses

Algebra	Geometry
Biology	Health
Chemistry	Math
Computer Applications	Physiology
Earth Science	Science

Related Majors

Agriculture	Pathology
Animal Science	Pharmacology
Biology	Physiology
Entomology	Veterinary Science
Environmental Science	Wildlife Management
Marine Biology	Zoology Education
Museology	

Related Occupations

See page 11 for detailed explanation of key.

Animal Breeder—V	Museum/Zoo Worker—AA
Animal Control Officer—AA	Nature Photographer—AA/B
Animal Laboratory Technician—AA	Park Ranger—B
Biochemist—B	Pathologist—D
Biologist—B/D	Pest Control Worker—AA
Curator—B	Pet Shop Manager—V
Ecologist—B	Public Health Specialist—B
Biological Technician—AA	Range Manager—AA/B
Farm/Ranch Manager—V/B	Taxonomist—B
Fishery Biologist—B	Technical Writer—B
Forester—B	Veterinarian—P
Humane Society Worker—AA	Veterinary Assistant—V/AA
Kennel Operator—V	Wildlife Biologist—B/P
Marine Biologist—B	Zookeeper—AA/B
Microbiologist—B/D	Zoologist—B/D

Leisure Activities

- Browsing through 4-H exhibits, pet shops, and science displays
- Attending animal shows or the circus
- Belonging to a zoological society, National FFA Organization, wildlife preservation group, or the Humane Society
- Visiting aquariums, museums, zoos, and nature centers
- Hiking, camping, nature photography, bird watching, fishing, or horseback riding
- Owning and caring for pets
- Working part time or as a volunteer for the American Society for the Prevention of Cruelty to Animals, a national park or forest, zoo, or veterinary office
- Watching animal shows on TV
- Reading animal-related publications
- Collecting shells, butterflies, insects, or other natural specimens

Skills

- Proficiency in observing, collecting, and analyzing data
- Ability to concentrate for long periods of time
- Proficiency in reading, writing, speaking, and memorization
- Ability to conduct and clearly explain scientific research
- Proficiency in problem solving and decision making
- Proficiency for accuracy and detail
- Ability to work with and relate to animals

HELPFUL INFORMATION
Zoologists and Wildlife Biologists
Growth Outlook (2006–2016)

Projected: Grow about as fast as the average (increase 7% to 13%)
Number Employed (2006): 20,000   **(By 2016)** 22,000 (+9%)
Salary Range (2006): $32,000–$84,600
Related Occupations: *AIN*

	SALARY RANGE:
*Microbiologists	$35,500–$108,300
*Veterinarians	$43,500–$133,100
*Biological Technicians	$23,700–$57,900
Biological Science Teacher, Post-secondary	$37,600–$145,600

*According to the BLS, workers in these occupations are currently in high demand and thus have been designated as "In Demand."

SOURCE CODE(S):
Department of Labor, Bureau of Labor Statistics = *BLS*
Occupational Outlook Handbook, 2008–2009 = *OOH*
America's Career InfoNet (Online) = *AIN*
O*NET (Online) = *NET*

- Intellectual capacity to perform well in most undergraduate and graduate college programs
- Thorough knowledge of general biology
- Good health, physical stamina, agility, and manual dexterity

Values and Attributes

- Achievement
- Desire to help others
- Creativity
- Courage, respect, and determination
- Deep appreciation for and kindness toward animals
- Interest in animal protection and preservation
- Curiosity
- Endurance
- Patience
- Perseverance
- Self-control
- Compassion

Resources

- **American Association of Zoo Veterinarians**
  581705 White Oak Road
  Yulee, FL 32097
  904-225-3275
  http://www.aazv.org/wildlife
  (offers student membership, job listings, and externship opportunities)
- **American Institute of Biological Sciences**
  1444 Eye Street NW, Suite 200
  Washington, DC 20005
  202-628-1500
  http://www.aibs.org
  (has information on careers in biology, scholarships, and more; see Education Office link)
- **Society for Integrative and Comparative Biology**
  1313 Dolly Madison Boulevard, Suite 402
  McLean, VA 22101
  703-790-1745
  http://www.sicb.org
  (offers student membership and educational programs; provides information, job listings, and fellowships)
- **U.S. Fish and Wildlife Service**
  698 Conservation Way
  Shepherdstown, WV 25443
  202-208-5611
  http://www.fws.gov
  (has information on conservation, jobs, and training)

SECTION V

College- and Career-Related Questions and Answers

College-Related Questions

1 How do I know if a program or institution is good?

While in some instances this may require considerable investigation, a general evaluation of an academic/training program or institution can be obtained by checking its accreditation status. Most college directories, such as Peterson's, include accreditation status. Accreditation procedures are usually thorough and comprehensive and normally include on-site observations and periodical evaluations. To obtain accreditation, an institution or program has to meet previously determined acceptable standards of quality in the following:

- Academic performance of students
- Competence level of the faculty and administration (amount of training, degrees earned, recognitions, etc.)
- Appropriateness of curriculum
- Quality of library and technology resources
- Quality of student support services (such as assistance for students with disabilities, tutoring, career development and job placement services, foreign student support, and student activities)
- Adequacy of physical facilities

In addition, you can evaluate a program or institution by the following:

- Seeing how closely it complements your personality attributes and helps you to realize your fundamental life values (determined with a self-assessment or by consulting a career counselor)
- Obtaining a sampling of opinions from current and past students and instructors
- Checking the institutions job placement records for information on how many of the recent graduates in your interest area are employed in related fields
- Ascertaining the institution's public image and credibility; in other words, what do professionals in your community, past and present students, friends, and community residents say about it?
- Taking note of the ratio of applicants accepted to students enrolled

2   What is a college major?

A college major is a specialized field of study that usually reflects your strongest interests and involves the largest number of courses you elect to take. While the term major applies to college and university study, its equivalent would be the largest concentration of related courses elected by a student engaged in any postsecondary educational experience (e.g., trade or vocational school, military, etc.).

3   What is a liberal arts major?

A liberal arts major refers to a concentration of courses in nontechnical, nonspecialized areas such as anthropology, art, foreign language, political science, communications, literature, religion, English, history, music, economics, journalism, philosophy, psychology, and sociology.

Students who have successfully completed liberal arts curricula normally demonstrate proficiencies in many, if not most, of the following knowledge and skill areas, which are important for occupational flexibility, advancement, and overall life fulfillment:

- Ability to analyze and synthesize information
- Critical thinking and reasoning ability
- Ability to read analytically and speak articulately
- Active listening
- Ability to make good judgments and keen observations
- Ability to solve problems and apply the steps of good decision making
- Interpersonal communication
- Tolerance for change and ambiguity
- Understanding underlying causes and ability to see the big picture
- Self-discipline and good organizational skills
- Flexibility
- Appreciation for diversity
- Identifying trends and implications
- Ability to get along with people of different racial and ethnic backgrounds and personalities

4   What should I know before selecting a major?

Choosing the appropriate major requires more preparation than many people realize. Contrary to what many think, most of the work needed to effectively select a major should be done prior to entry into a college or university. Ideally, the selection of a major should take place only after you have a fairly good grasp of the techniques for determining, monitoring, and adjusting to who you are and what is most important in your life. Your major area of study should represent only one of a number of important areas in your life, completing the broader life direction previously established. Unfortunately, this advance work is not done by most people, resulting in avoidable frustration due to frequent changes in majors as well as wasted time, energy, and money. You can significantly improve your chances of selecting the most appropriate major if you carefully do the following, in order, beforehand:

I. Identify who you are and what is most important to you in life. In other words, conduct a thorough self-assessment, and if necessary, seek the help of a qualified career counselor.

II. Learn the steps of good career decision making. A good decision-making model might be

Step 1. Become aware of the need to make a decision.

Step 2. Identify what you value and determine whether you need more information.

Step 3. Gather any additional information you believe you need to make a more informed and wise decision.

Step 4. After you have gathered this information, consider the possible results of each alternative.

Step 5. Select the one alternative that you believe will most appropriately complement the results of your self-assessment.

Step 6. Develop and implement a plan of action.

Step 7. If circumstances make it necessary, review and repeat steps 1 through 6.

III. Identify significant factors (including disability, need for more training, family problems, or recent job loss) that you must consider before deciding what to do.

IV. Applying the steps of good decision making, choose from the following alternatives:

- Enter college or trade school
- Enter and apprenticeship program
- Join the military
- Travel
- Work for VISTA or the Peace Corps
- Get a job
- Keep doing what you are doing

It is only at this point (assuming the results of your self-assessment clearly indicate the need for some type of additional training or education) that you are ready to address the next question.

5   How do I select a major?

Choosing a major is often one of the most important and difficult decisions you have to make during your lifetime. A genuine effort to determine a suitable major can serve as the catalyst for comprehensive career planning activities. The results can have lifelong implications in terms of learning how to establish and monitor life direction. There are four main steps in the decision-making process. (If you plan to enter a one- or two-year program of study, apprenticeship, or similar endeavor that requires that the major area of study be decided immediately, then you should complete steps 1, 2, and 3 before entry.)

Step 1. Apply the steps of good decision making to determine what type of curriculum most adequately complements your self-assessment. More than likely—particularly if you have elected to enter a four-year college program—after selecting a suitable curriculum, you will find that a number of related majors can possibly fit. A specific major preference may not crystallize until later.

Usually, this comes about after you have taken a variety of course, have had fulfilling experiences in certain courses, and have explored several options in depth through discussions with advisors and reading relevant materials

Step 2. As you continue to apply the steps of good decision making, select the training institution, college, or university you believe offers the curriculum and environment that best support your self-assessment and accommodate any significant influencing factors.

Step 3. Next, continue applying the steps of good decision making, select the major that best supports your self-assessment and accommodates any significant influencing factors.

Step 4. Finally, continue to monitor the results of your self-assessment. This is important due to the possibility that one or more significant influencing factors could alter your profile. You should always be ready and willing to reconfigure previous decisions.

6   What should I do if I want a college degree but don't know what to pick for my major?

Regardless of whether you are in high school or college, there are basic courses that are required to earn a diploma or degree. Take these first, as they are likely to apply to the curriculum or major you eventually select. (Be sure to check the basic requirements in the school's handbook or catalog.) In addition to the basics, you may want to take one or more liberal arts or practical electives (computer science, interpersonal communications, writing, speech) that are increasingly important in our changing society. Although these courses may not directly apply to your eventual major or profession, the information acquired can be applied to other areas of your life. Since you will take these courses, at least initially, as electives, it is recommended that you don't enroll in too many before you've reached a decision on your curriculum focus. The extra time you gain as a result will provide you with the opportunity to engage in unrushed self-assessment and other career planning activities. Then, the next time you select courses, you can make informed and wise decisions.

7   Should I "test" out of a required course?

It depends on your particular circumstance, but it may be to your advantage to test out of one or more of the following is true:

- You are thoroughly proficient in the basic knowledge and/or skills that will be covered in the course; to take the course would be a rehash of what you already know and thus may be a waste of valuable time. For example, if you've been a freelance writer for five years, testing out of a basic composition course in your degree program makes good sense.
- Extenuating circumstances, such as disabilities that keep you from taking on-campus courses or serious time conflicts due to family or job obligations, demand that an alternative to regular classroom attendance be explored.
- You have taken an advanced placement (AP) class during high school in the area you want to test out of, and you are quite knowledgeable and/or highly capable in that area. In this instance, testing out may allow you to move into advanced courses and thus shorten the time required to earn your degree. Remember, the rationale here for testing out is that you are already highly capable. If this is not true, then maybe taking the course would be the wiser choice. If in doubt, see a qualified counselor.

On the other hand, testing out may not be the best option if one or more of the following reflects your present situation:

- Due to lack of effort, knowledge, or ability, you have failed a required course and thus would like to test out of it to avoid taking it over again.
- You believe you can pass the test and are looking for a quick and easy way to obtain a degree. Not only is there a good chance you will not pass, but you may very well find out later that you have unnecessarily shortchanged yourself in terms of the enriching educational experiences that often result from classroom exposure.
- The course is in an important foundation area that will give you knowledge and skills you will later need to apply regularly and with significant proficiency. In such instances, it is recommended that you take the actual class. It is unlikely that a test will be able to duplicate the formal and informal discussions between instructor and student that a classroom experience affords. A great deal of learning, as well as valuable networking opportunities, can be lost if you are not exposed to such

experiences. To test out of courses that demand depth and breadth in all aspects could eventually put you at a disadvantage in the future.

If you are interested in testing out, contact your high school or college counselor and ask about Advanced Placement, CLEP tests, GED tests, and/or any Challege Tests (faculty made) that may be available.

8   I must register for a full load of classes tomorrow but I don't know what to take. What should I do?

There are many variables to consider. Do you plan to graduate from this institution? If so, have you completed all of the basic required courses? Do you have self-assessment results from recent career development activities? If so, what courses seem to complement what you know about yourself? Do you have room for electives? Do you want to attend days? Nights? Part time? Full time? Try to answer these questions first. Then, although it may be difficult to talk with someone on short notice, present this concern to a qualified career counselor or academic advisor. Some career counselors have short exercises, checklists, or tests that you can complete in an hour or less, which may point out some general directions. A discussion with a qualified counselor and/or the completion of such exercises may result in a tentative emergency decision. However, this should be viewed as a temporary measure only!

While it may be true that more comprehensive career development activities later will verify the general direction that you arrived at as a result of the above emergency efforts, it does not negate the need to engage in more comprehensive career development. While such Band-Aid measures are often required to meet the sometimes overwhelming demands of a fast-moving society, the most successful professionals will strongly recommend follow-up activities.

9   What should I do if I only want to pursue a short-term program of a year or less?

Most short-term programs are highly specialized, and courses taken rarely transfer to other programs. Entering into a short-term program without a clear indication that it will most realistically support your self-assessment would prove to be a significant waste of time, energy, and money. Therefore, comprehensive career planning activities are recommended before enrolling in any one- or two-year programs. (You can elect to do this yourself or seek help from a qualified career counselor.)

10   What are home-study (distance learning) courses?

Traditionally, home-study courses (sometimes referred to as correspondence courses or distance learning) have been off-campus courses taken by individuals via mail. However, the mode of delivery has changed dramatically due to computerization. A growing number of classes can now be taken via the correspondence route, from elementary through the graduate level. Correspondence courses can be particularly attractive to those who are shut-in. *Bear's Guide to Earning Degrees by Distance Learning* (Ten Speed Press, 2006) comprehensively covers this topic.

Pros
- Most home-study courses provide a one-on-one teaching experience.
- They are flexible and convenient for faculty and students.
- You can work at your own pace.
- You can usually enroll at any time.
- You can experience personal growth and satisfaction from achievements.
- You can save time and money (transportation, housing, etc.).
- There are no scheduling hassles.

Cons
- In-person interactions are reduced.
- You need strong self-discipline.
- There may be distractions at home.
- You may not be able to transfer course credits to a traditional program later.
- Your isolation is increased.

11 What is virtual education?

Virtual education can be considered an outgrowth of distance learning, resulting from widespread technological advances. In essence, it is taking academic classes and/or training electronically (primarily via the computer) instead of in an educational institution.

This form of educational training has experienced phenomenal growth and there is no end in sight for the foreseeable future. Various technologies are utilized, although the computer is the primary tool. Depending upon the school, program, and class, other methods or technologies used may include interactive TV, computer conferencing, audiographics, audiocassettes, telecourses, videotape courses, e-mail, teleconferencing, and fax machines. Colleges that offer entire programs of study online are now commonplace. Students at many of these virtual colleges can now access libraries around the world virtually.

For more information, contact the U.S. Distance Learning Association (USDLA) at http://www.usdla.org.

12 What is co-op education?

Co-op (short for cooperative) education is a joint venture between an educational institution and an employer to provide a learning experience for one or more students, combining classroom studies with related on-the-job work activities. Normally, the student is paid and the work experience is supervised by representatives from both of the parties involved. Co-op programs are widespread and are administered through many high school, college, and university job placement offices or business departments. The co-op student may spend part of his or her day or semester on the job while the other part is spent in the classroom. In some cases, students rotate between terms of full-time study and terms of full-time work. Many co-op programs grant academic credits.

Pros

- It may lead to a job with the employer.
- It prepares you for the real world due to the large block of time required for work.
- You can earn money for school fees and other expenses.
- A co-op program can help you determine your career direction.
- Work experience can enhance your résumé and interviews.
- Co-ops can help you develop work experiences and contacts.
- Co-ops can enrich your personal development.

Cons

- You may not be able to take other academic courses.
- You may find out that the area is not suited for you and thus waste valuable time and energy.
- You may not be able to participate in as many school-related or campus activities due to a full schedule.

13 What is an apprenticeship?

An apprenticeship is an arrangement between an employer and an individual (referred to as an apprentice) whereby the apprentice agrees to be trained and supervised by a skilled craftsperson for a specified period of time. Apprenticeship experiences combine classroom instruction and on-the-job training, which must add up to a minimum number of required hours (usually around 8,000 hours or four years of on-the-job experience and a minimum of 576 hours of related instruction). During this time, the apprentice is paid at a progressively higher rate of pay. If the apprenticeship is successfully completed, the apprentice usually applies for and receives his or her journeyworker certificate and card, which represents full status as a skilled craftsperson in a particular area of training. (However, be aware that one may acquire a journeyworker certificate and card, usually through a union, and not have completed an official apprenticeship program.)

Some occupations that offer apprenticeship training include: Automobile-Body Repairer, Electronics Mechanic, Automobile Mechanic, Emergency Medical Technician, Baker, Firefighter, Biomedical Equipment Technician,

Furniture Finisher, Boilermaker, Glazier, Butcher, Hazardous Waste Material Technician, Bricklayer, Instrument Mechanic, Cabinetmaker, Legal Secretary, Carpenter, Machinist, Cement Mason, Millwright, Cosmetologist, Painter, Drafter, Plumber, Electrician, and Sheet-Metal Worker.

14 What is an internship?

An internship is an experience offering an individual an opportunity to work in a real job situation for a prescribed period of time to gain knowledge, skills, and work experience. Internships are usually related to your area of study and can be served with or without financial compensation or other work benefits. While many internships take place during the summer months, they may take place anytime during the year and last for a much longer period of time. Some professional internships last a year or more. A growing number of college programs now require the successful completion of an internship before a certificate or degree is granted. Some internships offer academic credits.

Pros
- You can learn job-related skills, behaviors, and responsibilities.
- You can establish contacts for future employment.
- An internship can help you make career decisions.
- You can gain experience valuable on résumés and in interviews.

Cons
- An internship may offer reduced or no pay.
- It may take time away from paid work experience.
- You may find during the internship that the area is not for you and thus waste valuable time and energy.

15 What is mentoring?

Mentoring occurs when an experienced and/or skilled adult (often in an influential leadership position) takes another individual (or mentoree) who is less experienced, knowledgeable, and skilled under his or her wing for the purpose of:

1. Instructing, coaching, and advising to help the mentoree overcome potential obstacles and increase the chances for career success;

2. Sharing important inside information about a company, organization, agency, or institution; or

3. Being a contact and support person as well as an advocate for the mentoree in terms of future employment possibilities or promotions.

Having a mentor appears to be extremely advantageous for a growing number who seek to get a foot in the door and learn what it takes to experience upward career mobility within a particular organization. But mentoring relationships have both pros and cons:

Pros

- There is an increased chance to be noticed and thus permanently employed or promoted.
- You have an opportunity to learn from the inside of a company.
- You can pick up skills of use in other situations.
- You can learn valuable tips that will prevent mistakes later.
- You can cut down on the amount of time you need to move up.
- You can build a support base.

Cons

- There is danger of becoming too intimate with or dependent on your mentor.
- The relationship may create friction among your mentor's coworkers.
- Advice from your mentor may conflict with advice from others.
- You may be perceived as a threat by some.
- You may be unfairly used by your mentor.
- If the experience doesn't turn out well, it may hamper your prospects at the company.

16 What are "STEM" jobs?

According to the Bureau of Labor Statistics, STEM jobs are occupations related to science, technology, engineering, and mathematics. Workers in such occupations use science and mathematics to solve problems. An ability to think logically is necessary and educational requirements can range from a high school diploma up to a Ph.D. For a more detailed description along with specific examples of STEM jobs, see "STEM Occupations" by Nicholas Terrell (*Occupational Outlook Quarterly*, Spring 2007).

17 What is an MBA?

MBA stands for Master of Business Administration. Traditionally, the acquisition of an MBA, particularly if it has been earned at one of the nation's top business schools, signifies that you have been well-educated and are highly qualified to step into the world of business. For years, MBA candidates, as well as many professionals, have regarded this degree as the one to acquire if you expect to succeed in corporate America. The MBA has been touted as the key to higher salaries and upper-level executive positions. Indeed, some would probably say that the MBA is to business what the Ph.D. is to college teaching. While some have expressed concerns about this degree's significance in light of our changing times, the MBA remains a cherished goal for most aspiring business students and still appears to provide a competitive edge for many.

18 Should I go for an MBA?

This is probably a question that is asked by most, if not all, undergraduate business majors. Before you make a decision, carefully consider the following:

Age. Do you believe that the years you will have to benefit from having the MBA will outweigh the projected time and effort required to earn it?

Cost. Will you be able to recoup the expenses incurred from attending an MBA program for several years?

Values and Family Lifestyle. Will the pursuit of an MBA, as well as projected benefits later on, support your desired values and lifestyle?

The following is a brief summary of the pros and cons of pursuing an MBA:

Pros
- MBAs usually enjoy a higher salary than non-MBAs.
- In larger corporations, an MBA may improve your chances for advancement and promotion.
- MBA programs usually involve a broad-based (often including an international aspect) and future-directed perspective, which is greatly needed in an increasingly competitive and global market.
- The MBA saves job candidates the frustration of being passed over because of a lack of credentials.
- The MBA is still viewed by many as desirable and may provide opportunities in unrelated areas.

Cons
- Some employers may shy away from MBA grads, believing that they are overrated, lack technical skills, expect higher salaries, and that they may quickly move on to another company.
- An MBA program can be very expensive, possibly costing as much as two years of lost salary that may never be recouped.
- The pursuit of an MBA may place a significant strain on family time and finances.
- You may find out after completion of an MBA program that the sacrifice was not required, particularly if you start your own business or remain in a smaller one.
- If your MBA is not earned from a top business schools, you may experience difficulty in landing the type of position you desire.
- You may have unrealistic expectations regarding what the MBA will do for you.

19 Should I get a Ph.D.?

Whether you should go for the Ph.D. (Doctor of Philosophy)—or for that matter, any graduate degree—depends on how you answer the following questions:

- Do the values, lifestyle, and occupation your are seeking require that you go on to graduate school?
- Do you have the money and/or can you afford the expense of going on to graduate school?
- Will the outlay of money, time, and energy be worth the expected benefits later on?
- Are you willing to do the rigorous and time-consuming research usually required for the final dissertation?
- Do you have to work while you pursue this degree or can you quit work and attend school full time?
- What is the likelihood you will get a job related to your studies?
- Will the pursuit of a Ph.D. come into severe conflict with your other life values, particularly concerning your family?

These questions should be answered by the potential Ph.D. candidate prior to starting a program of study. A thorough self-analysis should be the first priority. If the results clearly point to areas such as university teaching, higher education administration, research, computer science, or engineering supervision, then a Ph.D. should be a definite consideration. To obtain the highest-level professional jobs in mathematics, physics, psychology, sociology, engineering, and many other academic disciplines, a Ph.D. is required. The Ph.D. might also be your goal if you have a continuing desire to learn and be intellectually stimulated through research, discovery, and publishing. You may choose this route to obtain the status and job advantages often associated with the Ph.D. However, you may want to avoid such a rigorous academic endeavor if you dislike or are weak in the areas of language, writing, and research. Listed below are some of the pros and cons of pursuing a Ph.D.

Pros

- A doctorate may open up many more professional and/or supervisory employment possibilities.
- A Ph.D. may increase your prestige and status; you may be considered an expert in your area.
- You may have an opportunity to earn more income.
- A Ph.D. usually increases your credibility in terms of published materials and research.
- A doctorate will probably put you in a good position to take advantage of an increasingly complex and knowledge-oriented society in terms of being able to apply skills learned.
- You have the satisfaction of learning at a highly specialized level.

Cons

- A great deal of time is normally required. It is estimated that the average candidate takes about six or seven years beyond the bachelor's degree to complete the Ph.D.
- After receiving a Ph.D., and if employed in a university setting, you may be pressured to "publish or perish."
- The cost of obtaining a Ph.D. can be very high.
- You may experience discrimination from some employers who consider you overqualified.
- The written dissertation is a major obstacle for many.
- You may not be able to find the most desired employment and thus may experience underemployment.

Finally, if you are seriously considering the pursuit of a Ph.D., be sure to get input from postdoctoral and current graduate students in your area of interest before making a decision.

20 What is networking and can it help me?

Networking is simply establishing as many relevant personal contacts as possible to enhance future career possibilities and personal growth. This could include a wide range of individuals, from family members, friends, and job or school associates to professional acquaintances developed at conventions and meetings and through referrals. Most people engage in networking, whether they realize it or not, through discussions about mutual interests, fellowship, and other interchanges. Networking is viewed negatively by some people because they feel the individual who seeks to network may selfishly take advantage of others. Unfortunately, this may be true of some. However, networking can and should be a give-and-take arrangement wherein both persons involved derive benefit from the interaction and each assists the other.

Career-Related Questions

1 What does the word "career" mean?

For many people, career means the part of life that is concerned with employment. From an occupational standpoint, it means the sum total of the various jobs you may hold during your lifetime. However, these definitions do not fully capture the meaning of career. Think of career not only as a job that pays well and provides fulfillment, but also as encompassing all of your major roles in life. When viewed in this manner, your career can be said to be all of what you are currently involved in that enables you to carry on with life.

2 What is career decision-making?

You can best understand good decision making by first defining the term *decision*. A decision is the act of choosing. A decision, whether you are aware of it or not, is a response to a question, concern, or problem. Appropriate career decisions can be further defined as the ongoing lifelong process of making choices that complement your personal attributes and help you to realize your basic life values. Indeed, career decisions (particularly those pertaining to an occupation) should be made with great care, for they will significantly influence your direction, personal satisfaction, and fulfillment in life.

3 What is *good* career decision making?

A good career decision usually includes the following basics:

Step 1. Become aware of the need to make a decision and then do something to make the decision happen.

Step 2. Determine or confirm who you are and what's most important to you in life. Gather information about yourself on the INSIDE.

Step 3. Gather necessary information OUTSIDE of yourself to better ensure you have considered the options available.

Step 4. Narrow down the alternatives to those that seem to be most realistic.

Step 5. Select the alternative(s) you believe to be the best fit for you at this time in your life.

Step 6. Continuously monitor the results of your decision(s) and, if necessary, repeat one or more of the previous steps.

4 What is career development?

Career development is primarily concerned with helping a person to establish or maintain appropriate direction and balance in life. It is, in essence, life development. Career development, from a positive standpoint, encompasses choices made and changes experienced that result in a person increasingly realizing a more satisfying and fulfilling life.

5 Is career development different for an older adult than for a younger person?

While the basics of career development (self-assessment, occupational awareness, exploration, decision making, and implementation) are the same regardless of age, variations in maturity and life experience necessitate different approaches. Some career specialists believe that most adults, like children and young people, go through a number of developmental stages. Consequently, they consider the life stage of a person before selecting a consulting strategy.

6 What is a career resource or information center?

A career resource or information center is an office or agency that provides you with career and life development information, materials, and services.

Career resource or information centers can be either public or private, and they can be independent or part of a larger institution. Many such centers are located on college campuses and within placement services. Others are found in libraries or high schools. The goal of most centers is to maintain accurate, up-to-date career information and provide support services such as seminars and workshops, which enable you to make more effective life and career decisions.

7 Are career development and job placement services the same?

Not really. However, career development and job placement services are often cited by many in the same breath. This is understandable in light of their close relationship. Services and programs often overlap and many colleges and universities offer career development and job placement functions jointly through the same office. Nevertheless, while there are a number of program similarities, there are several distinguishing characteristics. Career development is primarily concerned with helping someone make the most appropriate decisions to ensure a fulfilling life. Job placement, on the other hand, focuses on helping a person to locate suitable paid work. One might refer to career development as the beginning or foundation stage of the career development and placement process, while job placement is the final or practical application stage. However, particularly in the United States, both functions are usually intertwined in realizing a more meaningful life.

8 What are career development services?

Career development services often include the following:

- Life and career advising, consultation, and counseling
- Online career guidance activities
- Administration and interpretation of career interest and personality surveys, as well as ability and achievement tests
- Access to up-to-date occupational files and a career resource library
- Seminars and workshops related to self-awareness, decision making, goal setting, and other career development areas
- Development and distribution of career-related handouts and similar materials
- Access to test information files
- Career lectures presented to classrooms and community groups
- Career information for school administration, faculty, students, and the community at large
- Help in appropriately integrating home life, work, and leisure activities

9   What are job placement services?

Job placement services often include the following:

- Employment advice and counseling
- Information about local, state, and national job openings
- Placement of individuals into part-time and full-time jobs
- Creation and maintenance of individual qualification files
- Job hunting, résumé, and interviewing services including online résumé and job placement assistance
- On-campus interviews with potential employers
- Creation and maintenance of employer information files
- Information about career fairs and career days
- Help in establishing professional relationships with local employers
- Information about internships, co-ops, work-study experiences, and on-site visitations
- Follow-up studies related to job placement results and trends
- Lectures to groups on and off campus on job hunting, labor market trends, and other pertinent topics

10   What does a good career counselor do?

Most of the information cited here was developed by the National Career Development Association, which can be contacted at http://ncda.org.

A good career counselor:

- Conducts individual and group counseling sessions to help clarify life and career goals;
- Administers and interprets tests and inventories to assess abilities and interests and to identify career options;
- Encourages exploratory activities through assignments and planning exercises;
- Evaluates, organizes, and provides educational, occupational, and personal resources and information to clients engaged in life development;
- Utilizes career development and occupational information systems to help individuals better understand the world of work;
- Helps to improve decision-making skills;
- Assists in developing individualized career plans;
- Assists with job search planning and résumé development;
- Fosters and understanding of the integration of work and other life roles; and
- Provides support for persons experiencing job stress, job loss, or career transition.

11   What is a self-assessment?

A self-assessment entails a serious and honest look at yourself. Self-assessment is a process that requires prioritizing, deep thinking, discovery, and acceptance of personal realities. It may or may not include the help of a career counselor. However, if you want to conduct your assessment in a comprehensive manner, it is strongly recommended that you secure the assistance of a qualified professional. It is not always easy to identify personal aspects of oneself or to use the information discovered to make effective life-changing decisions. However, once you successfully start this process (and it is an ongoing process), it can result in more focused and fulfilling life. At minimum, self-assessment should include the accurate identification of physical and personal attributes, temperament, abilities and aptitude, strengths and weaknesses, attitudes, life values, work values, interests, and goals.

Once you have identified, defined, and summarized the above in writing, you will have a beginning blueprint of who you are and what you want in life. You can then compare your decisions with this self-assessment to determine how close they are. Keep in mind that you will need to continually monitor, revise, and update your blueprint. This will ensure that it stays current with your changing reality.

12   What are career tests?

It may help to first define *test*. Any procedure that attempts to measure or evaluate in order to determine quality, achievement, or ability level can be said to be a test. Career tests are actually surveys, in that they attempt to help you identify interests, skills, and various personality characteristics that will help you make appropriate career-related decisions.

13   Should the results of my career tests determine what I do in the future?

Absolutely not! This is an incorrect assumption that is believed by people far too often. Career tests results should only verify other information you have obtained about yourself so that you can make a better and more informed decision. The intricately complex nature of the human being as well as the highly technical and changing society we live in can never be fully measured by human-devised evaluations. However, when the appropriate career or aptitude test is used, it can be highly beneficial.

Even if it were possible to determine precisely what you should do in the future, it is probably more important to answer the following questions:

- Are my career interests or aptitude test results generally supportive of my most cherished life values?
- Do the results complement my personality attributes?
- Do the results provide me with enough additional information and insight to help me make a better decision about my career direction?

Once again, it is most important to remember to combine the results of any career assessment you take with as much additional information as you need to be able to make an informed and wise decision.

14 Should I accept career test results that point to a single field?

Possibly, although you should not act too hastily, even if the results seem to verify your career focus. Also, if you have not had a qualified career counselor assist you in your interpretation, I would strongly encourage you to do so. It is usually wise to have several indicators clearly point in the same direction. I would recommend three to five verifications of direction (e.g., career survey results, favorite school courses and/or those in which you have the highest grades, career worksheet results, feedback from credible others, your own personal beliefs, etc.). Multiple verifications usually minimize the tendency for you to doubt or have continuing second thoughts. They should increase your confidence as well as the chances for you to realize personal satisfaction in life. Finally, using several clear indicators may help you avoid spending time, effort, and money moving in an inappropriate direction.

15 What does it mean when the results of my career testing show that I am interested in just about everything?

While there are a number of possible reasons for such a profile, it is more than likely that one or more of the following is true:

- You may have purposely put down answers that would show a high interest in everything so as not to miss out on anything exciting or interesting.
- You have broad and strong interests in many different areas but may not know enough about yourself to identify those areas that represent the highest priority.
- You lack decision-making skills.
- You simply marked all of the items "favorable" in order to just get through.
- You genuinely have strong interests in many areas, but, unrealistically, want to do everything.
- You may have misunderstood or responded incorrectly.
- There may have been a mechanical (or computer) malfunction or a human recording error.

In such cases, if you cannot identify the reason (and eventually resolve your confusion) from among the above possibilities, you should seek the help of a qualified career counselor or do what you most want to do (given that other verifications support the decision).

16 Am I required to take a battery of tests to effectively plan my career?

No. A number of resources can help you determine career direction. Some people, because of family influences, their past experiences with counselors, and other career-directing activities, have developed a clear understanding of themselves and their values. Certain individuals have been fortunate to have had interested and knowledgeable teachers who continually encouraged them in self-analysis, exploration, and good decision making, or maybe a family member just happened to be a career counselor. Still others have benefited from a variety of career-oriented family friends or comprehensive home libraries or enriching trips and vacations. Consequently, they not only monitor change within and around themselves continually, but also they have learned effective decision-making skills.

Some find the results of career-related worksheets, exercises, and written questionnaires sufficient to make appropriate career decisions. Others simply develop over time the necessary motivation and direction by reading books and other publications and doing Internet research. Finally, certain individuals develop an effective system of career decision making through career-oriented audiovisuals; seminars, workshops, and conferences; clubs; classroom and community lectures and discussions; computer software programs; work, volunteer, co-op, or internship experiences; and talking to others.

As you can see, career tests represent only one of a variety of career development activities for you to consider. Testing may not be required or even appropriate for you due to time constraints, cost, language difficulty, reading level, or availability, just to name a few reasons. However, you will want to be absolutely sure you have enough information about yourself and the world around you to better ensure that you are making wise career decisions.

17 What is the difference between an aptitude test and an interest inventory?

While these two types of tests attempt to measure something quite different, I have found that many individuals do not know the difference and are confused. A frequently heard statement is, "I'd like to take one of those aptitude tests." This statement could be referring to an occupational interest inventory, abilities test, or a personality survey. Quite often, after some clarifying questions, it is discovered that the individual actually desired a more comprehensive test to help him or her make a better decision.

Aptitude Tests—According to Harcourt Brace Jovanovich, Inc., publishers of the popular *Differential Aptitude Tests* (DAT), aptitude is "the capacity to learn given appropriate training and environmental input." Aptitudes are considered by this leading test publisher as learned and not inherited. Its tests attempt to measure your degree of "readiness or potential to perform or do" in some identified area(s). An aptitude test seeks to establish if you have a strong, average, or weak tendency to perform well, based on natural and/or learned abilities in selected areas (e.g., spatial, verbal, numerical, mechanical, abstract reasoning, clerical, etc.). Normally, the results of an aptitude test do not provide enough diagnostic information for those seeking to establish career direction, unless they are added to other relevant data.

Interest Inventories (Surveys)—These tests are widely used and may be mistakenly perceived by some as having more comprehensive career development application than they have been designed for. Interest inventories attempt to identify significant trends toward or away from selected occupational areas, the objective being to compare the inventory-taker's interests with the general interests of individuals in designated occupations. Interest inventories are based on the premise that the more your interests are like/unlike individuals in selected occupations, the more compatible/incompatible the occupational area is likely to be. Nevertheless, just as it is true for aptitude tests, interest inventory results are limited, no matter how accurate, and represent only one of a number of important aspects that should be considered in career decision making.

18 Can occupational projections be trusted?

Some would answer, "Well, yes!" and others would say, "Probably not." Whatever position you take, it must be clearly understood that occupational projections are merely educated guesses, although they may be based on extensive research. No human being can foretell the future perfectly; many variables can and do, often unexpectedly, affect outcomes (e.g., supply and demand, technological advances, weather, war). Predictions have often been known not to hold up. Nevertheless, job projections can be quite helpful when coupled with other related data, particularly if information is obtained from a reliable source. A key resource, considered to be credible by most, is the U.S. Bureau of Labor Statistics (BLS), a government agency that specializes in occupational predictions. Many college and university career development and placement centers, as well as state employment service offices, maintain a file of updated labor market projections from the BLS and other sources. Also, many career specialists believe that jobs are available in most occupational areas, regardless of job predictions. However, to acquire these jobs, you must learn and effectively implement the skills of job hunting (including via the Internet) and self-marketing. I am inclined to agree.

19 What is career success?

Career success really depends on the individual. For some, career success is measured by financial and material accumulation. Others base career success on recognition and popularity. Still others believe that real career success comes only through helping others or making a contribution to society.

It is my belief that career success comes when you achieve inner satisfaction (reflected in a generally positive attitude) through the continuing realization

- of your deepest and most cherished life values in every major endeavor (home, work, school and leisure);
- that you have the opportunity and inspiration to use and develop current and desired skills; and
- that you are excited about what you have achieved, are achieving, and can achieve in the future.

20 What are the 4 "MUSTS" that can improve your chance for life success?

"MUST" #1 is knowing which way to go or proceed in life. In other words, one who has determined or confirmed his or her accurate and appropriate direction, purpose, or reason for being in life.

"MUST" #2 is having goals that, when acquired, help you to increasingly realize the desired results that lead you to fulfill your purpose or life direction.

"MUST" #3 is planning the specific steps you need to take to meet the goals you have set.

"MUST" #4 is the follow-up you do after you have made your plan(s) to meet your goal(s). This can include writing a cover letter and résumé, applying for a job, signing up for the military, applying for financial aid, registering for college, etc.

Appendix A

Self-Assessment Survey

One of the most important parts of Step 1 of the 4-Step Career Development Process is self-assessment. Self-assessment surveys, such as the one that follows, are activities used by many career counselors to help people focus on their inside to identify what is most important to them. Feel free to duplicate any of the following self-assessment sheets for your own personal use. Responses can also be simply written on a sheet of paper.

TEMPERAMENTS

Temperaments are personality attributes that relate to your way of thinking, feeling, and behaving and determine whether you are comfortable or uncomfortable in a given situation. Please read the directions and complete the temperaments profile below.

Directions: Weigh each of the temperaments below on a comfort scale of 1 to 12 (1 being the situation in which you feel the MOST COMFORTABLE). Place your rating on the black line beside the appropriate letter. If you feel equally comfortable about more than one, do not hesitate to use the number twice.

___A. Situations involving a VARIETY of duties often requiring frequent CHANGE (doing different activities).

___B. Situations involving REPETITION or REPEATING SOMETHING FREQUENTLY according to set procedures or sequences (doing the same task over and over).

___C. Situations involving DOING THINGS only UNDER SPECIFIC INSTRUCTION, allowing little or no room for independent action or judgment in working out job problems (little or no personal input required).

___D. Situations that involve DEALING WITH PEOPLE in actual job duties beyond giving and receiving instructions (high degree of interaction and cooperation with people).

___E. Situations that involve DIRECTING, CONTROLLING, and PLANNING of entire activities or the activities of others.

___F. Situations involving WORKING ALONE and apart from others although the activity may be integrated with that of others (doing most or all of your work by yourself although it may be done around others).

___G. Situations that involve INFLUENCING PEOPLE in their opinions, attitudes, or judgments about ideas or things (being able to persuade others in the way they think, act, and behave).

___H. Situations involving PERFORMING ADEQUATELY WHILE WORKING UNDER PRESSURE or when confronted with the critical or unexpected or when taking risks (being challenged, taking challenges and coming through on challenges).

___I. Situations that require you make an evaluation based on PERSONAL JUDGMENT (making decisions based on personal experiences and through the use of your senses, e.g., sight, smell, hearing, taste, or touch).

___J. Situations requiring you to make a decision using MEASURABLE OR VERIFIABLE CRITERIA (making decisions based on something that has been or can be measured based on facts, rules, or standards).

___K. Situations in which you INTERPRET AND EXPRESS FEELINGS, IDEAS, OR FACTS IN A PERSONALLY CREATIVE WAY (such as through song, acting, writing, painting, etc.).

___L. Situations involving PRECISION in terms of set limits, tolerances, or standards (being detailed and exact).

PRIMARY SOURCE: *Dictionary of Occupational Titles*

STRENGTHS Circle those you believe are most like you and rank order your strongest five.

Active	Enduring	Industrious	Punctual
Affectionate	Energetic	Intelligent	Respectful
Ambitious	Enthusiastic	Joiner	Self-confident
Analytical	Expressive	Kind	Sense of humor
Assertive	Fair	Like challenges	Sensitive
Caring	Faithful	Logical	Sharing
Charming	Flexible	Loyal	Speak well
Cheerful	Forgiving	Mannerly	Spontaneous
Comforting	Friendly	Neat	Steadfast
Compassionate	Generous	Objective	Tactful
Competent	Gentle	Observant	Talented
Cooperative	Good listener	Open-minded	Team player
Courageous	Good with hands	Optimistic	Thoughtful
Creative	Good-natured	Organized	Thrifty
Dedicated	Graceful	Patient	Tolerant
Dependable	Grateful	Peacemaker	Trustworthy
Determined	Helpful	Perform well	Understanding
Disciplined	Honest	under pressure	Unselfish
Discreet	Hospitable	Persistent	Witty
Efficient	Humble	Poised	
Encouraging	Independent	Productive	

WEAKNESSES Circle those that are most like you and rank your weakest five.

Aggressive	Disrespectful	Liar	Rarely finish
Apathetic	Do dumb things	Moody	anything
Argumentative	often	Not dependable	Rude
Bossy	Domineering	Obnoxious	Sarcastic
Braggart	Drug abuser	Often negative	Secretive
Can't concentrate	Easily offended	Overly critical	Selfish
Can't make	Fearful	Overly talkative	Shy
decisions	Flippant	Panicky	Stingy
Can't say no	Gullible	Perfectionist	Stubborn
Can't take	Hateful	Perform poorly	Sulky
criticism	Hostile	under pressure	Swear a lot
Clumsy	Impatient	Pessimistic	Tactless
Cocky	Impulsive	Picky	Uncouth
Complainer	Inflexible	Poor listener	Unrefined
Condescending	Insensitive	Poor loser	Wasteful
Confronter	Intolerant	Prejudiced	Whiny
Cruel	Irresponsible	Prideful	Wimpy
Deceptive	Jealous	Put things off	Worry a lot
Dependent	Judgmental	Quick-tempered	
Dishonest	Lack of courage	Racist	
Disorganized	Lazy		

Top Five Strengths

1. _____
2. _____
3. _____
4. _____
5. _____

Top Five Weaknesses

1. _____
2. _____
3. _____
4. _____
5. _____

SKILLS (ABILITIES and APTITUDES)

Skills can be divided into two major categories:

ABILITIES—An ability can be defined as something you can do as a result of rehearsal and/or practice. Abilities and skills are often thought of as being the same; being skilled, though, usually implies that you can do something well. A specific knowledge of your strongest abilities can greatly increase your sense of confidence.

APTITUDES—Aptitudes are those activities you have the potential to perform well and seem to come easily and naturally. Some people have aptitudes they are either unaware of or have been unable to develop to their fullest. Becoming aware of your aptitudes can help you to better understand who you are on the inside.

Directions: Place an "A" in front of the area(s) in which you believe you have ABILITY or APTITUDE. Feel free to write in any ability/aptitude you may have in addition to or instead of the sampling listed. Leave blank any area you are not sure of. As you go through, keep in mind that you will be asked when finished to list your five strongest abilities/aptitudes.

__/__Understanding instructions, facts, and underlying reasoning; being able to reason and make judgments

___Understanding the meaning of words and ideas; being able to present information or ideas clearly

___Doing arithmetic operations quickly and correctly

___Looking at flat drawings or pictures of objects and forming mental images of them in three dimensions or in terms of height, width, and depth (such as in reading blueprints, patterns, etc.)

___Observing details in pictorial or graphic material and effectively making visual comparisons; good at noticing differences in shapes, shading, etc.

___Observing details and recognizing errors in numbers, spelling, and punctuation in written materials, charts and tables; good at avoiding errors when copying

___Moving the eyes and hands or fingers together to perform a task rapidly and correctly

___Moving the fingers to work with small objects rapidly and correctly

___Moving the hands with ease and skill, as in placing and turning

___Moving hands and feet together in response to visual signals, etc.

___Seeing likenesses and differences in colors or shades; matching colors

___Finding errors in writing

___Following instructions

__/__Asking the right questions

__/__Improving what others have done

__/__Explaining things clearly

___Planning and organizing

___Operating mechanical equipment

___Expanding on what others have started

___Exploring and doing research

___Budgeting

___Being exact and to the point

___Spelling

___Accepting constructive advice

___Being creative

___Getting along with others

___Counseling others

___Doing artistic things

___Keeping records

___Leading and supervising others

___Teaching others

___Gardening

___Typing

___Giving others helpful advice

___Being flexible

___Drawing or designing things

___Mechanical things

___Training others to do things

___Driving vehicles

___Performing in front of others

___Taking risks

___Solving conflicts

___Noticing shapes, sizes, etc.

___Staying with a task until done

___Repairing and servicing computers

___Getting others to believe in something

___Making good decisions during emergencies

___Simplifying what appears to be complex

___Learning from mistakes and past experiences

___Working alone for long periods of time

___Understanding and reading blueprints, maps, drawings, etc.

___Listening or picking up on what others say

___Seeing the underlying reasons for behavior or events

___Estimating costs

___Interpreting the feelings and emotions of others

___Reading and comprehending

___Doing activities that require heavy physical work

___Writing

___Copying things or activities done by others

___Collecting things

___Constructing things out of wood or metal or other materials

___Speaking in public

___Working with numbers/solving accounting-type problems

___Operating computers

___Motivating others to perform or do something

___Being thorough

___Expressing feelings

___Managing time

___Distinguishing sounds

___Doing things for others

___Communicating to others

___Controlling own emotions

___Thinking before acting

___Team sports (basketball, football, etc.)

___Individual sports (tennis, golf, etc.)

___Leading and supervising people and activities

___Using your fingers to work with small objects or instruments

___Studying English or related subjects (name related subject(s))_____

_____

___Studying social studies or related subjects (name related subject(s)) _____

_____

___Studying science or related subjects (name related subject(s)) _____

_____

___Other (Include any additional or alternative skills.)

_____   _____

_____   _____

_____   _____

List your five STRONGEST abilities/aptitudes.

1. _____
2. _____
3. _____
4. _____
5. _____

The skills list represents just a sampling of possibilities. For a more comprehensive and personalized list, you may want to read the latest edition of Richard Nelson Bolles's *What Color Is Your Parachute?* (Ten Speed Press, 2007).

LIFE VALUES

Life values are those deeply cherished things, activities, or relationships you place the most importance on and aspire to obtain or engage in. Life values provide us with the necessary motivation to endure many of life's hardships. Read the directions and complete the life values survey below.

Directions: Read through the entire list. After reading, go back and place in the blank to the left of each value the code that best describes its level of importance to you:

NVI = Not Very Important   I = Important   VI = Very Important

Next, circle the items marked VI that you consider MOST IMPORTANT (identify at least five but no more than seven).

___ACHIEVEMENT (accomplishment; being able to see or experience results that have been brought about by persistence or hard work)

___AESTHETICS (the appreciation and enjoyment of beauty for beauty's sake, as in the arts and/or in nature)

___ALTRUISM (having a special regard for or dedication to the welfare of others; service to others)

___AUTONOMY (independence; the ability to make your own decisions; self-directed; not being dependent on others)

___CREATIVITY (being able to try out new ideas; being different from the traditional; being innovative)

___EMOTIONAL WELL-BEING (having peace of mind and inner sense of security; the ability to identify and resolve inner conflict; being relatively free from anxiety)

___HEALTH (maintaining an acceptable condition in terms of your physical body; being relatively free from pain, discomfort, sickness, etc.)

___HELPING MANKIND (engaging in activities or inventing, developing, or producing something that will positively influence the lives of many; making a significant contribution of lasting or continuing value)

___HONESTY (being frank, genuine, and truthful with yourself and others)

___JUSTICE (treating others fairly or impartially; holding to truth or reason)

___KNOWLEDGE (desire to learn or know; to seek truth; to acquire information about)

___LOVE (warmth, caring, and unselfish devotion that freely accepts others without conditions)

___LOYALTY (maintaining allegiance to a person, group, or institution; not abandoning; sticking with during difficult times)

___MORALITY (believing and keeping ethical standards; personal honor; integrity; doing what you truly believe is right)

___PHYSICAL APPEARANCE (concern for your attractiveness; being neat, clean, and well-groomed)

___PLEASURE (having satisfaction, fun, joy, gratification)

___POWER (having possession or control; authority or influence over others)

___RECOGNITION (to be regularly recognized and positively noticed; receive attention)

___RELIGIOUS FAITH (having religious beliefs; having a personal relationship with God)

___SECURITY (being sure of most endeavors or involvements in life; having visible or concrete support or back-up before taking risks)

___SKILL (being very good at something; being better than average; performing at a high proficiency level)

___WEALTH (having many possessions and plenty of money)

___WISDOM (having mature understanding; deep insight; good sense and judgment; being able to make appropriate and effective decisions)

WORK VALUES

Work values are those things, activities, and relationships you place the most importance on and aspire to obtain or engage in, relative to an occupation. While work values are often similar to life values, many are specifically related to an occupational setting. Work values tend to reflect much of who you are on the inside. Read the directions and complete the work values survey below.

Directions: Read through the entire list. After reading, go back and place in the blank to the left of each value the code that best describes its level of importance to you:

NVI = Not Very Important   I = Important   VI = Very Important

Next, circle the items marked VI that you consider MOST IMPORTANT (identify at least five but no more than seven).

___ACHIEVEMENT (accomplishing something everyone can't do or will not do; doing something that requires considerable effort and/or difficulty)

___ADVANCEMENT (the ability to advance and move up; opportunity for higher position or training or education, etc.)

___ASSISTING OTHERS (being directed and supervised by others; preferring not to have the responsibility of leading or directing people or activities)

___BENEFITS (having good hospital and life insurance, etc.; unemployment and vacation benefits)

___COMPETITION (being in an environment where you have to compete or be matched against in rivalry; being challenged to produce or perform)

___CREATIVITY (being able to try out new ideas; to be innovative)

___ENVIRONMENT (being in physical or social surroundings that are suitable to your temperaments and values, e.g., beautiful, neat, friendly, warm, etc.)

___HANDS-ON CONTACT (working with things, objects, and/or equipment; using hands and other body parts to perform tasks and activities that are primarily of a physical nature)

___HELPING OTHERS (engaging in activities that directly aid and assist others)

___INDEPENDENCE (having little or no supervision; freedom to guide your own activities and make your own decisions)

___INDUSTRY (work that keeps you busy and active continuously; could include physical and/or mental tasks; having little or no down time)

___INTERESTING (being positively excited and motivated most of the time in what you are doing; not likely to be bored for any significant span of time; doing something you can continuously enjoy with few exceptions)

___LEADERSHIP MANAGEMENT (being in a leadership, supervisory, or managerial position; being in charge of others)

___LEARNING (using mental abilities; gaining knowledge and understanding; being intellectually stimulated)

___MONEY (earning a high salary)

___NUMBER CONTACT (working with numbers; charting; doing statistical reports and summaries)

___PEOPLE CONTACT (high interaction and cooperation with people; being around people most of the time)

___POSITIVE RELATIONSHIPS (being able to get along very well with co-workers and supervisors; working with people whom you generally like; being in an environment that is characterized by warm and cooperative relationships)

___PRESTIGE (having a position that is recognized as being very important and influential by most; being in a position that commands great respect)

___RELIGIOUS FAITH (work that is in line with your religious beliefs; work that does not interfere with your ability to practice your religious principles)

___SECURITY (being relatively free from the fear of frequent layoffs, job loss, reduced hours, etc.)

___SELF-DIRECTION (being able to determine what you are going to do and how you are going to do it in terms of work tasks, procedures, pace, etc.)

___SKILL (having the ability to perform one or more tasks at an extremely high proficiency level; being able to do something that requires special effort or training or education)

___SUPPORT (being in a work environment where you receive emotional support, praise, and backing)

___TRAVEL (being able to travel within a local community as well as from city to city as a part of your job responsibilities; having a travel budget)

___VARIETY (doing different things or activities; not doing repetitive tasks)

___WHOLE LIFE SENSITIVITY (working in a situation that allows or provides reasonable flexibility and choice in terms of overtime, time off, vacation selection, length of workday, family priorities, and outside concerns; being able to engage in non-job-related activities without hindrances)

___WORDS/IDEAS INFORMATION (working with oral, visual, and written information, knowledge, facts, ideas, and/or symbols (may include numbers))

___OTHER (Include any value that has not already been mentioned. If you desire to add more, feel free to do so.)

_____

_____

INTERESTS

Interests are those things, activities, and experiences you enjoy and are excited about. Much of what we do during our leisure time tends to reflect our interests. Interests often reveal some of our most important values. Also, you can be interested in an activity, experience, etc., without actually being involved in it. A selected list of interests and/or leisure-time activities has been included below and on the next several pages. Read through the directions and complete the interests survey below.

Directions: Go through the entire list and circle those things, activities, or experiences that represent a STRONG INTEREST for you. Keep in mind that you will be asked when you finish to list your strongest interests.

being the leader

cooking

acting

gardening

solving math problems

visiting museums

organizing community events

working with people

water sports and games

canoeing, sailing, etc.

doing hard physical work

working with words or ideas

participating in church activities

drawing cartoons or real-life pictures

helping those who are poor

hunting, fighting, trapping, etc.

biology, life science, etc.

working on cars or other mechanical things

team sports (basketball, baseball, football, hockey, etc.)

individual sports (swimming, golf, jogging, tennis, racquetball, etc.)

reading

writing

beading

selling things

going to plays

driving vehicles

music

teaching

canning

parenting

earning money

competing with others

video games

electronic gadgets

board games

listening to the radio

watching TV

eating out

bowling

arts and crafts

traveling

antiques

talking

foreign languages

movies

politics

guns

knitting

collecting (butterflies, leaves, stamps, coins, etc.)

designing clothes

ham radio operation

interior decorating

backpacking

bird watching

camping

exploring

flying

hiking

horseback riding

nature walks

sailing

sightseeing

walking

yard work

Big Brother/Big Sister or similar program

charitable drives

counseling others

neighborhood associations

house plants and flowers

Peace Corps

military involvement

war games

Red Cross

spending time with the elderly or visiting the sick and shut in

VISTA

YMCA/YWCA

browsing through bookstores

conferences/conventions/workshops

debating

editing

jigsaw puzzles

lab experiments

lectures

organizing activities

preparing taxes

researching

science exhibits

studying and going to school

talk shows

working in a nursery or day care center

writing in a diary

antique shows

art galleries

auctioning

auto shows

religious study

boat shows

singing in a choir

playing or singing with a group

circuses

composing

concerts

macramé

needlepoint

photography

pottery

sculpting

typing

dancing

entertaining others

fairs

fashion shows

festivals

marching band

nightclubs

parties

pen-pal exchange

plays

poetry

talent shows

variety shows

visiting libraries

zoos

planetariums

4-H

archery

club leader

conservation

health

nutrition

investments

Junior Achievement

Masons

astrology

motorcycles

scouting

sororities/fraternities

broadcasting

doing housework

exercising

learning new things

comic books

magazines

newspapers

professional journals

sleeping

window shopping

shopping

teaching a craft or sport

visiting flea markets

viewing travelogues

auto racing

fitness activities

gymnastics

ice skating

skiing

weightlifting

fencing

cross country

In the blanks below, write any interests or leisure-time pursuits that you strongly enjoy but were not included above.

_____ _____

_____ _____

_____ _____

What do you like the most? Write your STRONGEST (at least five but no more than seven) interests below.

1. _____

2. _____

3. _____

4. _____

5. _____

6. _____

7. _____

Are there any things, activities, or experiences (listed in the sampling or not) that you strongly dislike? If so, write these in the blanks below.

1. _____

2. _____

3. _____

4. _____

5. _____

6. _____

7. _____

SELF-ASSESSMENT PROFILE SHEET (SAPS)

A Self-Assessment Profile Sheet appears on the next page. On this sheet record the summary information you were asked to identify in each section. If you feel there are items that should be added to the number requested because you believe they are of equal weight (or tied in terms of rank order), feel free to do so. A sample of a completed SAPS has been included.

Remember, your profile is subject to change in time due to Significant Influencing Factors (SIF). SIF are situations or events that significantly alter your thinking patterns, activities, and relationships and consequently motivate you to make adjustments in important occupational decisions. Examples of SIF include sickness, disease, accident, flood, famine, war, change in religious beliefs, divorce, drug abuse problem, loss of a job, new legislation, among others. Therefore, it is suggested that you periodically review this profile and, whenever necessary, update it.

After completing your SAPS you will probably want to identify the occupation and/or college major you believe the results most realistically reflect (minus the weaknesses and dislikes, of course). You can generate your own list of occupations and majors to pick from or take a Career Interest Survey, such as the Kuder or Strong-Campbell surveys, from a career counselor. It is my hope that after you complete the reading and exercises in this book, as well as follow the suggestions given, you will be well on your way toward a more directed and fulfilling life.

SELF-ASSESSMENT PROFILE SHEET

LIFE VALUES (p. 228) List the five to seven items you circled.

1.
2.
3.
4.
5.
6.
7.

WORK VALUES (p. 229) List the five to seven items you circled.

1.
2.
3.
4.
5.
6.
7.

INTERESTS (p. 231) List your five to seven STRONGEST interests.

1.
2.
3.
4.
5.
6.
7.

TEMPERAMENTS (p. 223) List in order from 1 to 12 your MOST COMFORTABLE temperaments.

1.
2.
3.
4.
5.
6.
7.
8.
9.
10.
11.
12.

SKILLS (p. 225) List your five STRONGEST abilities/aptitudes.

1.

2.

3.

4.

5.

STRENGTHS (p. 224) List your top five strengths.

1.

2.

3.

4.

5.

WEAKNESSES (p. 225) List your top five weaknesses.

1.

2.

3.

4.

5.

SELF-ASSESSMENT PROFILE SHEET

(Sample of Completed Form)

LIFE VALUES

1. Achievement
2. Emotional well-being
3. Love
4. Morality
5. Religious faith
6. Wisdom

WORK VALUES

1. Support
2. Variety
3. Words/ideas/information
4. Advancement
5. Money
6. Benefits
7. Achievement

INTERESTS

1. Being the leader
2. Sports
3. Making money
4. Biology
5. Talking
6. Religious study and prayer/meditation
7. Being with friends

TEMPERAMENTS

1. Measurable/verifiable
2. Directing/controlling
3. Variety/change
4. Influencing people
5. Precise

SKILLS

1. Solve conflicts
2. Doing for others
3. Knowing what to say/do
4. Leading/supervising
5. Being exact and budgeting

STRENGTHS

1. Independent
2. Dependable
3. Competent
4. Ambitious
5. Organized

WEAKNESSES

1. Moody
2. Perfectionist
3. Argumentative
4. Judgmental
5. Often negative

APPENDIX B

Descriptions of Selected Occupations

The following descriptions should encompass the least familiar occupations mentioned in this book. Most of the occupational definitions cited come from the *Occupational Outlook Handbook* and the Occupational Information Network (O*NET).

ABSTRACTOR—A worker who analyzes pertinent legal or insurance details or sections of statute or case law to summarize for purposes of examination, proof, or ready reference—may specialize as a title examiner.

ACCOUNTING CLERK—A clerical worker who performs any combination of routine calculating, posting, and verifying of financial information for use in maintaining accounting records.

ACQUISITIONS LIBRARIAN—A librarian who selects and orders books, periodicals, films, and other materials for a library.

ACTIVITIES SUPERVISOR—A recreation therapist who specializes in the organization, direction, and supervision of recreational activities for those individuals who are elderly, ill, or disabled to assist in their overall rehabilitation.

ACTUARY—A professional who applies knowledge of mathematics, probability, statistics, and principles of finance and business to various forms of insurance, annuities, and pensions.

ACUTE CARE NURSE—A nurse who provides advanced nursing care for patients with acute conditions such as heart attacks, respiratory distress syndrome, or shock.

ADJUDICATOR—A government worker who adjudicates (gives an opinion on) claims filed by the government against individuals or organizations.

ADMINISTRATIVE EXAMINER—A worker who supervises and oversees polygraph examiners who question and screen individuals to detect deception or to verify truthfulness using polygraph equipment and techniques.

ADMIRALTY LAWYER—A lawyer who specializes in legal matters pertaining to inland navigable waters or on the high seas.

ADULT AND VOCATIONAL EDUCATION TEACHER—A teacher who specializes in preparing students for a particular vocation such as welding, food service, or horticulture.

ADVERTISING ACCOUNT EXECUTIVE—A professional who plans, coordinates, and directs advertising campaigns for the clients of an advertising agency.

AERODYNAMIST—An engineering specialist who plans and conducts the analyses of aerodynamic, thermodynamic, aerothermodynamic, and aerophysics concepts, systems, and designs to resolve problems and determine suitability and application to aircraft and spacecraft.

AERONAUTICAL ENGINEER—An engineer who applies engineering principles and techniques to design, develop, and test aircraft, space vehicles, surface effect vehicles, and missiles.

AEROSPACE ENGINEER—An engineer who designs, develops, tests, and helps produce commercial and military aircraft, missiles, and spacecraft.

ARCHIVIST—A professional who appraises and organizes permanent records and historically valuable documents, participates in research activities involving archival materials, and directs the safekeeping of archival documents and materials.

ART THERAPIST—A health care specialist who plans, coordinates, and supervises art techniques, projects, and programs to assist in the rehabilitation of mentally or physically challenged patients.

ASTROPHYSICIST—A physicist who specializes in the study of the physical aspects of the heavenly bodies or space such as the sun, stars, and planets.

AUDIOLOGIST—A professional therapist who specializes in diagnostic evaluation of hearing, prevention research, and rehabilitative services for people with hearing problems and related disorders.

AUDITOR—An accounting professional who examines or audits financial records and controls operating procedures to determine effectiveness and efficiency; may specialize in internal, external, county, tax, or other kinds of auditing.

BACTERIOLOGIST—See Microbiologist.

BAILIFF—A court officer who maintains order in a courtroom during trials and guards the jury from outside contact, can arrest persons violating the law, and is responsible for overall security.

BAR EXAMINER—A professional who determines the qualifications of candidates seeking to practice law; prepares written exams, corrects and marks papers, announces those who pass, and makes recommendations.

BIBLIOGRAPHER—A professional who compiles lists of books, periodicals, articles, and audiovisual materials on specialized subjects.

BIOCHEMIST—A professional scientist who studies chemical processes of living organisms and conducts research to determine the influence of foods, drugs, serums, and other substances on tissues and vital processes.

BIOINFORMATICS SCIENTIST—A scientist who conducts research using bioinformatics theory/methods in areas such as pharmaceuticals, medical technology, biotechnology, computational technology, proteomics, computer information science, biology, and medical informatics.

BIOMEDICAL ENGINEER—An engineer who specializes in using medical and biological ideas and principles in the design, development, production, and supervision of medical equipment and devices.

BIOMEDICAL EQUIPMENT TECHNICIAN—A worker who specializes in the inspection, maintenance, calibration, and modification of the electronic, electrical, mechanical, hydraulic, and pneumatic equipment and instruments used in medical therapy.

BIOPHYSICIST—A biological scientist who studies the physical principles of living cells and organisms, their electrical and mechanical energy, and related phenomena.

BLACKSMITH—A worker who creates and repairs various metal articles such as tongs, edged tools, hooks, chains, machine and structural components, and agricultural articles.

BLOOD BANK SPECIALIST—A health care worker who specializes in both simple and advanced blood techniques such as drawing blood, classification, collection and transfusion, testing, evaluation, preservation and storage, and other related activities.

BOILERMAKER—A worker who assembles, analyzes defects in, and repairs boilers, pressure vessels, tanks, and vats by using power and hand tools.

BOOKBINDER—A worker who cuts, sews, and glues the pages of a book to its cover, using a sewing machine, hand press, and hand cutter.

BOTANIST—A biological scientist who studies the development and life processes, physiology, heredity, environment, distribution, anatomy, morphology, and economic value of plants for application in such fields as agronomy, forestry, horticulture, and pharmacology.

BUYER—A professional who purchases merchandise or commodities for resale, inspecting, selecting, ordering, and authorizing payment for them.

CABLE SPLICER—A worker who splices overhead, underground, or submarine multiple-conductor cables used in telephone and telegraph communications and electric power transmission systems.

CARDIOLOGIST—A medical doctor who specializes in the diagnosis, treatment, and prevention of diseases of the heart.

CARTOGRAPHER—A professional drafter who specializes in drawing maps of geographical areas to show natural and constructed features, political boundaries, and other features.

CATALOGER—A librarian who compiles information and materials, such as books and periodicals, and prepares catalog cards and computer records to identify materials and integrate information into a library's collection.

CATERER—One who coordinates the food service activities of a hotel, restaurant, or other similar establishment or at a social function; includes food preparation, budgeting, menu planning, managing staff, and maintaining food quality.

CERAMIC ENGINEER—An engineer who specializes in developing new nonmetallic, inorganic materials and new methods for making ceramic materials into useable products.

CHAMBER OF COMMERCE OFFICER—One who represents a local association of businesspeople who aim to promote commercial and industrial interests in the community; involves analyzing of market trends, economic conditions, and tax issues; advising businesses; supporting economic and civic growth; and other activities.

CHAPLAIN—A clergy worker who conducts and coordinates worship services, evangelism activities, and religious education endeavors in the armed forces, correctional institutions, hospitals, and on college campuses.

CHEMICAL LABORATORY TECHNICIAN—A worker who conducts chemical and physical laboratory tests and makes qualitative and quantitative analyses of materials, liquids, and gases for the purpose of research, new products, health and safety standards, criminology, environmental concerns, and more.

CHIEF EXECUTIVE OFFICER (CEO)—The top executive or administrator of a large corporation or government.

CHILD WELFARE WORKER—A social worker (caseworker) who aids parents with child-rearing problems and children who have difficulties in social adjustments; investigates home conditions; refers clients to community resources; coordinates foster care or adoption activities; provides counsel to families; and supervises and monitors placements.

CHIROPRACTOR—A physician, but not a medical doctor, who specializes in the adjustment of the spinal column and other body parts to improve health and correct abnormalities of the human body believed to be caused by interferences with the nervous system.

CHOREOGRAPHER—A dance director who creates and teaches original dances for ballet, musical, or revue to be performed for stage, TV, motion picture, or nightclub production.

CINEMATOGRAPHER—A photography director who plans, directs, and coordinates the filming of a motion picture.

CIRCULATION MANAGER—A manager who directs the sales and distribution of newspapers, books, and periodicals.

CITY MANAGER—A government administrator who directs and coordinates the administration of a city or county government in accordance with policies determined by a city council or other authorized officials.

CIVIL ENGINEER—An engineer who plans, designs, and directs the construction and maintenance of structures and facilities such as roads, railroads, airports, bridges, harbors, channels, dams, irrigation projects, pipelines, power plants, water and sewage systems, and waste disposal units.

CLIMATOLOGIST—A meteorologist who specializes in the study of climate and climate conditions.

CLINICAL CHEMIST—A biochemist who studies the chemical processes of living organisms and uses complex chemical tests and procedures to analyze body tissues and fluids.

COAL PIPELINE OPERATOR—A worker who controls, from a master panel, a semiautomatic processing plant that pulverizes and mixes coal with water and sends the resulting slurry into a pipeline for transportation.

COLLEGE DEAN—A college administrator who directs and coordinates a specific area of responsibility such as student affairs, academics, occupational programs, continuing education, men, or women.

COLUMNIST—An individual who analyzes news and writes a column or commentary based on personal knowledge and experience with the subject matter for publication or broadcast.

COMMERCIAL ARTIST—A professional artist who draws or paints illustrations for use by various media to explain or enhance the printed or spoken word.

COMMUNITY SERVICE AGENCY DIRECTOR—An individual who directs the activities of a community health or social service agency concerned with community problems such as teen pregnancy, child abuse, substance abuse, or disease.

COMPOSITOR—A worker who assembles and sets type by hand or machine and creates galleys for printed materials.

COMPUTER SECURITY SPECIALIST—An individual who evaluates the security of computer systems; also trained to prevent, safeguard against, and investigate computer-related crimes.

CONSERVATIONIST—A worker who is concerned with the protection and care of natural resources such as streams, rivers, lakes, and forests.

CONSULTANT—A professional who has developed a proficiency or expertise in a particular area and is consulted by clients to define a need or problem, conduct studies or surveys to obtain information, and analyze data to give advice on or recommend a solution.

CONTRACTOR—A manager who contracts to perform specified construction work in accordance with architectural plans, blueprints, and codes; may be classified as a building contractor, landscape contractor, engineering contractor, or other specialized contractor.

CONTROLLER/COMPTROLLER—An individual who directs the financial affairs of an organization such as a bank, hospital, governmental office, or hotel.

COOPERATIVE EXTENSION WORKER—An agricultural agent who organizes meetings to advise farmers and individuals engaged in agribusiness in application of agricultural research findings; may direct 4-H club activities, give lectures, and prepare articles; sometimes called an agricultural extension agent.

COPYWRITER—A professional who writes or revises material (copy) for use by print or broadcast media to promote the sale of goods and services.

CORONER—A medical examiner who directs investigations of death occurring within a particular jurisdiction as required by law. Coroners conduct inquests, perform autopsies and laboratory analyses, and may testify at hearings or trials.

CORRECTIONS OFFICER—An individual who is responsible for guarding inmates in jails and prisons in accordance with established policies, regulations, and procedures.

COURT REPORTER—A clerk who performs clerical duties in a court of law, including preparing a calendar of cases, examining legal documents, explaining procedures, securing information, recording minutes of court proceedings, and other tasks.

CREDIT MANAGER—A worker who directs and coordinates the activities of a federal or state chartered credit union that provides savings and loans services to members.

CRIMINOLOGIST—A professional sociologist who specializes in the study of crime and criminal behavior.

CRITICAL CARE NURSE—A nurse who provides advanced nursing care for patients in critical or coronary care units.

CURATOR—A professional who oversees the collection, research, authentication, preservation, maintenance, and information dissemination activities of operating and exhibiting institutions such as museums, botanical gardens, arboretums, art galleries, herbariums, and zoos.

CURRICULUM SUPERVISOR—A professional educator who supervises and oversees the implementation of an instructional materials program in an elementary, junior high, or high school in accordance with guidelines.

CUSTOMS INSPECTOR—A government worker who inspects cargo, baggage, and articles worn or carried by persons on vessels, vehicles, or aircraft entering or leaving the country to enforce customs and related laws.

CYTOLOGIST—A biological scientist who studies plant or animal cells.

CYTOTECHNOLOGIST—A health care specialist who assists pathologists through the process of staining, mounting, and studying cells of the human body to determine pathological conditions.

DANCE THERAPIST—A specialist who plans, organizes, and directs dance activities and learning experiences as part of the care and treatment of patients to produce positive behavioral changes.

DATABASE MANAGER—A worker who supervises and manages the designing, creating, and operating activities in the formulation of a computerized information storage bank.

DATA-ENTRY EQUIPMENT OPERATOR—A worker who enters information into a computer system.

DENTAL HYGIENIST—A health care worker who specializes in removing plaque and tartar from teeth and beneath the gumline; also does preliminary examinations for the dentist.

DENTAL LAB TECHNICIAN—A health care worker who builds and repairs full and partial dentures (sets of teeth), bridges, crowns, and other dental apparatus using hand tools, molding equipment, and bench fabricating machines.

DERMATOLOGIST—A medical doctor who specializes in the diagnosis and treatment of diseases and conditions of the skin.

DESIGN/BUILDING SPECIALIST—An architect who specializes in both the design and physical building aspect of a project; may work with a contractor or make modifications on his or her own.

DESKTOP PUBLISHER—A professional who produces printed materials via computer using the techniques of layout and graphic design.

DIAGNOSTIC MEDICAL SONOGRAPHER—A health care specialist who uses ultrasound diagnostic procedures, which make use of sonic energy to identify or determine the extent of disease or injury in body tissue.

DIETETIC TECHNICIAN—A worker under the direction of a dietitian who assists in food service management, nutrition education, and dietary counseling.

DIETITIAN—A health care specialist who directs, plans, and supervises programs for menu planning, food preparation, nutritional care, serving of meals, and specialized diets.

DIRECTOR OF ADMISSIONS—A professional who directs and coordinates a student admissions program at private schools or public and private colleges or universities according to policies developed by a governing board, determines who will be accepted, prepares and distributes materials about the institution and its programs, and conducts recruitment programs.

DIRECTOR OF CAREER PLACEMENT—A professional who directs and supervises job placement services for students and employees; usually arranges for interviews, posts or publicizes listings of job openings, supervises and coordinates campus work-study programs, offers seminars and workshops related to job seeking/holding skills, develops and distributes occupational information, etc.

DIRECTOR OF GUIDANCE—A professional counseling administrator who directs and coordinates educational and vocational guidance and counseling programs for students and graduates.

DISPATCHER—A worker who dispatches buses, cabs, trains, airplanes, trucks, and other transporting vehicles; supervises, coordinates, and relays schedules and instructions regarding movement and location; also maintains an operational log.

DISTRICT ATTORNEY—A lawyer who conducts prosecutions in court proceedings on behalf of the city, county, state, or federal government;

presents evidence against the accused to a grand jury and before a judge or other judiciary or jury.

DRAFTER—A worker who prepares clear, complete, and accurate working plans and detail drawings from rough or detailed sketches or notes for engineering or manufacturing purposes according to specified dimensions; may specialize in architectural, aeronautics, electrical, or other area.

ECOLOGIST—A biological scientist who studies the relationship between organisms and their environments and the effects of pollutants, rainfall, temperature, altitude, and other variables on organisms.

ECONOMIST—A professional who plans, designs, and conducts research to aid in interpretation of economic relationships and develops solutions for problems arising from the production and distribution of goods and services; may specialize in health, agriculture, labor, or other areas.

EDITOR—A person who prepares materials for publication or release, making revisions or other modifications.

EEG (ELECTROENCEPHALOGRAPHIC) TECHNOLOGIST—A health care worker who measures impulse frequencies and differences in electrical potential from the brain for use in diagnosis of brain disorders using the electroencephalograph.

EKG (ELECTROCARDIOGRAPH) TECHNICIAN—A health care worker who records electromotive variations in the action of heart muscle, using the electrocardiograph machine, to help determine the causes of heart complications.

EMERGENCY MEDICAL TECHNICIAN—A health care worker who administers first aid, including life support, while transporting sick or injured persons to a medical facility.

ENDOCRINOLOGIST—A doctor who specializes in diseases that affect glands (thyroid, parathyroid, pancreas, ovaries, testes, adrenal, pituitary and hypothalamus).

ENDOSCOPY TECHNICIAN—A worker who maintains a sterile field to provide support for physicians and nurses during endoscopy procedures.

ENERGY ENGINEER—An engineer who designs, develops, and evaluates energy-related projects and programs to reduce energy costs or improve energy efficiency during the designing, building, or remodeling stages of construction.

ENGINEER—A professional who applies mathematical and scientific principles in an economical and efficient manner to the design, planning, development, production, supervision, repair, and maintenance of the products, equipment, structures, processes, systems, and programs of industrial societies. The main branches of engineering are civil, electrical/electronics, mechanical, industrial, metallurgical, chemical, aerospace, agricultural, and nuclear.

ENTOMOLOGIST—A professional scientist who studies insects and their relation to plant and animal life, identifies and classifies insects, and helps to develop pesticides and other methods to control pests.

ENTREPRENEUR—An individual who starts and owns his or her own business.

ENVIRONMENTAL ENGINEER—Usually a civil, chemical, or mechanical engineer who specializes in some aspect of the environment (e.g., soil testing, air pollution, water pollution, toxic substances, etc.).

ENVIRONMENTAL HEALTH TECHNICIAN—A worker who conducts tests and field investigations to obtain information for use by environmental engineering and scientific personnel in determining sources and methods of controlling pollutants in air, water, and soil.

ENVIRONMENTALIST—A professional who studies, analyzes, and evaluates environmental problems and applies scientific knowledge to prevent pollution, solve problems, and make predictions about the air, water, land, noise, and radioactivity.

ERGONOMIST—A professional who specializes in designing products and arranging work environments to adapt to the behaviors of human beings and to ensure their health and safety on the job.

ESCROW OFFICER—A professional worker who holds in escrow (safekeeping) funds, legal papers, or other collateral posted by contracting parties to ensure fulfillment of contracts or trust agreements.

ESTIMATOR—An accounting specialist who prepares cost estimates for products or services requested to aid management in bidding on jobs or determining the price of those products or services.

EXECUTIVE HOUSEKEEPER—An administrator who directs an institutional housekeeping program to ensure clean, orderly, and attractive conditions; may be employed by hospitals, hotels, or motels.

FINANCIAL AID DIRECTOR—A professional who directs the scholarship, grant, and loan programs at a college or university to provide financial assistance to students.

FINANCIAL ANALYST—A worker who conducts statistical analyses of information affecting an investment program of a public, industrial, or financial institution such as a bank, insurance company, brokerage, or investment house.

FINANCIAL PLANNER—A professional who specializes in helping individuals and companies invest their income in the most efficient and economical manner to better prepare for future needs, goals, and emergencies.

FLORICULTURIST—A professional horticulturist who specializes in the research, breeding, production, storage, processing, and transit of flowers.

FOOD AND DRUG INSPECTOR—A government worker who inspects establishments where food, drugs, cosmetics, and similar consumer items are manufactured, handled, stored, or sold to enforce legal standards of sanitary conditions and health and hygiene habits of persons handling such products.

FOOD SCIENTIST—A professional scientist who applies scientific and engineering principles in the research, development, production technology, quality control, packaging, processing, and utilization of foods; may specialize in dairy products, poultry, cereal, grains, etc.

FOOD SERVICE MANAGER—An individual who manages, supervises, and coordinates a program of serving food in a hospital, nursing home, college, or other institution.

FOREIGN SERVICE OFFICER—A government worker who represents the interest of the United States government and citizens by conducting relations with foreign governments and international organizations, protecting and advancing political, economic, and commercial interests, and rendering personal services to Americans abroad and to foreign nationals traveling to the United States; may be termed diplomat, consultant, ambassador, etc.

FORESTER—A professional who manages and protects forest lands and their resources for economic, educational, and recreational purposes.

FORESTRY TECHNICIAN—A worker who gathers information pertaining to size, content, condition, and other characteristics of forest tracts and under the direction of a forester, leads workers in forest propagation, fire prevention and fighting, and maintenance of facilities.

4-H CLUB AGENT—A worker who organizes and directs the educational projects and activities of a 4-H club; recruits farm volunteer leaders; directs selection of projects such as sewing, woodworking, photography, and livestock raising; and develops and arranges exhibits in county or state fairs.

FRAUD EXAMINER, INVESTIGATOR, OR ANALYST—A worker who obtains evidence, takes statements, produces reports, and testifies to findings to resolve fraud allegations.

FREELANCE WRITER—A self-employed writer who submits his or her work to various sources for publication and/or writes on a contract basis.

FUNERAL DIRECTOR—An individual who arranges, coordinates, and directs burial preparations and funeral services.

GENEALOGIST—A historian who conducts research into the background of an individual or family to establish descent or to discover and identify forebears of the individual or family.

GENERAL PRACTITIONER—A medical doctor who treats a variety of medical problems without specializing in any one area.

GENERAL SUPERINTENDENT—A manager who directs the activities of workers in the construction of buildings, dams, highways, pipelines, or other structures; usually directs and oversees other supervisory personnel.

GENETICIST—A professional scientist who studies the hereditary variation of characteristics in forms of life; may specialize in molecular, population, human, medical, animal, or plant genetics.

GEODESIST—A professional who studies the size, shape, and gravitational field of the earth.

GEODETIC SURVEYOR—A worker who measures large areas of the Earth's surface using satellite observations, global positioning systems (GPS), light detection and ranging (LIDAR), or related sources.

GEOGRAPHER—A professional who studies nature and the features of the earth, relating and interpreting interactions of physical and cultural phenomena.

GEOMORPHOLOGIST—A geologist who specializes in the history, structure, and changes of the earth's surface.

GEOPHYSICIST—A physical scientist who studies the physical aspects of earth, including its atmosphere and hydrosphere. Specialties include oceanography, glaciology, and volcanology.

GEOSPATIAL INFORMATION SCIENTIST/TECHNOLOGIST—A worker who conducts research and develops geospatial technologies.

GEOSPATIAL INFORMATION SYSTEMS TECHNICIAN—A worker who assists scientists, technologists, and related professionals in building, maintaining, modifying, and using geographic information systems (GIS) databases.

GEOTECHNICAL ENGINEER—A civil engineer who specializes in the evaluation of soil and rocks that support structures and assists in the design and construction of foundations, dams, tunnels, and other structures.

GERIATRIC CASE MANAGER—A professional social worker who specializes in diagnosing the physical and mental health needs and arranging for the proper care of the elderly.

GERONTOLOGIST—A sociologist who specializes in the study of aging and older adults.

GLAZIER—A construction worker who installs glass in windows, skylights, store fronts, display cases, building fronts, interior walls, ceilings, and table tops; may specialize in auto glass, aircraft, plate glass, etc.

GRAPHIC DESIGNER—An artist who designs books, magazines, newspapers, packaging, and other printed materials as well as artwork for TV and other media.

GREENSKEEPER—A worker who oversees a staff in preserving the grounds and turf of golf courses.

GROUNDSKEEPER—A caretaker who maintains the grounds of industrial, commercial, or public property and performs a combination of tasks such as cutting lawns, trimming hedges, pruning trees, fertilizing and spraying, raking and planting, watering, and shoveling snow.

GYNECOLOGIST—A medical doctor who specializes in the diagnosis, treatment, and prevention of diseases and disorders of the female genital, urinary, and rectal organs.

HAND MOLDER—A worker who tends a stuffing machine that fills molds with meat emulsion to form meat loaves; may stuff bologna and sausages into casings by hand.

HEALTH ADVOCATE—A health care professional who serves as a liaison between patients and health care institutions; provides a link to appropriate services.

HOME ECONOMIST—A professional who organizes and conducts consumer education services or research programs for equipment, food, textile, or utility companies utilizing principles of home economics (preparing food, recipe testing, using household equipment and products, home management, etc.); may specialize as a nutritionist, equipment specialist, or in another area.

HOME HEALTH AIDE—A worker who cares for elderly, convalescent (recovering from illness), or people with disabilities in their homes, performing any combination of tasks such as changing beds, ironing, washing, purchasing food items, giving massages, assisting patients in walking, and monitoring their patients' conditions.

HORTICULTURIST—A professional who conducts experiments and investigations in the breeding, production, storage, processing, and transport of fruits, nuts, berries, vegetables, flowers, bushes, and trees.

HOTEL/MOTEL MANAGER—A person who manages a hotel or motel to ensure it is an efficient and profitable operation and is meeting the guests' service needs.

HYDRAULICS ENGINEER—A civil engineer who specializes in the area of hydraulics (operation or motion by means of water or liquid).

HYDROGRAPHER—An individual who analyzes hydrographic data to determine trends in movement and utilization of water.

HYDROLOGIST—A geologist who studies the distribution, circulation, and physical properties of underground and surface waters.

ILLUSTRATOR—A worker who creates drawings or other images for display, book or magazine illustration, or advertising purposes using pencil, pen, charcoal, watercolors, air brush, or computer.

INDUSTRIAL DESIGNER—A professional who conceives and designs the forms of manufactured products.

INDUSTRIAL HYGIENIST—A health care professional who develops, conducts, and evaluates the health program in an industrial setting or governmental organization in an effort to identify, eliminate, and control health hazards such as dust, gases, vapors, lighting, noise, ventilation, and diseases.

INDUSTRIAL TRUCK OPERATOR—A worker who drives a gasoline, natural gas, or electric-powered industrial truck equipped with lifting devices (forklifts, boom, scoop, lift beam, swivel hook, fork-grapple, clamps, elevating platform, or trailer hitch) to push, pull, stack, tier, or move products, equipment, or materials in a warehouse, storage yard, or factory.

INFORMATION SCIENTIST—A professional who designs computerized information systems to provide management or clients with specific electronic data utilizing data processing principles, mathematics, and computer capabilities.

INSTRUMENT REPAIRER—A worker who repairs and calibrates speedometers and other automotive gauges and meters using hand tools and test equipment.

INSTRUMENTATION TECHNICIAN—A skilled worker who develops and operates electronic equipment and related apparatus to test mechanical and/or electrical equipment.

INSURANCE ADJUSTER—A worker who investigates claims against insurance or other companies for personal, casualty, or property loss or damages, and attempts to effect an out-of-court settlement with the claimant; may be called a claims adjuster.

INTERIOR DESIGNER—A professional who plans, designs, and finishes interior environments of residential, commercial, and industrial buildings; may specialize in the decorative aspect and be called an interior decorator.

INTERNAL REVENUE AGENT—A government officer who conducts independent field audits and investigations of federal income tax returns to verify or amend tax liabilities.

INTERNIST—A medical doctor who specializes in the diagnosis, treatment, and prevention of diseases, conditions, and injuries of human internal organs and systems.

JOB ANALYST—A professional who collects, analyzes, and prepares information on various occupations; observes jobs and interviews workers; writes job descriptions and specifications; may specialize in classifying positions.

JOB SETTER—A machinist who sets up and adjusts various machine tools such as lathes, milling, and boring machines, drill and punch presses, etc.; usually works by blueprint, job order, and other specifications.

LANDSCAPE ARCHITECT—A professional who plans and designs the development of land areas for parks, airports, highways, parkways, hospitals, schools, factories, housing projects, business establishments, and other projects.

LANDSCAPE GARDENER—A worker who plans and executes small-scale landscaping operations and maintains grounds of businesses and private residences.

LATHER—A construction worker who fastens wooden, metal, or rockboard (lathe) to walls, ceilings, and partitions of buildings to provide supporting base for plaster, fireproofing, or acoustical material, using hand tools and portable power tools (not to be confused with someone who uses a tool called a lathe).

LAYOUT WORKER—A worker who lays out metal stock or work pieces such as castings, plates, or machine parts to indicate location, dimensions, and tolerances necessary for further processing; analyzes specifications and computing dimensions; and follows blueprints.

LEGAL INVESTIGATOR—A legal assistant who researches and prepares cases relating to administrative appeals of civil service members; also presents arguments and evidence to support appeals hearings.

LEGAL SECRETARY—A secretary who prepares legal papers and correspondence of a legal nature such as summonses, complaints, motions, and subpoenas.

LIBRARY TECHNICIAN—One who provides information services, including answering cataloging questions, assisting users with research tools, filing cards, answering routine inquiries, and making referrals.

LICENSED PRACTICAL NURSE—A health care worker, licensed by the state, who provides direct bedside care for those who are sick, injured, or elderly in hospitals, clinics, private homes, convalescent homes, and other institutions.

LINE INSTALLER—A worker who, using electrician's hand tools, installs and repairs telephone and telegraph lines, poles, and related equipment according to diagrams and other specifications.

LINGUIST—A professional who studies the components, structure, nature, and modification of language and speech and may help to prepare language teaching materials, dictionaries, and handbooks.

LITHOGRAPHER—A worker who transfers positive or negative images to offset printing plates using various methods.

LOBBYIST—A public relations specialist who contacts and meets with members of the legislature and other public officials to persuade them to support laws that are favorable to a client's interest.

LOGISTICS ENGINEER—An engineer who analyzes and designs operational solutions for projects such as transportation optimization, network modeling, process and methods analysis, cost containment, capacity enhancement, routing and shipment optimization, and information management.

LOGISTICS MANAGER—A worker who plans, directs, or coordinates purchasing, warehousing, distribution, forecasting, customer service, or planning services.

LOSS PREVENTION MANAGER—A worker who plans and directs policies, procedures, and systems to prevent merchandise loss.

MACHINIST—A worker who, applying knowledge of mechanics and machinery procedures, sets up and operates machine tools and fits and assembles parts to make or repair metal parts, mechanisms, tools, or machines.

MAITRE D'HOTEL—The head waiter or steward of a hotel or restaurant.

MANPOWER DIRECTOR—An administrator who directs and supervises employees and activities aimed at securing qualified temporary workers to fill job vacancies.

MANUFACTURER SALES WORKERS—A salesperson who sells single, allied, diversified, or multiline products to wholesalers or other customers for one or more manufacturers on a commission basis.

MARBLESETTER—A construction worker who cuts, tools, and sets marble slabs in the floors and walls of a building and repairs and polishes existing slabs.

MARKET RESEARCH ANALYST—A professional who researches marketing conditions and trends in a local, regional, or national area to determine the potential sales of a product or service.

MECHATRONICS ENGINEER—An engineer who applies knowledge of mechanical, electrical, and computer engineering theory and methods to the design of intelligent systems or industrial control.

MEDICAL ASSISTANT—One who serves as a secretary, receptionist, and/or bookkeeper and performs duties such as arranging for X-rays and other medical procedures, billing and collecting fees, and filing insurance claims.

MEDICAL ENGINEER—An engineer who works with physicians and scientists to apply engineering principles to medical diagnosis, surgery, and rehabilitation.

MEDICAL/SCIENTIFIC ILLUSTRATOR—An artist who sketches, draws, paints, and develops diagrams and models illustrating medical and scientific findings for use in publications, exhibits, consultations, research, and teaching.

MEDICAL LAB TECHNICIAN—A health care worker who performs routine laboratory tests, such as taking blood samples, for use in the treatment and diagnosis of disease.

MEDICAL OFFICER—A public service worker who plans and participates in medical research programs in hospitals, clinics, or other public medical facilities to provide medical services to those who qualify.

MEDICAL RECORDS TECHNICIAN—An individual who specializes in compiling and maintaining medical records of hospital and clinic patients.

MEDICAL TECHNOLOGIST—A medical specialist who performs chemical, microscopic, serologic, hematologic, immunohematologic, parasitic, and bacteriologic tests to provide information for use in treatment and diagnosis of disease.

MENTAL HEALTH TECHNICIAN—A health care worker who assists, treats, works with, and directly supervises emotionally ill and mentally disabled patients.

MENTAL HEALTH WORKER—Any individual, from a secretary to a counselor or an administrator, who works in a hospital or agency that provides treatment and/or services to individuals who experience mental or emotional difficulties.

MERCHANDISE DISPLAYER—A worker who displays merchandise such as clothes, accessories, and furniture in windows, in showcases, and on sales floors of retail stores to attract the attention of prospective customers.

METALLURGIST—A person who researches the physical characteristics, properties, and processing of metals.

METEOROLOGIST—A physical scientist who analyzes and interprets meteorological data gathered by surface and upper-air stations, satellites, and radar to prepare weather reports and forecasts.

MICROBIOLOGIST—A scientist who studies the growth, structure, development, and general characteristics of bacteria and other microorganisms; may specialize in viruses, fungi, or in other areas.

MILLWRIGHT—A skilled worker who installs machinery and equipment in industrial plants, according to a layout plan, blueprint, and other drawings, using hoists, lift trucks, hand tools, and power tools.

MINERALOGIST—A geologist who examines, analyzes, and classifies minerals, gems, and precious stones.

MODEL MAKER—A skilled worker who constructs scale models of objects using clay, metal, wood, fiberglass, or other substances, depending on the industry for which the model is being constructed.

MULTIMEDIA SPECIALIST/TECHNICIAN—A worker who skillfully blends audio, video, graphics, and text to communicate information, often working solely on a computer.

MUSIC THERAPIST—A health care specialist who plans, organizes, teaches, and supervises music and related activities for a more integrated and successful rehabilitation of patients.

MYCOLOGIST—A scientist who studies the life processes of edible, poisonous, and parasitic fungi to determine which are useful to medicine, agriculture, and industry.

NATURALIST—A professional who specializes in the study of plants or animals (e.g., zoologist, botanist, etc.).

NATUROPATHIC PHYSICIAN—A physician who diagnoses, treats, and helps prevent diseases using a system of practices based on the natural healing capacity of individuals.

NEUROLOGIST—A medical doctor who specializes in the diagnosis and treatment of organic diseases and disorders of the nervous system.

NUCLEAR ENGINEER—An engineer who engages in the design, development, monitoring, and operation of nuclear power plants to generate electricity and power navy ships; may also conduct research on nuclear energy and radiation.

NUCLEAR MEDICINE TECHNOLOGIST—A medical specialist who prepares, administers, and measures radioactive isotopes in therapeutic, diagnostic, and tracer studies, utilizing a variety of radioisotope equipment; prepares stock solutions of radioactive materials and calculates doses to be administered by a radiologist.

NURSE ANESTHETIST—A professional health care specialist who administers anesthetics or drugs (via fluid, gas, etc.) to lessen or alleviate pain during surgical, dental, or other medical procedures.

NURSE-MIDWIFE—A nurse who specializes in providing medical care to women under the care of an obstetrician; delivers babies and provides patients with health care during pregnancy as well as for a period of time following childbirth.

NURSE PRACTITIONER—A professional health care specialist who usually works with a physician to provide general medical care and treatment to assigned patients; may work independently.

NUTRITIONIST—A professional who conducts and organizes consumer education service or research programs involving food and nutrition.

OBSTETRICIAN—A medical doctor who specializes in the treatment of women during prenatal, natal, and postnatal periods; concerned with the mother's as well as the infant's health and comfort during pregnancy.

OCCUPATIONAL THERAPIST—A health care specialist who plans, organizes, and conducts a comprehensive rehabilitation program to help mentally, emotionally, or physically disabled persons to return to work and resume daily activities.

OCEANOGRAPHER—A specialist who studies oceans, seas, marine life, and related areas.

OPERATING ENGINEER—A heavy equipment operator of one or more types of power construction equipment such as compressor pumps, hoists, derricks, cranes, shovels, tractors, scrapers, or motor graders to excavate, move, and grade earth; erect and reinforce steel; or pour concrete or other hard surface material.

OPHTHALMOLOGIST—A medical doctor who specializes in the diagnosis, treatment, and prevention of diseases and injuries of the eyes.

OPTICIAN—A specialist who makes or orders and sells eyeglasses and contact lenses according to individual prescriptions.

OPTOMETRIST—One who specializes in eye examinations to determine visual efficiency, performance, diseases, and conditions, and prescribes corrective lenses or procedures.

ORTHODONTIST—A dentist who specializes in the prevention, diagnosis, and correction of abnormalities in the arrangement and growth of teeth.

ORTHOTIST—An individual who, in cooperation with a physician, fits and prepares devices for patients with disabling conditions of the limbs and spine.

OSTEOPATH—A medical doctor who specializes in the diagnosis, treatment, and prevention of diseases and injury through an integrated or holistic approach using drugs, surgery, radiation, physical and/or manipulative therapy; particular focus is on the correction of musculoskeletal disorders.

OTOLARYNGOLOGIST—A medical doctor who specializes in the diagnosis, treatment, and prevention of diseases of the ear, nose, and throat.

OUTPLACEMENT SPECIALIST—A professional who assists workers in transitions, particularly those from executive and management backgrounds who have been laid off or fired, to find other employment; may help with career planning and job hunting techniques and by providing referrals.

PALEONTOLOGIST—A professional who studies the fossilized remains of plants and animals found in geological formations to trace the evolution and development of past life and identify geological formations according to nature and chronology.

PARALEGAL—A law clerk who studies law, researches facts, and prepares documents to assist lawyers.

PARASITOLOGIST—A professional scientist who studies characteristics, habits, and life cycles of animal parasites such as protozoans, tapeworms, roundworms, and flukes to determine how they attack and affect humans and animals.

PARK RANGER—An officer who enforces laws, regulations, and policies in state or national parks.

PAROLE/PROBATION OFFICER—A professional social worker involved in the conditional release of juvenile or adult offenders from correctional institutions; establishes relationships, provides supervision, and evaluation, and performs other duties.

PATENT AGENT—A professional worker who prepares and presents patent applications to the U.S. Patent Office and in patent courts.

PATENT LAWYER—A lawyer who specializes in advising clients such as inventors, investors, and manufacturers concerning the patentability of inventions, infringements, validity, and similar items; prosecutes and defends clients.

PATHOLOGIST—A medical doctor who specializes in determining the nature, cause, and development of diseases, structural and functional changes caused by them, cause of death, and effects of treatment.

PEDIATRICIAN—A medical doctor who specializes in the general medical care of children through adolescence.

PEDODONTIST—A professional dental specialist who specializes in the treatment of children's teeth.

PENOLOGIST—A professional sociologist who specializes in research on punishment for crime, crime control and prevention, management of penal institutions (jails and prisons), and rehabilitation.

PERFUSIONIST—A health care worker who operates equipment designed to support or temporarily replace a patient's circulatory or respiratory functions.

PERSONNEL DIRECTOR—An individual who plans and carries out policies relating to all phases of personnel activity; recruits workers, interviews, fills vacancies, plans and conducts new employee orientations; keeps records of promotions, insurance, transfers, and hires; may be called a human resources manager.

PETROLOGIST—A professional who studies the composition, structure, and history of the rock masses that form the earth's crust.

PHARMACIST—A medical professional who specializes in mixing chemical compounds and dispensing medications prescribed by physicians, dentists, and other health care professionals; also makes recommendations regarding over-the-counter drugs.

PHARMACOLOGIST—A biological scientist who specializes in the study of drugs, gases, dusts, and other materials and their effect on the tissue and physiological processes of animals and human beings.

PHOTOENGRAVER—A worker who photographs copy, develops negatives, and prepares photosensitized metal plates, such as copper, zinc, aluminum, and magnesium, for use in printing using photography and developing equipment and engraver's tools.

PHOTOGRAMMETRIST—A surveyor who specializes in the preparation of maps and drawings by measuring and interpreting aerial photographs using analytical processes and mathematical formulas.

PHOTO-OPTICS TECHNICIAN—A worker who sets up and operates photo-optical instrumentation to record and photograph data for scientific and engineering projects.

PHYCOLOGIST—A life scientist who specializes in the study of seaweeds or algae.

PHYSIATRIST—A medical doctor who specializes in the clinical and diagnostic use of physical agents and exercise to provide physiotherapy for physical, mental, and occupational well-being.

PHYSICAL THERAPIST—A health care specialist who plans and administers medically prescribed treatment programs to relieve pain and treat malfunctions in the neuromuscular and other systems caused by disease, injury, or loss of body parts.

PHYSIOLOGIST—A professional scientist who conducts research on cellular structure and organ-system functions of plants and animals, studying growth, respiration, circulation, excretions, movement, reproduction, and other functions.

PIPEFITTER—A plumbing specialist who lays out, builds, assembles, installs, and maintains piping and piping systems, fixtures, and equipment for steam, hot water, heating, cooling, lubricating, sprinkling, and industrial processing systems.

PLANT BREEDER —A professional who plans and conducts breeding studies to develop and improve varieties of crops; seeks to improve size, quality, yield, maturity, and resistance to disease, frost, and pests.

PLASTERER—A construction worker who applies coats of plaster to the interior walls, ceilings, and partitions of buildings to produce a finished surface.

PLASTIC SURGEON—A medical doctor who specializes in skin grafts and bone tissue replacement and restoration and repair of lost, deformed, or injured parts of the face and body.

PLAYWRIGHT—A professional who writes original plays, such as tragedies, comedies, or dramas, or adapts themes from fictional, historical, or narrative sources for dramatic presentation.

PODIATRIST—A medical doctor who specializes in the diagnosis, treatment, and prevention of foot diseases, conditions, and deformities.

POLICE COMMISSIONER—A professional government worker who administers a municipal (city) police department.

PROCTOLOGIST—A medical doctor who specializes in the diagnosis and treatment of diseases and disorders of the anus, rectum, and colon; performs surgical removal of diseased or malfunctioning parts; and prescribes medication or other procedures when necessary.

PRODUCTION SUPERINTENDENT—A manager who, using knowledge of product technology, production methods and procedures, and capabilities of machines and equipment, directs and coordinates other supervisory personnel in activities concerned with the production of a company's products.

PROSTHETIST—A worker who, working with a physician, provides care to patients with partial or total absence of limbs by planning the construction and fitting of devices.

PSYCHIATRIC SOCIAL WORKER—A professional social worker who specializes in providing psychiatric social work assistance to mentally or emotionally disturbed patients at hospitals, clinics, and other medical centers, as well as to their families, collaborating with a psychiatric and allied team in providing a diagnosis and treatment plan.

PSYCHIATRIST—A medical doctor who specializes in the study, diagnosis, and treatment of mental, emotional, and behavioral disorders.

PSYCHOLOGIST—A professional who specializes in the research, collection, interpretation, and application of scientific information about human behavior and mental processes; may specialize in experimental, educational, social, clinical, counseling, school, industrial, engineering, or developmental psychology.

PSYCHOMETRIST—A professional who administers, scores, and interprets intelligence, aptitude, achievement, and other psychological tests.

PUBLIC HEALTH EDUCATOR—An individual who plans, organizes, and directs health education programs for groups and communities; prepares and distributes educational information materials; conducts surveys; and offers workshops.

PUBLIC HEALTH SERVICE OFFICER—A health care professional who administers a public-health program for a county or city; inspects public facilities for health hazards; may help establish free clinics, impose quarantines, or close establishments for safety reasons.

PUBLIC RELATIONS SPECIALIST—A professional worker who specializes in the planning and conducting of a public relations program designed to create and maintain a favorable public image for an employer or client.

PUPPETEER—An entertainer who stages puppet shows, moving controls of puppets to animate them; also may design and construct puppets.

PURCHASING AGENT—A professional worker who purchases raw materials or other unprocessed goods for processing machinery, equipment, tools, parts, produce, or other supplies, or services necessary for the operation of an organization or business.

RADIATION THERAPY TECHNOLOGIST—A health care specialist who assists radiologists in the treatment of disease by exposing the affected areas to prescribed doses of X ray or other ionizing radiation; maintains operation controls; assists in treatment responsibilities and record keeping.

RADIOGRAPHER—A health care specialist who applies roentgen rays and radioactive substances to patients for diagnostic and therapeutic purposes; X-ray technicians may do the actual equipment operation and body positioning.

RADIOLOGIST—A medical doctor who specializes in the diagnosis and treatment of disease using X rays and radioactive substances to examine organs, make diagnoses, and administer treatments.

RECREATIONAL THERAPIST—A health care specialist who plans, organizes, and directs medically approved recreation programs for patients in hospitals and other institutions.

REGISTERED NURSE—A professional health care worker who specializes in providing those who are sick, injured, or elderly with direct personal care, support, and ongoing medical supervision.

REGISTRAR—A professional who directs and coordinates registration activities at a college or university, handling transcripts and credit evaluations, coordinating class schedules, and preparing statistical reports.

RELIGIOUS BROTHER/RELIGIOUS SISTER—In the Roman Catholic Church, a member of a religious community (e.g., Benedictines, Carmelites, etc.) living vows of poverty, chastity, and obedience in the service of God; religious brothers may or may not be priests.

RESEARCH ANALYST—A professional who analyzes management and operational problems and develops solutions using mathematics and computer simulation.

RESPIRATORY THERAPIST—A health care worker who administers respiratory therapy and life support to patients with deficiencies and abnormalities of the cardiopulmonary system under the supervision of a physician and by prescription.

RIGGER—A worker who assembles rigging (material used to hold something together) to lift and move equipment or material at a manufacturing plant, shipyard, or a construction site.

SAFETY ENGINEER—An engineer who specializes in the design, development, implementation, and evaluation of safety programs, apparatus, and other equipment to prevent or correct unsafe environmental working conditions utilizing knowledge of industrial processes, mechanics, chemistry, psychology, and industrial health and safety laws.

SANITARY ENGINEER—A public health engineer who designs and directs the construction and operation of hygienic projects such as waterworks, sewage systems, garbage and trash disposal plants, drainage systems, and insect/rodent control projects.

SCHOOL SUPERINTENDENT—An administrator who directs and coordinates the activities and administration of a state, city, or county school system in accordance with board of education standards; the highest ranking administrator in a school system.

SECURITIES CLERK—A worker who compiles and maintains records of a firm's securities (stock purchases) transactions.

SECURITIES SALES AGENT—One who buys and sells in a trading division of an investment and brokerage firm.

SECURITY OFFICER—A worker who plans and establishes the security procedures for a company engaged in manufacturing products or processing duty or materials for the federal government.

SEISMOLOGIST—A geologist who studies and interprets seismic (earthquake) data to locate earthquakes and earthquake faults.

SHEET METAL WORKER—A worker who fabricates, assembles, installs, and repairs sheet metal products and equipment such as control boxes, drainpipes, ventilators, and furnace casings according to a job order or blueprint.

SILVICULTURIST—A professional who establishes and cares for forest stands and manages tree nurseries and other forests to encourage natural growth of sprouts and seedlings of designated variety.

SOCIAL WORKER—A professional worker who provides assistance through counseling, activities, referrals, and other means to individuals and groups challenged by poverty, illness, family troubles, antisocial behavior, financial mismanagement, inadequate housing, and other concerns; may specialize in medical, psychiatric, industrial, school, child welfare, family, or other areas.

SOCIOLOGIST—A professional who researches the developmental, structural, cultural, and behavioral patterns of human beings and societies; may specialize in criminology, industrial, rural, social problems, gerontology, urban, medical, or other areas.

SOFTWARE SALESPERSON—A worker who sells, either wholesale or retail, computer programs and/or related materials.

SOIL CONSERVATIONIST—A professional who plans and develops coordinated practices for soil erosion control, moisture conservation, and efficient soil use.

SOIL SCIENTIST—A scientist who studies soil characteristics, maps soil types, and monitors results of soil management techniques.

SOUS CHEF—A chef who supervises and coordinates the activities of cooks and other workers in preparing and cooking foodstuffs.

SPECIAL AGENT—An investigator of alleged or suspected criminal violations of federal, state, or local laws who determines if evidence is sufficient to recommend prosecution; obtains evidence, maintains surveillance, performs undercover work, makes reports, testifies, etc.

SPECIAL EDUCATION TEACHER—A teacher who specializes in the education of students with mental, emotional, behavioral, developmental, learning, or physical disabilities.

SPEECH PATHOLOGIST—A professional who specializes in the diagnosis, treatment, and prevention of speech and language problems; may also research human communications.

SPORTS MARKETER—A public relations and advertising specialist who works to increase and/or maintain spectator patronization of a particular sporting endeavor.

SPORTS MEDICINE PHYSICIAN—A physician who diagnoses, treats, and helps prevent injuries that occur during sporting events, athletic training, and physical activities.

STATISTICIAN—A professional mathematician who plans information collection; analyzes and interprets numerical information from experiments, studies, surveys, and other sources; and applies statistical methodology to provide for further research or statistical analysis.

STOCKBROKER—A professional who buys and sells stocks and bonds for individuals and organizations as a representative of a stock brokerage firm applying knowledge of securities, market conditions, government regulations, and financial circumstances of customers.

STONE MASON—A construction worker who sets stone to build stone structures such as piers, walls, and abutments or lays walks, curbstones, or other special types of masonry using mason's tools.

STRATIGRAPHER—A professional who studies the relative position and order of succession of deposits that contain or separate archaeological fossil or plant material.

STRUCTURAL ENGINEER—An engineer who directs or participates in developing, designing, and reviewing building plans to determine load, size, shape, strength, and material requirements necessary for structural integrity.

SURGICAL TECHNICIAN—A health care worker who performs such tasks as washing, shaving, and sterilizing before, during, and after surgical operations.

SURVEYOR—A worker who specializes in the inspection of the earth's surface by measuring angles and distances to determine location, elevation, lines, areas, and contours for purposes of construction, mapmaking, land divisions, title claims, mining, etc.

SYSTEMS ANALYST—A professional who analyzes business or operating procedures to devise the most efficient methods of accomplishing work.

SYSTEMS PROGRAMMER—A professional who develops and writes computer programs to store, locate, and retrieve documents, data, and information for science, engineering, medicine, language, law, military, library science, and other purposes.

TAILOR—A worker who applies principles of garment design, construction, and styling to the construction of new clothing or, more commonly, to the alteration of ready-made apparel.

TAXONOMIST—A plant or animal scientist who specializes in the identification and classification of species and organisms.

TECHNICAL ILLUSTRATOR—A drafter who lays out and draws illustrations for reproduction in reference works, instructions, brochures, and technical manuals showing the assembly, installation, operation, maintenance, and repair of machines, tools, and equipment.

TECHNICAL WRITER—An individual who develops, writes, and edits materials for reports, manuals, briefs, proposals, instruction books, catalogs, and other technical and administrative publications.

TECHNICIAN—A worker who, in direct support of engineers or scientists, uses theoretical knowledge of scientific, engineering, mathematical, or draft design principles to solve practical problems.

TERRAZZO WORKER—A construction worker who applies cement, sand, pigment (color), and marble chips to floors, stairways, and cabinet fixtures to create durable and decorative surfacing according to specifications and drawings.

TISSUE TECHNOLOGIST—A medical specialist who cuts, stains, mounts, and prepares tissue for examination by a pathologist; may assist in autopsies.

TITLE ATTORNEY—A lawyer who specializes in examining abstracts of titles, leases, contracts, and other legal documents to determine ownership of land, gas, oil, and mineral rights; may assist in related trials.

TOOL-AND-DIE MAKER—A skilled worker who analyzes specifications, lays out metal stock, sets up and operates machine tools, and fits and assembles parts to make and repair metal-working dies, cutting tools, jigs, fixtures, gauges, and machinist hand tools.

TOOL PROGRAMMER—A skilled worker who plans a numerical control tape program to control contour-path machining of metal parts on automatic machine tools by means of magnetic or perforated tape.

TOXICOLOGIST—A professional who studies the nature and effects of toxins (poisons) and the treatment of poisoning.

TRAFFIC MANAGER—An individual who directs and coordinates the activities of an organization, including the routing and transportation of goods and products, scheduling, and loading.

TREE SURGEON—A worker who prunes and treats ornamental and shade trees in yards and parks to improve their appearance, health, and value.

TRUST ADMINISTRATOR—A professional who directs and coordinates the creation and administration of private, corporate, probate, and guardianship trusts (safeguarding of goods or items) in accordance with a trust, will, or court order.

TUTOR—A teacher of academic subjects such as English, mathematics, and foreign language to pupils requiring private instruction, adapting the curriculum to meet their needs.

TYPESETTER—A worker who arranges type by computer or by hand in preparation for printing.

UNDERWRITER—A worker who reviews individual insurance applications to evaluate the degree of risk involved and either declines or accepts them.

UPHOLSTERER—A skilled worker who engages in spreading, marking, cutting, and sewing fabric padding, covering, and trimming to articles such as furniture, mattresses, and vehicle seats; may work on new furniture or the renovation of older items.

URBAN PLANNER—A professional who develops comprehensive plans and programs for the utilization of land and physical facilities of cities, counties, and metropolitan areas.

UROLOGIST—A medical doctor who specializes in the diagnosis, treatment, and prevention of diseases and disorders of the urinary or urogental tract.

VIROLOGIST—A microbiologist who specializes in the study of viruses and the diseases they cause.

VOCATIONAL REHABILITATION COUNSELOR—A professional counselor who specializes in counseling individuals with disabilities in job readiness, placement, preparation, and training.

WEBMASTER—A computer specialist who is responsible for overseeing all aspects of a company's or organization's Web site (includes design, development, operations, performance, and maintenance).

WELDER—A worker who is skilled in joining, surfacing, building, or repairing structures or parts of weldable materials using such processes as arc, gas, resistance, solid state, and others.

WHOLESALER—One who manages a store that sells a specific line of merchandise such as groceries, meat, liquor, apparel, jewelry, appliances, furniture, or other items to retailers, who then sell directly to consumers.

WIRELESS SPECIALIST—A technician who specializes in the design and service of small high-tech instruments such as cellular phones, fax machines, and pagers.

APPENDIX C
Definitions of Selected Skill Statements

ABSTRACT REASONING—The ability to work with and apply ideas and concepts that are difficult to understand; also, the ability to think through that which is not concrete or easily understood from a practical perspective.

AGILITY—Quality of nimbleness or being quick and light-footed; performing body movements with ease.

ANALYZE—To effectively look at an item, event, or situation to determine its nature and how to gain a better understanding.

ANALYZE OR LISTEN INTROSPECTIVELY—To examine and understand the various aspects of your own or another's behavior; to interpret feelings, thoughts, and behaviors effectively.

APPROPRIATE DECISION MAKING—The ability to make effective decisions at the right time, usually resulting in a suitable outcome.

APTITUDE FOR ACCURACY AND DETAIL—The ability to carefully perform tasks that involve much detail.

CHARISMA—The ability to draw or attract others to listen, observe, or follow.

FINGER DEXTERITY—The ability to move one's fingers rapidly or accurately when handling small items or objects.

FORM PERCEPTION—The ability to notice details in objects, pictures, or other materials and to see fine differences in shape, shading, figures, and widths and lengths of lines.

FORMULATE AND DEFEND POSITION—To effectively present and back up with factual evidence a belief, opinion, or position.

INTERPERSONAL COMMUNICATION—The ability to skillfully give, listen to, and understand messages to and from other people through the use of words, listening techniques, eye contact, body language, actions, etc.

INTERPRET—To provide a definition for something in a manner that can be more clearly understood by others.

KEEN OBSERVATION—Alertness; the ability to pick up detail and notice things others may miss.

LOGICAL THINKING—Thinking in which opinions and decisions are based on factual evidence; the ability to arrive at a decision following standard and predictable reasoning procedures.

MAINTAIN COMPOSURE IN STRESSFUL SITUATIONS OR UNDER PRESSURE—To remain rational and calm in the face of danger, frustration, fear, disaster, or unexpected events.

MAKE ANALOGIES—To make connections, often revealing similar events, situations, and problems that occurred under different circumstances.

MANUAL DEXTERITY—The ability to work skillfully with one's hands, accomplishing tasks deftly and accurately.

MOTOR COORDINATION—The ability to work one's fingers or hands in coordination with one's eyes to accomplish tasks deftly and accurately.

OBJECTIVITY—The ability to listen or react to a statement, event, or situation in a factual manner without allowing negative or positive impressions to interfere with one's reaction; the tendency to keep responses relatively free from biased emotions and feelings.

PHYSICAL STAMINA—The ability to physically endure periods of sickness, disease, fatigue, etc.

READ OR SPEAK ARTICULATELY—To read aloud or speak clearly using correct pronunciation.

SOLVE QUANTITATIVE PROBLEMS—To figure out answers to problems that involve numbers, measurements, or mathematics.

SOUND JUDGMENT—The ability to look at an event, situation, or problem from all angles, using decision-making techniques along with your education, training, and experiences to determine what is occurring and how to react to it.

SPATIAL PERCEPTION—The ability to look at blueprints, flat drawings, or diagrams and accurately visualize how the structure will appear in physical form, including height, width, and depth.

SYNTHESIZE INFORMATION—To integrate or put together parts to arrive at a solution or answer or to create a whole.

Definitions of Values and Personal Attributes

ACHIEVEMENT—Making progress; successfully completing or accomplishing a goal or task.

ADAPTABILITY—The ability to adjust to and fit into different situations; the ability to alter one's behavior or thinking in order to suit circumstances.

AESTHETIC AWARENESS—The ability to grasp and appreciate the beauty of an event, performance, situation, or physical or social environment; the ability to relate to the beauty in music, song, dance, pictures, structures, nature, and behavior.

ALERTNESS—The ability to quickly recognize details and things that others miss; tendency to observe closely and remain watchful.

ANALYTICAL AND LOGICAL THINKING—The ability to look at and understand the various aspects of an event, situation, or item and arrive at a decision using standard and predictable reasoning procedures.

COMPETITIVE DRIVE—The spirit of challenging and contesting others in order to win or gain something desired; a liking for rivalry and competition with others.

CONSCIENTIOUS—Aware of what you do and sensitive to how your behavior may be affecting another.

CURIOSITY AND ENTHUSIASM FOR GADGETRY—The tendency to handle, take apart, ask questions, and be excited about manipulating items and objects (machines, etc.).

DECISIVENESS—The ability to decide without delay; making a decision to act firmly and without doubt.

DEDICATION—Strong commitment to something to the extent that you are willing to go through much discomfort, if necessary, to achieve the end result; loyalty; giving your total effort.

DEPENDABLE—Trustworthy, reliable, and responsible; can be counted on to come through and to behave as expected.

DILIGENCE—The quality of working steadily at a task until done.

DIPLOMATIC—Careful to do what is appropriate and to consider the various sides of an issue; having the ability to manage and negotiate with others without hurting their feelings.

DISCREET—Showing good judgment; not likely to do something without thoughtful consideration; capable of keeping quiet about a private or controversial matter.

EMPATHY—The ability to genuinely relate to other people by imagining their emotions and feelings; the ability to put yourself in another person's shoes.

ENDURANCE—The ability to withstand discomfort, painful circumstances, hardship, boredom, or stress.

FRAME INQUIRY AND RESPOND OBJECTIVELY—To ask questions that can be logically and scientifically researched as well as respond to others relatively free from biased emotions and feelings.

IMAGINATION—The ability to think and form images of things, events, or ideas that do not presently exist or have never existed.

INDEPENDENCE—The desire to think or perform tasks and activities without being helped, controlled, directly supervised, or assisted; liking to do things on one's own; freedom from authority and confining rules.

INDUSTRIOUS—The ability to work hard continuously, steadily; diligent; to keep busy.

INITIATIVE—The ability to take the lead; to move ahead or take the first step.

INQUISITIVE—Curious; wanting answers; desiring to gain knowledge.

INTEGRITY—Honesty; truthfulness and desire to do what is morally right; uprightness; can be trusted to follow through without corruption.

INTELLECTUAL GROWTH—The ability and desire to continually gain knowledge, understanding, and wisdom without stagnation or hindrance.

LINGUISTIC ABILITY—The ability to analyze and understand the structure of languages, make comparisons, etc.

LOYALTY—A strong sense of commitment or unbroken support; faithfulness.

MENTAL AND EMOTIONAL WELL-BEING—The ability to remain calm, make appropriate decisions, and control one's emotions in stressful or extremely difficult circumstances; not easily shaken emotionally or mentally.

PERSEVERANCE—The quality of not quitting; never giving up; steadfastness; to persist in spite of difficulties.

PERSUASIVE—The ability to influence and draw others to think or behave in a certain way.

POISE AND COMPOSURE UNDER CLOSE PUBLIC SCRUTINY AND CRITICISM—The ability to maintain control over your thoughts and actions and calmly continue in your tasks or activities while being observed (or having something you are responsible for observed) and/or criticized by others.

PRACTICAL—The tendency to take effective action instead of theorizing or speculating; pragmatic.

REFLECTIVE NATURE—Thoughtful; making mental connections between disparate situations.

RESOURCEFULNESS—The ability to solve problems and get through difficult situations, particularly when standard resources are scarce or nonexistent.

RESPONSIBLE—Trustworthy and dependable; having the ability to adequately carry through, oversee, or supervise; can be relied on to perform as expected.

SECURITY—Safety from danger, hurt, discomfort, or instability; firmly fixed and sure; occupationally, the relative assurance of a steady income and job stability.

SELF-DISCIPLINE—The ability to control and positively direct one's emotions, feelings, thoughts, and behavior.

SENSITIVITY TO MULTIPLE PERSPECTIVES—Openness and understanding in terms of different viewpoints, techniques, methods of operation, uses, etc.

SENSITIVITY TO THE INCONSISTENCIES OF HUMAN BEHAVIORS—Understanding, helpfulness, and patience with those who demonstrate abnormal, antisocial, and/or self-defeating behaviors.

SPIRIT OF SCIENTIFIC INQUIRY—Thinking and questioning in a manner and spirit that reflect a preference for and use of scientific laws and procedures.

TACTFULNESS—The ability to say and do the appropriate things at the appropriate times; being sensitive to the feelings of others.

THOROUGHNESS—The tendency to bring an endeavor to completion with attention to detail; leaving nothing undone.

VERSATILITY—The ability to readily change or move into something different; the ability to easily adapt to many circumstances or environments.

WISDOM—Good judgment; the ability to make appropriate decisions; applying knowledge to do what is right and true; using knowledge rightly.

Index of Occupations

About the Author

Paul Phifer has more than 35 years of experience as an educator at both the high school and college levels. He currently serves as the director of Career Development Services at Grand Rapids Community College in Michigan. Phifer holds a master's degree in guidance and counseling from Western Michigan University and is a Licensed Professional Counselor (LPC), a National Certified Counselor (NCC), and a Master Career Counselor (MCC). A father of four, Phifer has long been active in his community, first as a Big Brother and now as a Christian Career Development Facilitator for his church.